400 Trees and Shrubs for Small Spaces

400 Trees and Shrubs for Small Spaces

Diana M. Miller

Timber Press
Portland | London

To all the members of the Royal Horticultural Society's Woody Plant Committee for their inspiration for over 35 years.

← *Malus* 'Evereste'

All photographs are by the author except: Jonathan Buckley/The Garden Collection 24, 32 left; Liz Eddison/The Garden Collection 20, 22; John Hillier 73 left, 86, 115, 140 left, 163 left; Andrew Lawson/The Garden Collection 10, 25; Gary Rogers/The Garden Collection 33; Derek St Romaine/The Garden Collection 26, 30; Nicola Stocken Tomkins/The Garden Collection 29, 32 right; Graham Titchmarsh 45, 48 right, 52 top, 53, 56, 58, 82, 85, 92 bottom, 98, 101 left, 107, 117 left, 126 right, top & bottom, 128, 134, 137, 140 right, 146, 169, 177 top.

Published in 2008 by
Timber Press, Inc.
The Haseltine Building
133 S.W. Second Avenue, Suite 450
Portland, Oregon 97204-3527, U.S.A.
www.timberpress.com
For contact information regarding editorial, marketing, sales, and distribution in the United Kingdom, see www.timberpress.co.uk.

Design by Dick Malt
Printed in China

Library of Congress Cataloging-in-Publication Data

Miller, Diana M., 1940-
400 trees and shrubs for small spaces / Diana M. Miller.
p. cm.
Includes bibliographical references and index.
ISBN-13: 978-0-88192-875-4
1. Woody plants--Great Britain. 2. Woody plants--United States. 3. Small gardens. 4. Trees--Identification. 5. Shrubs--Identification. I. Title. II. Title: Four hundred trees and shrubs for small spaces.
SB435.6.G7M55 2008
635.9'77--dc22
2007036183

A catalogue record for this book is also available from the British Library.

Contents

Foreword

For many years until her retirement in 2005, Diana Miller was the hard working and highly respected secretary of the Royal Horticultural Society's Floral Committee B, now known as the Woody Plant Committee. This committee's duties include the assessment of those woody plants, including climbers, conifers and bamboos, suitable for cultivation in British gardens and parks. Members of this committee are also called upon to judge those nursery exhibits featuring woody plants at the Society's many shows including the world famous Chelsea Flower Show in London. A special subcommittee has the additional responsibility of judging the Woody Plant Trials held at the Society's Wisley Garden and at various other sites countrywide. One important outcome of this work is the recommendation of awards to those plants considered the best of their kind. Such information is helpful to all gardeners especially those new to gardening as well as the more experienced.

Like the Society's other Floral and Trial committees, membership of the Woody Plant Committee is drawn from the most experienced and knowledgeable gardeners, amateur and professional in Britain. It is no wonder then that Diana Miller should have accrued so much information from her exposure to such expertise over so many years. But this isn't all. She is an avid and experienced gardener herself and is fully aware of the many temptations as well as the potential pitfalls that await new gardeners as they pick their way through today's nursery catalogues or wander through the Aladdin's Cave displays of plants found in garden centres and specialist nurseries, not to mention plant fairs and the like.

It is one thing admiring or desiring a tree or shrub, quite another growing it successfully in your own garden. Diana Miller has long experience of the joys and the disappointments of growing woody plants and without dampening the excitement of trying something new or adventurous, seeks in the following pages to guide her reader through what, to beginners certainly, can often seem a minefield of do's and don'ts.

Trees and shrubs are perhaps the most important of all ornamental plants in the garden, especially in today's increasingly smaller gardens, if only because they generally take up the most space. This does not mean, however, that small gardens should contain only small trees and shrubs. A single large tree or shrub if chosen wisely, planted intelligently and cared for sensitively can make a huge contribution to a garden without it taking over or requiring major surgery. I know this from my own experience in a relatively small suburban garden confined by neighbours' hedges. Mind you, I am passionate about plants and an avid collector which can bring its own problems and pleasures.

One outstanding fact about choosing woody plants for the garden, and this is amply demonstrated in Diana Miller's book, is the bewildering choice available today. Her selection and it can only be such, brings the best of the old and the most promising of the new together in a catalogue of delights. Few gardens today could accommodate all she recommends but in the choosing of a few personal fancies the adventurous gardener can look forward to an enjoyable journey encouraged by this most knowledgeable and reliable guide.

Roy Lancaster OBE VMH FIHORT

Acknowledgements

A book is the result of years of acquired knowledge from so many sources and people over a lifetime that it is almost impossible to remember and mention everyone. However, having spent my career as a botanist for the Royal Horticultural Society, I must thank all the RHS botanists and gardeners past and present, as well as the librarians of the Lindley Library, for all I have learned about plants and their nomenclature.

As secretary for the RHS Woody Plant Committee (Floral Committee B), I have worked with many of the most eminent British horticulturalists, who served as committee members and plant exhibitors; several, sadly, are no longer alive. This provided me with the opportunity to encounter an enormous range of woody plants and the chance to learn from their tremendous breadth of knowledge. To them I owe an immense debt of gratitude, especially to Christopher Brickell for teaching me so much in my early years and Roy Lancaster for his unquenchable enthusiasm for all plants. I am particularly grateful to Peter Catt of Liss Forest Nursery who has developed so many of the new cultivars in gardens today, with whom I have had numerous invaluable discussions and who has allowed me to photograph in his nursery. Robert and Suzette Vernon of Bluebell Nursery grow and introduce an amazing number of new and rare cultivars and have suggested several of the newer plants which have been included. Thank you also to John Gallagher for his advice on magnolias and camellias.

A book on plants is nothing without photographs and for these, many thanks are due to John Hillier for images of several of the more unusual species and to Graham Titchmarsh for many others. Thanks also to Madame d'Andlau who has created a beautiful garden at Rémalard in France and kindly allowed me to photograph her garden. My daughter Helen is responsible for the line drawings, and both she and my son David have helped with technical computer problems. Thank you to both and to my husband for their patience and support over the past few months.

Finally, thank you to my many friends for allowing me to photograph their plants and gardens and for their encouragement and comments on the text as the ideas progressed. And last, but not least, to Anna Mumford, Rom Kim and everyone at Timber Press for their support from the beginning and throughout the project.

Introduction

A garden without trees scarcely deserves to be called a garden.

Canon Ellacombe 1790–1885

← *Acer japonicum* 'Vitifolium' and *Hydrangea macrophylla* 'Gentian Dome' provide attractive autumn colour.

The aim of this book is to introduce the wealth of trees and shrubs which could be grown in a smaller garden. When the subject of trees or shrubs is raised, the initial thought is of the enormous forest examples such as oaks or beeches, but hundreds of smaller tree groups can be used in the average garden as well as smaller cultivated varieties of the woodland giants. The idea here is to include woody plants suitable for small gardens. It is not simply a book about small woody plants.

One of the first questions gardeners ask is "what is a small garden?" This answer depends on to whom one is addressing the question. More than 30 years ago, a garden of less than a tenth of a hectare (¼ acre) would have been described as small. Today this would be thought of as large. With a much higher density of buildings and many more people spending so much of their time working and commuting, the size of gardens is much reduced. So for the purposes of this book a small garden is well under this size. It does not, however, include tiny courtyard or patio gardens, although some of the shrubs listed would be suitable.

The second question is how to define a woody plant. A woody plant is a tree or shrub which has woody branches and does not normally die back in winter. Size is not important as some shrubs such as the prostrate thymes reach only 5 cm (2 in.) tall. Some might more correctly be classed as subshrubs like certain *Phygelius* species with stems which are woody at the base but also have softer, less woody stems and which in colder areas may die back each winter behaving like herbaceous perennials. There is some overlap between trees and shrubs and in several species the distinction becomes blurred. Trees growing wild at high altitudes may well have a shrublike habit and some smaller cultivars have been selected for this reason. In general, the definition has nothing to do with size, although in most cases trees are taller. A tree has a single stem or trunk whereas shrubs are multistemmed from the base. However, several shrubs such as *Buddleja alternifolia* can be pruned and trained to create very effective small trees while several trees such as *Eucalyptus* and *Salix* behave as shrubs if coppiced.

Whatever their size or shape, trees and shrubs are long-lived plants which will provide enjoyment for many years. It is possible to create a wonderful garden containing only woody plants selected for their flower, fruit and foliage colour throughout the year, not forgetting coloured bark and stems for winter effect. Differently shaped leaves give texture, and trees can provide shade, height and structure to a design. Alternatively, woody plants might be chosen to provide a backdrop for a mixture of herbaceous plants and bulbs during the spring and summer months. The choice may be for fewer larger trees and shrubs or numerous smaller sized ones.

Even quite small gardens can accommodate one or two carefully chosen trees. Perhaps choose one with multiple features of attractive bark for winter, showy scented flowers for spring, unusual leaves for summer and colourful foliage and berries for autumn.

Many woody plants need little attention but some plant groups, such as roses, do need regular pruning. Some trees and shrubs are naturally small, while other more vigorous plants can be grown in a limited space with judicious pruning or training. Most will tolerate this if done at the right time. Several larger shrubs and even small trees can be grown in a container but extra feeding and watering will be needed in these conditions. This may be an option for favourite plants which are ordinarily too large, but with the restriction of the roots, growth can be kept small enough for the garden. Others might be too tender for growing outdoors all year round but if pot grown, they can be moved to a more sheltered position in winter. Whatever the preference of plants and their arrangement, it is important to use the right plant in the right soil and the right position for the best effect and for them to thrive.

There are so many thousands of wonderful and exciting plants that it has been impossible to mention them all, and choosing which to exclude has been exceedingly difficult. Some more tender species have been described that could be grown in a container, and several will tolerate a slight frost, especially if grown in a sheltered area or against a wall. The climate does appear to be warming and certainly it seems possible to grow plants now that years ago would have been ignored. This book is simply a selection of species and cultivars, and for the larger genera such as roses and camellias, only a very small percentage of those which could have been chosen.

Many new and interesting species, and selections and hybrids of known species, are being introduced by specialist nurseries. Some of these are smaller in size or of a more compact or narrow and erect habit which can be accommodated in a limited space. For example, 'Sonoma', a new cultivar of *Davidia*, flowers when young so that it is not necessary to wait for perhaps 20 years to see the first flowers, but it is as yet not widely available in the trade. Other species are so exceedingly slow growing that although they may take many, many years to reach a large size, they are worth considering. Oaks in time can reach to over 30 m (100 ft.) but small weeping or pencil-slim, erect cultivars might be of use in certain situations.

This book features examples of both old and well-established species and cultivars, as well as the newly introduced ones, but many other worthy contenders could have been described. In the list of suggestions for further reading at the end of the book, the monographs include many more species and cultivars.

For simplicity, as few technical terms as possible have been used so that those planting a garden for the very first time may appreciate the plant descriptions as much as would the seasoned gardener. Terms that are unavoidable for clarity are explained in the glossary.

Several other significant groups of plants have been excluded but this does not diminish their importance in gardens. Conifers serve an essential role but the choice is endless and several books are devoted simply to this subject. Similarly, fruit trees can provide shade and structure to the garden and a spectacular flower display in addition to their edible fruits. They can be grown as standard trees, grafted onto dwarfing root stocks to create smaller plants, or even several different cultivars can be grafted onto a single trunk for a choice of fruits from a single individual. Trained in various ways, a number can be accommodated in a small space but again this is a specialist subject. A third group of woody plants which have been left out are the bamboos. These are wonderful and varied plants which provide structure and height in the garden as well as shades of green and restful rustling sounds in the wind. Some are very large and invasive but others are smaller and clump forming or could be suitable as pot-grown plants. For these again there are new and excellent monographs.

Ideas about design and cultivation have been covered briefly, but the main objective of this book is to highlight the breadth of variation within the woody plant world which can be used in a relatively small area. Many of the plants mentioned could be planted in pots in small courtyards or patio gardens but this is not the main purpose. This is not a book for identification, but I hope that it will inspire you, highlighting old favourites as well as new and more unusual or rare trees and shrubs. These are just some ideas.

1 Names of Woody Plants

← *Davidia involucrata* var. *vilmoriniana*, a variety of *D. involucrata* which has less hairy leaves.

As botanical names are used throughout this book, this chapter offers a simple explanation of the conventions of plant naming. A question frequently asked is "why do gardening books and plant nurseries use botanical (Latin) names?" The answer is very simple. It is so that there can be no confusion about the identity of each plant. In principle, every plant has a unique botanical name which is recognized internationally but it may have any number of English (common or vernacular) names and even more names in different languages. A simple example is *Davidia involucrata* which is known as the dove tree, handkerchief tree or ghost tree in English, whereas a *Eucalyptus* is known as a ghost gum which could easily be misrepresented as a ghost tree. Often gardeners use the botanical name quite naturally without realizing that it is not an English name, usually because there is no commonly accepted one, as, for example, with cotoneaster, rhododendron and clematis.

English names may be descriptive, but botanical names are, with a little knowledge, just as interesting. Many names commemorate well-known botanists (*Davidia* in honour of a French botanist and missionary to China), or may be derived from an older name (*Jasminum* from the ancient Persian name for the plant) or from mythology (*Daphne*, the nymph fleeing from the god Apollo). The second part of the name is often descriptive such as *Cornus alba*; "alba", meaning white, because the shrub has white berries, or *Camellia japonica*, a camellia growing wild in Japan. Books are available which will help take the mystique out of the botanical names and give insight into their origin and may even help with memorizing a plant name.

The botanical name of a plant consists basically of two parts, a system first introduced by Carl Linnaeus in 1753 and used in the classification of plants (and animals). Each plant is placed in a genus (plural genera) which contains closely related plants. *Rosa* is the generic name for all roses and *Syringa* for all lilacs. However, for example, within the genus *Rosa* many distinct roses are found wild all over the world. These are separated into species and given a specific name. *Rosa canina* is the pink-flowered English dog rose and *Rosa hugonis* is a yellow-flowered species from China. Occasionally the species is further subdivided into subspecies (subsp.) or forma (f.) or variety (var.). *Cercidiphyllum japonicum* f. *pendulum* is a name used for the weeping forms of a normally upright tree.

Plant names are written according to an international convention. The botanical name, including the genus, species, subspecies and forma, is always

↑ *Rosa canina*

↗ *Rosa hugonis*

written in italics or underlined for clarity. If there can be no confusion over the generic name, it may be shortened to the initial letter as in *R. canina*.

Hybrids are the result of either the deliberate or natural crossing of two species and are recognized by "×" inserted after the genus name and before the hybrid name as in *Laburnum* ×*watereri* which is a cross between the two species *L. alpinum* and *L. anagyroides*. For a cross between two genera, the "×" is placed before the hybrid generic name as in ×*Fatshedera lizei*, a cross between *Hedera* and *Fatsia*.

Genera are grouped into families and the family names are easily recognized as they always end in "aceae". Rosaceae, the rose family, includes related plants such as pyracantha, medlar and crab apples as well as roses. There are about half a dozen older family names such as Compositae, the older name for Asteraceae, the daisy family. These names do not end in "aceae" and may be encountered but they are used less and less frequently nowadays.

Garden plants pose certain problems with names because of the minor variations which are selected from species for ornamental use. A white variant of *Ceanothus rigidus* has been given the name 'Snowball' to distinguish it from similar blue-flowered types. This name is known as the cultivar name which is never Latinized but may be in the language where the plant originated, whether it be Russia, Brazil, Japan or an English-speaking country. The plant 'Snowball' is called a cultivar, a term which is a simple contraction of "cultivated variety".

↖ *Calycanthus floridus* and ← *Sinocalycanthus chinensis*, the parents of ×*Sinocalycalycanthus raulstonii* 'Hartlage Wine'.

↑ ×*Sinocalycalycanthus raulstonii* 'Hartlage Wine', a bigeneric hybrid between *Sinocalycanthus* and *Calycanthus*.

← *Laburnum* ×*watereri* 'Vossii' is a hybrid between *L. alpinum*, the Scotch laburnum, and *L. anagyroides*, the common laburnum. 'Vossi' is a free-flowering selected cultivar with very long racemes.

Cultivars come about in many different ways but are the result of the selection and maintenance of a distinct new plant which is named and propagated. By convention these names are not written in italics or underlined but enclosed in single quotation marks with an initial upper case letter. Sometimes a number of related cultivars are included in a Group.

↑ *Choisya ternata* SUNDANCE 'Lich'

For cultivated plants there is a further complication as a result of the registration of some for Plant Patents (United States of America) or Plant Breeders' Rights (United Kingdom and many other countries) by their breeders. These registrations give protection from unlawful propagation and sale for a determined period of time but not indefinitely. The plants are often registered under a different name to that used when the plant is sold. The yellow-leaved *Choisya ternata* was first registered for Plant Breeders' Rights as 'Lich' which is treated as the cultivar name and enclosed in single quotation marks. By law, this name must always be used when this plant is sold. However, 'Lich' is not a name which would appeal to the gardening public and the plant is sold (by approved retailers) by the much more attractive selling name SUNDANCE. So that the names can be distinguished, the selling names are written in a different script. Although the gardener will call a plant Sundance, the correct style of the name in any publication, including nursery catalogues and plant labels, is *Choisya ternata* SUNDANCE 'Lich'. Some plants may have several selling names in different countries which makes the use of the cultivar name even more important.

However, as much as botanists would like to retain the name of a plant, there are times when names change because plants are re-identified or reclassified or it is discovered that a plant's name is already being used for different plants elsewhere in the world. Name changes are never undertaken without a great deal of thought and discussion and these alterations can be controversial. Gardeners especially do not appreciate too many changes. The plant names used by *Plant Finder* of the Royal Horticultural Society are followed in this book for stability. However, in a few cases the names have been slightly shortened for simplicity, but they are still botanically correct and the plants are more often found under these names in plant nurseries. Where more than one name has been used for a plant in recent times, these synonyms have been included.

The rules for plant names may appear to be complicated but they do ensure that when applied correctly there can be no confusion in the identity of any particular plant anywhere in the world. Fortunately for garden plants, as long as the meaning is quite clear, the name may be simplified. *Callicarpa bodinieri* var. *giraldii* 'Profusion' may be shortened to *Callicarpa* 'Profusion' as there should be no other *Callicarpa* with the same cultivar name.

2 Selecting Woody Plants for the Garden

It is worth considering a number of factors which should influence the selection of plants for a smaller garden, some of which need serious thought, whereas others will be obvious and automatically encompassed or dismissed without further reflection. It is easier to choose plants suitable for the garden than to try to adapt the garden conditions to suit the requirements of the plant. There is really no more point in trying to grow lime-hating plants such as rhododendrons on chalk than planting lavenders in a shaded corner in heavy clay soil. In our busy modern lives, time for the garden may be limited, so it is important to ask how, why, when and by whom is the garden to be used. Perhaps the plants themselves are the primary consideration and all other factors less significant? These are some of the decisions that will need to be made when creating any new garden but especially one based on the longer-lived woody plants.

← Despite its considerable size, *Viburnum plicatum* 'Mariesii' provides a light touch in an enclosed courtyard garden.

Design by Chris Beardshaw

Use of the Garden

Everyone wants different things from a garden and the choice of plants and their arrangement need to accommodate these needs. If it is a space for children to play, at least while they are young, it would be prudent to avoid plants with attractive but poisonous fruits or those with sharp spiny leaves. If privacy is important, taller shrubs and trees may be used at strategic points, on the boundaries and elsewhere.

For some, a garden is simply a place to relax with friends, have a barbeque or sunbathe; therefore, easy, low-maintenance shrubs as a simple background, flowering during the warmer months of the year, are important. Higher maintenance plants which need annual pruning and regular deadheading and hedges which need trimming are perhaps best avoided in this instance. Bedding plants, hanging baskets and plants grown in pots need to be planted up each season and regularly fed and watered but a garden of carefully selected shrubs and a tree or two could be a solution for those who have little time or inclination for garden maintenance.

For many, however, it is the plants that are the main focus of the garden. The foliage, texture, flower colour, scent, season, plant shape and size should all be taken into consideration when making a selection. Think how the colours and shapes complement one another to provide interest for the times when the garden will be used and enjoyed. Winter-flowering plants are best placed near

the house where they can be enjoyed from the windows. Plants with scented foliage are appreciated if positioned where the leaves are brushed in passing and scented-flowering plants placed so they can be easily sniffed.

A garden does not need to be full of colour at all times to be interesting. Plants with foliage in different shades of green or with a range of leaf textures and colours can be very effective and restful to the eye. Foliage plants provide a foil for bulbs, herbaceous perennials and bedding plants.

If creating a haven for wildlife is of importance, choose plants with flowers which produce pollen and nectar for butterflies, bees and other pollinating insects. Pollination is necessary for the production of fruits and seeds which in turn provide food for birds and some small mammals. Avoid too many double-flowered cultivars which more often than not have extra petals at the expense of nectar, stamens with pollen and the ovaries for seed and fruit production. As well as food, trees and shrubs provide essential shelter and nesting sites for birds, and even places to hang nesting boxes. Selections of cultivars of native species will be beneficial, but in general, the more variety, the greater the usefulness. Hedges are especially important, but check for the ideal time for hedge trimming before starting the operation to ensure that the potential for maximum flowers and fruit is not lost and also that there are no nesting birds.

Whether the garden is of only woody plants or is a mixture of trees, shrubs, herbaceous plants and bulbs, each garden is unique and a reflection of its creator. There are many books on design with guides to basic rules, but in the end, rules can be broken with great results. After all, design is a personal preference and the garden should be planted to be enjoyed by its owner and not simply to follow a set of rules or even to impress the neighbours.

← A small, densely planted area features many shrubs including a Japanese maple, clipped box, clematis and *Lavandula pedunculata*.

Plants for Different Purposes

Trees give height, create an interesting three-dimensional structure and give a focal point to a garden. Trees also provide dappled shade and, unless they have dense, large and evergreen leaves and do not cast too deep a shadow, will allow for the planting, underneath their canopy, of smaller shrubs, herbaceous plants and bulbs which relish conditions out of direct sunlight. Carefully placed, they will create a screen, but to avert potential conflict, avoid planting too close to a boundary or where they might shade a neighbouring garden. It is also wise not

↑ A graceful focal point is created with this single specimen planting of *Cornus controversa* 'Variegata'.

to plant too close to the foundation of a house where, in some instances, the roots could cause damage. For maximum interest, choose a tree with interesting foliage, flowers, fruits and perhaps coloured bark as well. A columnar or weeping tree may be an interesting feature occupying less space, but one with a spreading canopy will provide a shaded sheltered place to sit during the heat of the day. The speed of growth is another consideration. A naturally slow-growing tree may be the answer in a small space but it will take many years to grow to a sufficient size to provide shelter, whereas a faster-growing tree may become too large too quickly. There are many naturally smaller trees such as *Malus* or *Sorbus* from which to choose, to name but two.

Climbers are useful for covering fences or walls and hiding less attractive structures such as sheds. They take up little ground space and the number and

← The strong yellow flowers of *Brachyglottis* contrast with the grey foliage of *Pyrus salicifolia* 'Pendula' to make a striking underplanting.

variety of species and cultivars in a garden can be increased by using these vertical spaces. A pergola or arch covered with colourful climbers could add an interesting additional feature.

The right species of climber might be allowed to scramble through other shrubs or trees. A flowering climber will extend the period of interest of a tree

↑ Wall shrubs and climbers are particularly valuable in small gardens as they provide colour and interest and take up little ground space as shown in this example where *Clematis* 'Lawsoniana' and *Ceanothus* 'Cascade' cover a wall and archway.

if it flowers at a different time. Alternatively, choosing two flowers in which the colours of the host and the climber are complementary can create stunning effects. A silver-leaved tree like *Pyrus salicifolia* 'Pendula' might perhaps provide support for a clematis with a deep purple coloured flower. It is, however, important that the host tree is not smothered by a very vigorous climber with dense foliage.

Hedges have their own special value in a garden and a selection of suitable shrubs can provide colourful flowers and fruits as well as privacy, a wildlife haven and a background to other borders. Thorny or spiny species have the added bonus as a potential deterrent to unwanted intruders. Sometimes the deeds of a house restrict the hedge height so a check may avoid future disputes.

Dwarf shrubs might be grown in a rock garden or on a wall and the most prostrate species such as thymes can be used between paving stones or slabs.

← Using all available space by growing *Clematis* 'Iola Fair' up a columnar pear tree in the garden La Petite Rochelle in France.

Shade-loving, low-growing, spreading species provide ground cover under other shrubs. Some can be quite vigorous and need vigilance to prevent them from growing out of control.

Shrubs with an enormous range of size, colour, season, fragrance, foliage, flower and fruits provide the basic backbone to a garden of woody plants.

Conditions in the Garden

The conditions in a garden are the result of a combination of different physical factors such as soil, light, water and temperature, and all affect the growth of plants. Many of these factors are interrelated; so, for example, some plants may survive a cold winter more readily if the soil is dry but not if it is too wet. Wild plants have adapted to their natural environment over thousands of years, and, although when brought into a garden they no longer have the competition of other plants that they experience in the wild, they do have some conditions which need to be fulfilled. Choosing plants which more closely match the garden environment will ensure more success than trying to grow something in a totally unsuitable situation.

Soils differ in their texture, their moisture retention and their pH (acidity or alkalinity). Clay soils are usually fertile and hold more water in dry spells but are cold and take longer to warm up in spring. Digging with the incorporation of compost will help. Sandy soils are porous and warmer but normally have fewer nutrients and can be very dry. They will also benefit from the addition of organic material such as compost or manure. A mulch on the surface will help reduce water evaporation.

The correct acidity of a soil, measured by pH, is vital for a number of plants. Inexpensive kits can be bought to test the pH and are easy to use. It is worth testing the soil of a new garden because the soil pH is not necessarily obvious. The average pH of a soil is very slightly acidic, if it is around 6.5, in which the majority of trees and shrubs will thrive. Most will tolerate a greater degree of acidity, and also a slight degree of alkalinity, just above 7, without showing signs of chlorosis, manifested as a yellowing of the foliage. However, some trees and shrubs are more exacting in their requirements. Alkaline- (chalk or lime) loving plants can usually cope with some acidity, but lime-intolerant plants such as heathers will not endure any degree of alkalinity.

Light is another significant issue in the choice of plants. Some need full sun and for others shade is preferable. There are few gardens totally in full sun all day and a certain amount of shade is rarely a severe problem. Each wall of a house has a different aspect and can be utilised to good effect by selecting suitable wall shrubs or climbers. Whereas a wall facing south provides the lightest position, it may be too hot and cause too great a water loss, by evaporation, for certain species. A west facing wall, sheltered from cold easterly winds, might be more suitable for early-flowering camellias whose flowers could be damaged by early morning sun while still covered in frost. Therefore, consider the aspect before selecting plants for each position.

Water is essential to plant life but few trees or shrubs will survive in cold water-logged soils. Where rainfall is sparse, choose drought-tolerant plants. Even if there is sufficient rainfall, drying winds or very porous soils may cause stress to plants which some accept more than others. Those with shallow rooting systems such as rhododendrons need a more water-retentive soil to endure hot weather or drying winds.

↑ *Pyrus salicifolia* 'Pendula' and clipped box continue to provide interest through the winter.

Understanding the local minimum temperatures is vital in deciding on the plants for a garden, but this is not, however, as easy a decision as might initially be perceived. Local factors can dramatically change the local climate even within 100 m (300 ft.). The north side of a hill may be considerably colder than the south and is made even colder by the fact that cold air flows downhill in winter. Frost pockets can further reduce the temperatures and will be found where the cold air cannot escape because of hollows or barriers such as buildings and fences. Land near a large expanse of water, on the other hand, will be warmer in winter. A garden sheltered by walls or trees will also be warmer than one totally exposed to northerly winds. Local microclimates may be very different to what might be anticipated from the altitude or latitude. So the hardiness of a particular plant is one of the most difficult concepts to define. A tender plant might survive in a sheltered corner grown against a wall but be killed elsewhere in the garden. Winter rain and humidity is sometimes more problematic than severe cold. On the other hand, if shrubs have been stimulated to flower or come into leaf early following a mild winter, they can be seriously damaged by late frosts.

The hardiness zone maps at the back of the book give a guide but do not account for local microclimates. The plants described in this book have been allocated a zone which indicates the minimum temperature they will endure. The maximum temperature is rarely as important. Therefore, a shrub with Zone 7 can be hardy in most of the British Isles but one of Zone 9 will only grow in the milder areas around the southern coast or sheltered gardens elsewhere.

However, with some thought about the positioning of plants and winter protection, if necessary, some surprising species can be grown in some unlikely places.

Tips for Smaller Plants

When thinking about the selection of trees and shrubs, it is not necessary to choose only naturally small plants, although, of course, these will be of prime consideration. *Caryopteris*, *Santolina* and *Sarcococca*, for example, rarely exceed 1.5 m (5 ft.) but a garden of shrubs of this height or less would create no sense of dimension and would be much too uniform. A range of sizes and shapes provides a more interesting environment.

Many of the larger genera contain garden-worthy plants of both tall and shorter species. The genus *Rhododendron* is a good example. Many species of *Rhododendron* with some reaching a massive size to 12 m (35 ft.) tall and wide with leaves to 45 cm (1 ½ ft.) long would be quite out of the question in a smaller garden. However, more reasonably sized species such as *R. yakushimanum* and many cultivars such as *R.* 'Elizabeth' are totally suitable.

Breeders and nurseries are continually creating, selecting and introducing new and smaller cultivars of all kinds of species to meet the demands of the modern market. Other woody trees are so slow growing that it is possible to consider them; however, do be aware that in the longer term, they may need to be removed. Although not the subject of this book, many so-called dwarf conifers have far exceeded their allotted space in a time frame far shorter than anticipated and have become a problem.

Many larger shrubs need not be discounted because most can be pruned to keep to a reasonable size. *Buddleja davidii*, for example, can grow several metres or feet in a season but can also be pruned hard each year in early spring to keep it within bounds. The suckers of *Kerria japonica* can be regularly removed to prevent it from spreading too far, and large camellias, for example, can be cut hard with no untoward effect if they become unwieldy. Most shrubs will tolerate pruning, although some, like lavender, do not easily sprout from the older wood, and so should not be cut back to the mature stems.

Coppicing is an extreme method of severe pruning but can be very effective for allowing some large trees to be grown for their ornamental foliage or for the attractive effects of their stems in winter.

Topiary is yet another way of reducing the size of some evergreens such as *Buxus* or *Osmanthus*, but it does require a certain amount of time, patience and skill to achieve a satisfactory result.

← Even in the depths of winter *Acer davidii* 'Serpentine' earns its keep providing interest with its striking bark.

↑ *Cornus alba* 'Sibirica', grown for its attractive coloured winter stems and seen here with an underplanting of *Galanthus* 'Atkinsii', is improved by coppicing every two to three years.

Design by Glen Chantry

It is possible to select narrow upright or weeping cultivars of several trees. The Japanese cherry, *Prunus* 'Amanogawa', takes up much less space and creates less shade than *Prunus* 'Shirotae' with its wide spreading canopy. Unless this has already been undertaken when the tree is purchased, the ultimate height of weeping trees can be determined by training the leader (the main stem) up a cane in the early years until the required height is reached, then allowing the branches to weep. This is very successful, for example, with *Buddleja alternifolia*.

Finally, growing shrubs in a container is a way of keeping them smaller by, in effect, reducing their root growth and hence the uptake of nutrients. It is also a means by which plants could be grown in a garden with unsuitable soil or for finding that extra space for yet another choice plant. Bonsai take root restriction to the ultimate.

Therefore, it is not always necessary to ignore all the favourite woody plants

← *Ilex crenata* responds well to being clipped into an interesting shape to provide stature and presence in a small garden.

↑ A sculptural tree trunk and containers of neatly clipped box set off the softer underplanting of lavender to create a pleasing year-round scene at Casa Nova, Italy.

Design by Mr. & Mrs. Cesare Settepassi

because they are too large. There are often ways of circumventing the problem by the selection of more appropriate varieties or by some other trick such as pruning.

Garden centres provide an opportunity to see plants in flower and to appreciate their colour and form before choosing which to buy, but remember that they will often have been grown with some protection and flower slightly early. The staff should be aware of local conditions and be able to give advice on suitable plants, their requirements and size as well as their care. Specialist nurseries will have knowledge of particular groups of plants, and can supply the more unusual species and cultivars. Many have mail-order services and nowadays a Website as well.

Enjoy planning and selecting some exciting and new trees and shrubs. The choice is endless and it is yours.

3 Looking After Woody Plants

The selection of a healthy plant suitable for the site in which it will grow, as well as careful preparation, planting and aftercare, will ensure that your trees and shrubs have the best chance to thrive and to resist any pests or diseases.

← Roses trained by tying onto wires which are permanently fixed onto the wall.

Purchasing Plants

When looking for plants choose a good healthy plant and, if possible, choose a nursery with a quick turnover so that the plants have not been kept in less than ideal conditions for too long. Avoid any which show signs of insect damage such as nibbled leaves, or those with any aphids or other insects on the plant. Choose a bushy plant which is not lopsided and has shoots arranged as evenly as possible all around. Beware of plants which have mildewed, discoloured or contorted leaves or shoots with dead tips. If the plant is growing in a container, make sure that the compost is moist, not waterlogged, and is not shrinking from the sides of the pot. If possible, examine the roots. If they are coiled around within the pot, or large roots are escaping, this could indicate that the plant is pot-bound and possibly starved. Roots that have become accustomed to encircling a container do not readily readapt once planted in the ground, and if they do not become well established, the plant may die unexpectedly at a later date. Also make sure that the compost does not fall away when the plant is removed from the pot. If it does fall away, this suggests that the roots are not well established or the plant was recently repotted. For bare-rooted plants check that the roots are evenly spread and not coiled or one-sided. If the plant has a root ball covered in hessian or some other type of netting, check that it is firm and the covering is not split.

For plants growing in a container, the time of purchase is less significant as these may, with care, be planted at almost any time of year, unless the ground is frozen or a prolonged drought is likely. For bare-rooted plants, the time of planting is more important. Deciduous trees and shrubs should be planted between autumn and spring when the ground is not frozen. Evergreen plants and those bought with a rootball are best planted either in autumn or midspring. Plants that are slightly tender should be planted in spring so that they have more of a chance to harden off and grow well before the onset of winter. If the plant has been bought through mail-order, unpack it straight away. Larger, more mature specimens, which are often available from specialist nurseries, will provide a more instant effect but they will need a little more aftercare for a longer period of time, whereas smaller plants generally become established more quickly.

Once the tree or shrub is purchased, plant it as soon as practical. In the meantime, store it in a shaded place and remember to water regularly. If the plant is bare-rooted, it should be heeled into the ground temporarily and watered until planted in its permanent position. For plants purchased with a rootball, keep the roots moist and if there is to be some delay, remove the covering and heel the plant into the ground.

Preparation, Planting and Aftercare

Before planting a tree or shrub, prepare the ground well. The area should be cleared of weeds, especially perennial ones which are more difficult to eradicate once their roots are entangled with those of your chosen plants. Dig the area thoroughly and deeply to loosen the soil so that the roots may penetrate more easily and so that air and water can enter, both of which are essential for healthy roots. Incorporate garden compost into the ground.

For shrubs, a hole should be dug deep enough to contain the roots and about twice as wide as the root spread of the new plant. For trees, the hole can be more than three times as wide as the root spread. Fork over the base, loosen the sides of the hole and add some compost and possibly fertiliser. Also mix the soil removed from the hole with compost before refilling.

Position the plant in the centre of the hole and spread out the roots of bare-rooted plants. For container plants, tease out the roots once the plant is removed from the pot. Refill the hole, firming the soil thoroughly. Ensure that the plant is placed at the same depth as when it was in the container or lifted from the ground for sale. In soils which tend to hold excess water and become waterlogged, raise the plant very slightly to assist in drainage and in poor dry soils create a slight hollow so that water tends to flow towards the centre of the plant. Water well. Mulching the ground around the plant helps to conserve water, reduce the weeds and make any that do appear easier to remove.

For the first season after planting, and for longer in dry conditions, water regularly until the roots are well established. A thorough soaking less frequently is more effective than a sprinkle of water every day. Watering in the evening en-

sures that any applied water does not evaporate in the heat of the day and that water droplets do not remain on the leaves in full sun causing leaf scorch.

Keep the area around the base of the plant free of weeds which will compete for water and nutrients and also, when the plant is small, for light as well. If the ground around the plant becomes compacted, loosen with a fork to allow air and water to penetrate. For the first few years, organic fertilizers such as manure or inorganic fertilizers will help a new tree or shrub grow away quickly, but, except in very poor soils, regular feeding should not be essential once the plant is established. Excessive fertilizer is not necessarily beneficial.

Shrubs rarely need staking, but for trees, a short stake or cane for the first year or two will help the roots become well established. Use tree ties, which can be expanded as the tree grows in girth, to fasten the trunk to the stake. In areas where rabbits might damage the bark, a tree guard will help protect the trunk but remember to loosen it and remove it when it is no longer necessary.

If it is practical and if the plant is not being grown for its ornamental fruits, removing the faded flowers can be an advantage, as by not producing seed, the plant will have more energy to grow and develop flowering buds for the following season. It is also worth watching for any shoots of a variegated plant which have reverted to green. These will be more vigorous and eventually take over from the variegated branches. Cut out these reverted shoots as far back as to

⇖ A young tree which has been staked using a cane and tied with string. The cane will be removed once the roots are well established.

↑ Many branches of this variegated *Elaeagnus* have reverted to green. Any green shoots should have been removed as soon as they appeared.

where they emerge from the stem. Likewise, in a plant that has been grafted, remove any of the shoots growing from below the graft which will be from the rootstock and not the cultivar which has been selected. For trees, suckering shoots which appear on the trunk can also be cut away.

If the plant is growing in a container, regular watering and feeding with an all-purpose, slow-release fertilizer will be much more important. If possible repot the plant every two to three years. In between time, the top few centimetres or inches of soil can be loosened and removed and replaced with new compost. Climbers grown in containers are especially greedy for food and water. If tender plants in large containers need to be protected in a warmer place during winter, consider using a trolley or pot holder on wheels to make moving easier.

For plants, especially climbers, grown against a wall, pergola or trellis, it will be necessary to train them while young to the shape required and tie the shoots to the support or onto wires or trellis attached to the wall or fence.

For hedges, the spacing will depend on the species chosen, but between two properties, plant away from the exact boundary to allow for the growth in width and consider beforehand how both sides can be trimmed.

Pruning

Pruning is a subject about which some gardeners become very concerned, but by following a few basic rules, it is not difficult to do it successfully. Even if it is done incorrectly, very few plants will die as a result and most will grow back into shape. A few plants benefit from annual pruning to encourage flowering and vigour, but not every tree or shrub needs regular pruning, and for the majority, all that is necessary is an occasional tidying up.

Pruning is carried out for a number of reasons. The most usual is to cut out any dead, weak or diseased branches to maintain the health of the plant and to remove any potential source of infection. Alternatively, it may be necessary to remove any crossing or crowded branches which are spoiling the shape, such as perhaps an upward-growing shoot on a pendulous tree. Thinning will also allow light and air to penetrate into the tree or shrub so the remaining branches can grow to their full potential. The plant may need to be pruned to keep it small and within the bounds of the garden. For hedges or topiary, pruning is essential, as it is for shrubs and climbers trained against a wall, trellis or pergola. Pruning also encourages the plant to produce more branches and, therefore, a bushier habit so a spindly shrub can be improved by cutting the main stems to increase the amount of branching below.

For pruning, it is important to use clean tools which will not transmit any potential disease, and sharp tools to avoid tearing the shoots causing jagged and untidy cuts. It is no longer considered essential to seal the cut surfaces.

Timing is exceedingly important to avoid cutting off all the future flower buds or fruits. Pruning is usually carried out after flowering unless the fruits are ornamental, in which case it is usually possible to wait until later in the season. In general, for plants that flower in the spring and early summer on the older branches from the previous year (for example, *Hamamelis* and *Daphne*), the buds are formed during the previous summer, so if pruning is required, it should be carried out as soon as possible after the plant has finished flowering. For plants which flower during the summer on the new branches produced that spring (for example, *Spiraea japonica* or *Lavatera*), any pruning is usually carried out in early spring or sometimes in autumn after flowering. There are, of course, a few exceptions which should be checked.

Clean cuts should be made immediately above the point at which the leaves emerge from the stem. For plants where the leaves are opposite one another, make the cut straight but in those where the leaves are arranged alternately up the stem, make the cut a slanting one.

Several shrubs may be large for a small garden but are very tolerant of hard pruning and can be grown very successfully in limited spaces. *Forsythia*, *Heptacodium*, *Philadelphus* and *Weigela* are examples of shrubs which if allowed to grow naturally may become very large but by cutting back each year, once they have reached a suitable size, can be grown in quite small areas. Certain plants, such as wisteria, need annual and more specialist treatment not within the scope of this book.

A number of large trees and shrubs have ornamental foliage or coloured stems and can be grown in smaller areas by regular coppicing. This forces the plant to produce a number of stems of similar age and size to grow from the stool (the base of the plant). Some species of *Cornus*, *Salix* and *Rubus* are grown in this way for the effect of their coloured stems in winter, whereas others, such as *Eucalyptus* and *Catalpa*, are used for their attractive foliage. Coppicing is usually undertaken in late winter or early spring, annually or biennially, cutting the old stems to within a few inches of ground level. Pollarding is simply coppicing at a predetermined height above the ground.

Hedges, once established and which have reached the required height, need regular trimming to maintain their size and to keep them dense and bushy. The timing and number of cuts required annually will depend on the species but check carefully before starting, to avoid disturbing nesting birds during the process. For plants with large leaves, prune with secateurs rather than shears to avoid ugly cuts and damage to the foliage.

Propagation

There are several different methods of propagation including budding, grafting, layering, cutting and seeding. For each plant, some methods are more reliable than others; some plants require more specialist knowledge and some are simply more difficult to propagate in the garden situation.

Propagation methods may be divided into two main types—sexual or vegetative. In sexual propagation, by seed, the new plants are the result of pollination of the flower and the resulting seedlings will not necessarily be identical in all aspects to the parent(s). In the second type, shoots or roots are used to produce new plants so that the new offspring are identical to the parent. Whether or not this factor is important will influence the choice of propagation method.

Seeds are produced by most species and may be germinated in suitable seed composts. If the fruit is a dry capsule, the seeds can be removed and any unwanted parts of the pods or husks discarded. If the fruit is fleshy, the seeds can be washed out and dried before sowing. Most cleaned seeds may be stored in a refrigerator or a cool dry place. Some may need treatment before they will germinate. For example, seeds of plants which naturally grow in areas with very cold winters may need stratification (periods of cold or even freezing) to germinate successfully. Others from places such as Australia, where fire is frequent, may require the seed coat to be weakened to allow germination, because in wild conditions, the fire and the chemicals in the smoke would normally induce germination. It is possible nowadays to buy products which imitate smoke. Species with large seeds and tough seed coats, including members of the pea family, often benefit from scarification which involves nicking the seed coat with a sharp knife or, alternatively, soaking them in hot water to weaken the seed coat. Finally, other species germinate more easily if given gentle heat. When growing from seed, do not be surprised if the seeds take several months to germinate or appear erratically. Remember that the resultant seedlings may be slightly different to the parent plant and produce a better (or worse) selection.

If the plant to be propagated is a cultivar, which will have been selected for a particular characteristic such as flower colour or size, a vegetative method of propagation will ensure the continuity of these characters. Budding and grafting are more specialist techniques but layering and taking cuttings are not difficult.

Plants which have a tendency to sucker or send out long shoots which root themselves when they touch the ground, can be increased by layering. A shoot is deliberately pegged into the ground and allowed to root before detaching it from the parent plant and potting it into suitable compost. Slightly wounding the shoot at the point where it is buried in the ground can increase the speed at which it roots. Alternatively, a sucker or self-rooted piece of stem may be cut away from the parent and potted up until it is established as an independent plant.

Cuttings can be taken from stems of different ages. Softwood cuttings are made from the young green stems, which are still flexible, in early summer. Semi-ripe cuttings are made of slightly woodier material taken later in the summer or early autumn. Hardwood cuttings are made in late autumn or even early winter after the leaves have dropped. Cuttings may also be nodal, that is, the cut is made immediately below the node (the joint where the leaves join onto the stem), or internodal, where the cut is made between the two nodes. Many climbers are more successful from internodal cuttings.

A large percentage of woody plants can be successfully propagated by semi-ripe cuttings. Cuttings should be about 5–10 cm (2–4 in.) long for most trees and shrubs. A sharp, clean cut should be made and the lower leaves removed leaving two to three leaves at the top of the cutting. Large leaves may be cut in half to reduce water loss. If using hormone-rooting powder or gel, dip the cut end into the compound and shake off the excess. Place the cuttings into a pot or propagator of prepared rooting compost containing a mixture of sharp sand and peat or a peat-free equivalent. Water gently, but not excessively, and cover with a glass sheet or clear plastic film. Bottom heat will assist in the rooting of most plants.

Hardwood cuttings can be about twice as long to 20 cm (8 in.) or more and the cuttings can simply be inserted into a trench in the ground or in a container where they are left through the winter until they begin to show signs of growth. Keep out of direct sun and water when necessary. Even if the leaves develop, it may be several months before the roots are sufficiently well established to repot the new plant.

Softwood cuttings can be about 5 cm (2 in.) in length and by their nature, are more liable to damage and will wilt more rapidly.

As with pruning, it is important to use sharp and clean secateurs or knives when preparing cuttings or layers.

Pests, Diseases and Other Problems

Good healthy trees or shrubs, planted carefully and growing in ideal conditions with the basic requirements of the right soil and sufficient water, light and space, are likely to recover more quickly from an attack by pests and less likely to succumb to disease. Sun-loving plants such as *Cistus* will not thrive in shade or moist soils, but others such as *Desfontainia* will not appreciate a very free-draining poor soil in full sun. Plants in the wrong position will be weaker and less resistant to pests or disease.

One common problem is when lime-intolerant plants are grown in an alkaline soil. In this case, the leaves become yellowish and the plant will fail to grow strongly. Commercial products can be used to overcome this lime-induced chlorosis but they need continual use and this can prove expensive. If a lime-hating plant must be grown and if it is not excessively large, why not consider growing it in a container in a lime-free compost, using rain water when watering if the tap water contains lime?

Fungicides can help with many fungal diseases such as mildew, but they become impractical if the tree or shrubs are too large.

Encouraging birds, frogs and hedgehogs into the garden will help to reduce certain pests such as slugs and snails. Many beneficial insects such as ladybirds will attack aphids and other harmful pests. Pesticides do not discriminate between useful and harmful insects and so are best used, following the manufacturers' instructions carefully, as a last resort.

For larger pests such as rabbits and deer which can cause serious damage by eating the bark and foliage of trees and shrubs, fencing together with tree guards for tree trunks is the only real solution. Squirrels and a few birds are not as easy to control and can damage young shoots and flower buds, although some deterrent chemicals are available.

Growing a mixture of different species is helpful in avoiding the spread of pests or disease because different plants are sensitive to different organisms. A mixed border is far less vulnerable than a bed of one type of plant such as roses.

On the whole, woody plants are quite tolerant but there are a few devastating diseases such as honey fungus. In these unfortunate cases, it is advisable to remove the infected plant as quickly as possible and either burn it or dispose of it away from the garden. If the disease is specific to a particular group of plants, plant a different species in the place of the sick plant, but if it is a general disease, change the soil in the area and try more resistant plants. Even with honey fungus, there are plants which are less susceptible; your local nursery should be able to advise on alternatives.

4
A to Z of Trees and Shrubs

← *Hamamelis ×intermedia* 'Orange Peel'

These accounts of genera, species and cultivars include a representative selection of the thousands of trees and shrubs which might be grown. The sizes given are on the generous side but the vigour of a plant can be affected by soil nutrients, temperature, light and water, so the exact size of any one plant in any one situation is difficult to predict accurately. The hardiness zone maps at the back of the book give an indication of where different plants can be grown. However, local microclimates might allow plants to thrive where in theory they should not live, whereas elsewhere normally tougher species may unexpectedly not survive.

The Award of Garden Merit 🏆 is given by the specialist committees of the Royal Horticultural Society to plants considered to be excellent, reliable for garden decoration and which are not prone to disease or reversion and do not require highly specialized care.

Abelia (Caprifoliaceae)

Deciduous and evergreen shrubs grown for their long-lasting, funnel-shaped flowers. The coloured calyx of many species persists after the flowers drop giving an added attraction for several weeks. A number of newer species and cultivars, some sweetly scented, are being introduced into cultivation and should come onto the market in a few years. Grow in a sunny position. If necessary, prune deciduous species in early spring and evergreens after flowering.

***Abelia* 'Edward Goucher'**, a popular hybrid with lilac-pink flowers, is semi-evergreen and exceptionally free-flowering from summer to autumn. Size: 1.5 × 2 m (5 × 6 ft.). Zone 8.

↑ *Abelia floribunda*

Abelia floribunda 🏆 from Mexico is evergreen or semi-evergreen with tubular, bright pinkish red flowers to 5 cm (2 in.) long. It is less hardy than other species but is effective if grown against a warm wall. Size: 2 × 3 m (6 × 10 ft.). Zones 8–9.

Abelia ×grandiflora 🏆 is a vigorous semi-evergreen shrub with clusters of white, funnel-shaped flowers tinged with pink from summer to autumn and enclosed in pink calyces which last long after the flowers have fallen. This can be used as a hedging plant but be careful to clip immediately after flowering to ensure flowers for the following season. 'Compacta' is a smaller neater plant. CONFETTI 'Conti' 🏆 has white-margined foliage which becomes pink in autumn. Size: 3 × 4 m (10 × 12 ft.). Zone 8.

Abelia schumannii 🏆 from China is deciduous with slightly scented, mauve-pink flowers marked with orange in the throats and pinkish brown calyces throughout the summer. The plant may be affected by severe winters but will usually regrow from the base. Size: 2 × 3 m (6 × 10 ft.). Zone 8.

Abelia triflora, a deciduous shrub from northwestern Himalayas, is slightly less common but worth growing for its dense clusters of sweetly scented, pink-tinged white flowers contrasting with bronze-coloured calyces in early summer. Size: 5 × 3 m (15 × 10 ft.). Zone 8.

Abeliophyllum (Oleaceae) white forsythia

Abeliophyllum distichum from Korea, the only species in this genus, is becoming rare in its native country. The branches of this fairly slow-growing, hardy, deciduous shrub are covered in late winter and early spring with clusters of white, scented, 4-petalled forsythia-like flowers, about 1 cm (½ in.) across. Plants with pale pink flowers belong to the Roseum Group. Prune after flowering. Trained against a sunny wall is an ideal site as the plants need heat to ensure prolific flowering. Size: 2 × 1.5 m (6 × 5 ft.). Zone 5.

↑ *Abeliophyllum distichum* Roseum Group

Abutilon (Malvaceae) flowering maple, Indian mallow

Most of the members of this genus are tropical shrubs or herbaceous plants but some deciduous species can be grown outdoors in milder areas in sheltered positions. They bear masses of large, brightly coloured flowers which are either bell- or saucer-shaped. Most have leaves somewhat like a maple in shape. Prune in spring.

Abutilon megapotamicum 🏆 from Brazil is a delicate, rather graceful, semi-evergreen or evergreen shrub with thin branches. Through the summer and early autumn, it bears pendulous, bell-shaped flowers to 4 cm (1½ in.) long, with inflated bright red calyces enclosing golden-yellow petals and protruding purple stamens. 'Variegatum' has leaves mottled and splashed with yellow. *Abutilon* 'Kentish Belle' 🏆 has slightly more yellow-orange petals. All are suitable for containers or conservatories and need winter protection in all but the mildest areas. Size: 1.5–2.5 × 1.5–2.5 m (5–8 × 5–8 ft.). Zones 8–9.

↑ *Abutilon* 'Kentish Belle'

A number of more tender evergreen hybrids can be grown in a conservatory to be put out in summer. The pendulous flowers produced from summer to autumn are large, about 7 cm (3 in.) across and bell-shaped. *Abutilon* 'Ashford Red' has red flowers, 'Boule de Neige' white flowers and 'Canary Bird' 🏆 yellow flowers. Size: 3 × 3 m (10 × 10 ft.) but less if restricted by a container. Zone 10.

Acacia (Mimosaceae) mimosa, wattle

Most of the species of this very large, mainly Australian genus of evergreen and deciduous trees and shrubs are tender and very tall. A few, including the florists' mimosa, can be grown in sunny sheltered gardens and fertile, lime-free soils. The leaves are either finely and repeatedly pinnately divided into fine leaflets or they are replaced by leaflike structures formed from modified flattened stems known as phyllodes. The fragrant flowers without petals are in fluffy, yellow balls made up of numerous stamens. Grow in sun. Prune immediately after flowering to restrict growth.

Acacia dealbata 🏆 (mimosa, silver wattle) is known best as a florists' flower but can be grown as a large shrub or small tree for its finely divided, silvery green, feathery leaves to 13 cm (5 in.) or more long. In late winter, numerous golden-yellow flowers in large flower heads to 20 cm (8 in.) across are formed. Size: 15 × 6 m (50 × 18 ft.) in favourable conditions. Zones 8–9.

Acacia pataczekii (Wally's wattle), a species only named in 1974, is not yet widely available but worth trying because it has proved to be hardier than many other species. It has flattened blue-green phyllodes 5 cm (2 in.) or more long and lemon-yellow flowers. Final size in cultivation is not yet certain. Zone 8.

Acacia pravissima 🏆 (Oven's wattle) has curious flattened, blue-green, triangular phyllodes under 2 cm (3/4 in.) long with a single spine on one point. The late winter flowers are bright yellow. Size: 3 × 3 m (10 × 10 ft.). Zones 8–9.

Acer (Aceraceae) maple

This is a very large genus and most of the species are deciduous trees, too big for smaller gardens. A few species are worth considering but bear in mind that some, such as *Acer pseudoplatanus*, seed freely and grow very quickly. Most

↑ *Acer griseum*

have palmately lobed or divided leaves often turning a good autumn colour. The flowers are small and are followed by the typical 2-winged fruits shaped like small propellers. The Japanese maples include small shrubs with an astonishing range of foliage, some of which could be grown in a container. A moist but well-drained fertile soil in sun or partial shade is best, and, although these are hardy, the roots of container-grown plants may need to be protected during severe frosts. Japanese maples need some protection from cold winds and the early leaves may be affected by late frosts. Prune in winter if necessary.

Acer campestre 🏆 (field maple, hedge maple) from Europe including the United Kingdom has 3- to 5-lobed leaves turning a good clear yellow in autumn. It is useful as an informal hedge. There are a number of cultivars, some

↑ *Acer palmatum*. A dissected-leaved cultivar in autumn.

with variegated foliage. 'Carnival' is slow growing, its leaves edged with creamy white. Size: 12 × 12 m (35 × 35 ft.). Zone 4.

Acer griseum 🏆 (paperbark maple) from central China, is grown for its wonderful peeling, cinnamon-coloured bark especially showy in winter when grown as a specimen tree. The leaves are trifoliate becoming scarlet and orange in autumn. Size: 10 × 10 m (30 × 30 ft.). Zone 5.

Acer japonicum (Japanese maple) from Japan is a small tree with light green leaves and attractive small red flowers. 'Aconitifolium' 🏆 has leaves deeply divided into narrow lobes becoming crimson in autumn, and 'Vitifolium' 🏆 has less divided leaves turning red and gold. Size: 10 × 10 m (30 × 30 ft.). Zone 5.

Acer palmatum (Japanese maple) from China and Japan is one of the most useful maples for small gardens with such a range of cultivars differing in their size, habit, leaf shape and colour that makes it difficult to decide which to choose. Those of the Atropurpureum Group have purplish red foliage through the summer, while those of the Dissectum Group have leaves which are more finely divided into feathery lobes. They are usually dome-shaped shrubs but if trained when young by removing the lower branches, they can be encouraged to form standards with a single trunk. 'Bloodgood' ♀ has foliage which remains deep reddish purple through the summer until it changes to red in autumn. 'Orange Dream' is a rather upright plant with 5- to 7-lobed leaves, orange-yellow turning yellow in autumn. 'Osakazuki' ♀ has slightly larger 7-lobed, green leaves and is one of the most vivid red plants in autumn. 'Sango-kaku' ♀ (synonym 'Senkaki; coral bark maple) not only has soft yellow autumn leaves but coral-red stems attractive throughout the winter. Variety *dissectum* 'Filigree' has a pendulous habit and very finely divided, light yellowish green leaves turning to gold. Size depends on the cultivar. Zone 5.

Acer pseudoplatanus **'Brilliantissimum'** ♀, a selection of the sycamore and a favourite of many, is a small, slow-growing tree with pink young leaves turning to yellow then green in summer. Size: 6 × 8 m (18 × 25 ft.). Zone 5.

Acer shirasawanum **'Aureum'** ♀ (synonym *A. japonicum* 'Aureum') is one of the most popular of the small maples with 7- to 11-lobed, bright yellow leaves turning red in autumn. Grow out of full sun which can scorch the leaves. Size: 6 × 6 m (18 × 18 ft.). Zone 6.

Acer tataricum **subsp.** ***ginnala*** (synonym *A. ginnala*; Amur maple) from China and Japan is a large shrub or small tree with deeply 3-lobed leaves turning brilliant orange and red in autumn. Size: 2 × 2.5 m (6 × 8 ft.). Zone 4.

Acer tegmentosum from northeast Asia is one of the smaller snake-bark maples with jade green bark streaked with silver. Size: 8 × 8 m (25 × 25 ft.). Zone 5.

Acradenia (Rutaceae) whitey wood

Of the two species in this genus, ***Acradenia frankliniae*** from Tasmania may be cultivated for both its aromatic foliage and late spring flowers. It is an erect, evergreen shrub with dark green, glossy, trifoliate leaves and clusters to 5 cm (2 in.) across, of numerous white, star-shaped flowers. In colder areas, protect from frost in severe winters. It thrives in moist but well-drained soils in partial shade. Prune after flowering. Size: 3 × 1.5 m (10 × 5 ft.). Zone 8.

↓ *Acradenia frankliniae*

↑ *Actinidia kolomikta*

Actinidia (Actinidiaceae)

A group of mainly twining, deciduous shrubs grown for their fruit or ornamental foliage. Grow in sun. Prune in late winter or early spring.

Actinidia deliciosa (often grown as *A. chinensis*; kiwi fruit, Chinese gooseberry) from China is not fully hardy and both male and female plants are required for the production of the edible fruits. These are not reliably produced in temperate climates. 'Jenny', a self-fertile cultivar, is worth trying. Height: 10 m (30 ft.). Zone 9.

Actinidia kolomikta ♕ from eastern Asia has clusters of fragrant, white flowers to 2 cm (¾ in.) across in early summer. These often go unnoticed because of the very striking dark green leaves to 15 cm (6 in.) long which quickly become variegated with white and pink towards their tips after unfolding. This plant is ideally trained against a sunny wall to display the foliage. The leaves may not develop their striking colours until the plant is well established. Height: 5 m (15 ft.). Zone 8.

Actinidia pilosula is much less common with narrow pink, green and white leaves.

Agapetes synonym *Pentapterygium* (Ericaceae)

Evergreen shrubs from warm temperate regions of which ***Agapetes serpens*** ♕, a rare shrub from the eastern Himalayas, is sometimes cultivated. It has small, narrow, deep green, glossy leaves on arching stems. In spring, numerous, pendulous, narrow, bell-shaped flowers, each about 2 cm (¾ in.) across, red with V-shaped darker markings, hang from the stems. It is a spreading shrub and the long branches may be trained to climb. Grow in a container and protect when there is a danger of frost. A moist but well-drained, lime-free soil is necessary. Remove weak or dead branches after flowering. Size: 1 × 2.5 m (3 × 8 ft.). Zone 9.

Akebia (Lardizabalaceae) chocolate vine

A genus of vigorous, semi-evergreen, twining climbers from Japan and China grown both for foliage and flowers. The leaves are palmate with oblong leaflets on long stalks which are an attractive light green, sometimes bronze-tinged as they unfold in spring, contrasting with the scented flowers in pendulous racemes. In hot summers, fleshy, purple, sausage-shaped fruits about 10 cm (4 in.) long may be produced.

↑ *Akebia quinata*

These plants will quickly cover a shed or pergola in moist, but not wet, soil, in sun or shade. They need to be cut back regularly after flowering in a confined space. Height: 9 m (30 ft.). Zone 5.

Akebia quinata has leaves with 5 leaflets and reddish brown flowers. 'Shirobana' is a new and rare white-flowering cultivar.

Akebia trifoliata has leaves with 3 leaflets and dark purple flowers.

Aloysia synonym *Lippia* (Verbenaceae)

Aloysia triphylla 🏆 (synonym *Lippia citriodora*; lemon verbena) from Chile is the only species of this genus to be commonly grown. It is a deciduous shrub with long, narrow, very strongly lemon-scented leaves in whorls of 3, which may be used in cooking or dried for potpourri. The minute flowers are pale purple formed in large branching inflorescences in late summer. It is not reliably hardy but can be grown against a warm sunny wall or, in colder areas, kept smaller in a container and given protection in winter. Position the plant where it can be brushed in passing to release its scent. Prune in spring after late frosts. Size: 3 × 3 m (10 × 10 ft.) if not confined. Zone 9.

Amelanchier (Rosaceae)

snowy mespilus, juneberry

Deciduous trees or large shrubs grown for their white, apple-blossom-like flowers in spring and their brilliant autumn colours. The juicy purplish or reddish black fruits, very attractive to birds, reach 1.5 cm (½ in.) across and are edible, although those of some species are rather insipid. Moist but well-drained, lime-free soils are best, in sun or partial shade. Prune if required in winter or after flowering. Zone 4.

The hybrid ***Amelanchier ×grandiflora*** includes two cultivars. 'Ballerina' 🏆 is a shrubby, multistemmed plant reaching about 6 m (18 ft.) with large flowers and large sweet fruits, while 'Robin Hill' is a larger but dense shrub with pink buds opening to very pale pink flowers.

↑ *Amelanchier lamarckii*

↓ *Amicia zygomeris*

Amelanchier laevis from North America is similar to *A. lamarckii* 🏆 but differs in the hairless young leaves and slightly fragrant flowers. Size: 8 × 8 m (25 × 25 ft.).

Amelanchier lamarckii 🏆, the most commonly grown species, which is found wild in several parts of northern Europe, is a graceful, spreading tree with drooping racemes of pure white flowers contrasting with the silky, hairy, coppery young foliage. In autumn, the fruits are sweet and the foliage turns a dramatic orange and red. Size: 10 × 12 m (30 × 35 ft.).

Amicia (Papilionaceae)

A genus of subshrubs of which **Amicia zygomeris** from Mexico is the only species, normally

cultivated for its foliage and flower. In cooler areas, it will behave as a herbaceous plant dying down in autumn but usually regrowing from the base unless the winter is very severe. The pinnate leaves have 4-leaflets to 7.5 cm (3 in.) long and 2 large and conspicuous, purple-tinged, rounded leaflike structures (stipules) at the base of the leaf stalk. The early to midautumn pea-like flowers are bright yellow to 3 cm (1½ in.) across with purple markings. Grow in sun and moist but well-drained soil. A mulch in winter will protect it from some frost. Cut back any frost affected shoots in spring. Size: 1.5 × 1 m (5 × 3 ft.). Zone 9.

Amorpha (Papilionaceae)

Deciduous shrubs with pinnate leaves and curious flowers which, although related to peas, have only one petal. They need a light, dry soil and a sunny position to thrive. Cut back flowering stems once they are over.

Amorpha fruticosa (bastard indigo, false indigo) from North America grows and spreads quickly. It has bold, fresh green leaves to 30 cm (1 ft.) long. In summer, it bears dense heads to 15 cm (6 in.) long of numerous purplish blue flowers with contrasting orange anthers. Size: 5 × 5 m (15 × 15 ft.). Zone 4.

Anisodontea synonym *Malvastrum* (Malvaceae)

Evergreen shrubs or woody perennials of which ***Anisodontea capensis*** (sometimes sold incorrectly as *A.* ×*hypomadara*) from South Africa is a useful small erect shrub. It flowers over a long period from summer to autumn and is becoming popular as a container or conservatory plant. The pale to deep pink, saucer-shaped flowers, 2.5 cm (1 in.) across, have dark red veins. It will grow outside all year in very sheltered gardens in sun but elsewhere needs winter protection. Prune if necessary in spring and take the tips out of young growth to encourage bushiness. Size: 60 × 40 cm (24 × 16 in.). Zone 10.

↑ *Arbutus unedo* f. *rubra*

Arbutus (Ericaceae)

A genus of medium sized, evergreen trees with attractive bark. Sprays of white, urn-shaped flowers about 6 mm (¼ in.) across provide food for bees and develop into orange or red strawberry-like fruits to 3 cm (1½ in.) across. Like other plants related to heathers, a lime-free soil is essential, although *Arbutus unedo* is slightly less fussy. Prune in spring only if necessary.

***Arbutus* 'Marina'** has exceptionally good cinnamon-coloured bark which peels off in curls as it ages. The flowers are pink and bell-shaped. It will grow into a tree unless pruned to create a rounded bush. Size: 8 × 8 m (25 × 25 ft.). Zone 8.

Arbutus unedo 🏆 (strawberry tree) grows wild in southern Ireland and the Mediterranean regions. The peeling red-brown bark is attractive throughout the year while the flowers and edible, red, warty fruits to 2 cm (¾ in.) across are produced exceptionally at the same time in late autumn. This is a useful, spreading, slow-growing tree for coastal districts where some other trees may not thrive. 'Atlantic' flowers freely even on young plants and forma *rubra* 🏆 has pink flowers. Size: 8 × 8 m (25 × 25 ft.). Zone 8.

Aronia (Rosaceae) chokeberry

A genus of small, hardy, deciduous shrubs from North America resembling *Crataegus* (hawthorn) but thornless and with larger, ovate leaves. The white or pink-tinged flowers, in clusters about 6 cm (2½ in.) across in spring, are followed by red or black fruits and amazing autumn foliage colour. These are very tolerant plants growing in most places except on shallow chalky soils. They may sucker. Prune from winter to spring, removing some of the older shoots.

Aronia arbutifolia (red chokeberry) has red fruits with leaves, hairy underneath, turning orange, yellow and red in autumn. 'Erecta' is a compact, more upright cultivar with exceptionally good autumn colour. Size: 3 × 1.5 m (10 × 5 ft.). Zone 4.

↑ *Aronia melanocarpa*

Aronia melanocarpa (black chokeberry) has glossy black fruits and glossy dark green leaves turning purple-red in autumn. Size: 2 × 3 m (6 × 10 ft.). Zone 4.

Artemisia (Asteraceae) wormwood, sage bush, mugwort

The woody plants of this genus are grown for their attractive, aromatic, usually finely divided, silvery, deciduous or evergreen leaves. The flowers are less significant. They grow best in full sun. Regular cutting back in spring retains the shape of the plants if they become straggly.

Artemisia abrotanum 🏆 (lad's love, old man, southernwood) from southern Europe has been grown since the sixteenth century for its fine, silver-grey foliage and in the past as a medicinal plant. Size: 1 × 1 m (3 × 3 ft.). Zone 5.

Artemisia afra from South Africa is fairly new to cultivation and is slightly less hardy. Even if it is cut back by severe winters, it normally grows again the following spring. The upright stems bear foliage which is particularly delicate and very silver. Size: 1.5 × 1 m (5 × 3 ft.). Zone 8.

***Artemisia* 'Powis Castle'** 🏆 was selected for its good compact and short habit and especially silvery leaves. Size: 1 × 1.5 m (3 × 5 ft.). Zone 8.

Asteranthera (Gesneriaceae)

Asteranthera ovata is an unusual evergreen climber which grows up trees in humid forests in the Chilean Andes and bears tubular, red, 2-lipped flowers 6 cm (2½ in.) long in early summer. This is a beautiful plant in the right conditions but slightly fussy, needing a damp and humid atmosphere, a lime-free soil and protection both from sun and frost. Prune after flowering only if necessary to remove weak or dead shoots. Height: 4 m (12 ft.). Zone 9.

Atriplex (Chenopodiaceae)

Of this large genus, one or two semi-evergreen shrubs are grown for their silvery foliage rather than their inconspicuous yellowish or greyish green flowers. Cut back in early spring to maintain bushiness.

Atriplex halimus (tree purslane) from southern Europe has been cultivated for over 300 years for its silvery grey almost diamond-shaped leaves. It is hardy and will thrive in sun and well-drained, poor soils and tolerate the salty winds of coastal districts. It is also suitable for use as low, informal hedges. Size: 2 × 2.5 m (6 × 8 ft.). Zone 8.

Aucuba (Cornaceae) spotted laurel

These tough evergreen shrubs are large and dense but very tolerant of almost all conditions and are therefore useful in difficult shaded sites in poor and dry soils. The added advantage is that they can be clipped, shaped or used for hedging, as specimen plants or in containers. They are usually grown for their glossy, dark green and often variegated foliage rather than their small reddish purple flowers. Male and female flowers are found on separate plants and when both are grown in close proximity, the female plants produce ovoid red berries about 1 cm (½ in.) long. The plant is mildly poisonous if eaten. Prune or trim hedges in early spring. Old and straggly plants can be cut back hard to encourage new growth.

Aucuba japonica from Japan has many cultivars; those with variegated foliage will brighten a dark corner. Any variegated shoots which revert to green should be removed. 'Crotonifolia' 🏆 (female) and 'Golden King' 🏆 (male) have large glossy leaves blotched and spotted with gold. 'Rozannie' 🏆 has plain green leaves and is said to be hermaphrodite so does not need a partner to produce fruits. 'Variegata' (synonym 'Maculata') (female) with gold speckled leaves is the original introduction from Japan and still very common in gardens. Size: 3 × 3 m (10 × 10 ft.). Zone 7.

Azara (Flacourtiaceae)

Most of the cultivated species are slightly tender evergreen shrubs with attractive, often glossy foliage. The clusters of tiny, fragrant petal-less flowers consist of numerous bright golden-yellow stamens. Grow as free standing plants or trained against a wall in a sunny position in a moist fertile soil. Prune if necessary after flowering.

Azara microphylla ♕ from Chile and Argentina is the hardiest species and in ideal conditions can eventually form a small tree with arching branches bearing tiny dark green leaves and masses of vanilla-scented flowers in early spring. It may also be clipped as a topiary specimen, although some flowers will be lost. 'Variegata' is slower growing with cream-edged foliage. Size: to 10 × 4 m (30 × 12 ft.) in ideal conditions or against a wall. Zone 8.

Azara serrata ♕ from Chile has toothed leaves to 6 cm (2½ in.) long and scented bright yellow flowers in early summer. 'Andes Gold' is the cultivar usually sold as *A. serrata*. *Azara dentata* is often confused with this species but differs in the hairy underside to the leaves. Size: 4 × 3 m (12 × 10 ft.). Zone 8.

Baccharis (Asteraceae) bush, tree groundsel, cottonseed tree

This large genus includes herbaceous and woody plants one of which, ***Baccharis halimifolia*** from eastern North America, is a useful plant for coastal areas as it tolerates salt spray. It forms a large bush with attractive grey-green leaves and in autumn bears large heads to 15 cm (6 in.) across of small white flowers followed by fluffy, silvery fruits. Cut back in early spring to maintain bushiness. Size: to 4 × 4 m (12 × 12 ft.). Zone 5.

↑ *Ballota pseudodictamnus*

Ballota (Lamiaceae)

Most of the species of this genus are herbaceous plants but ***Ballota pseudodictamnus*** ♕ from the eastern Mediterranean is a small evergreen shrub with yellowish green, almost round leaves

3 cm (1½ in.) across covered, like the stems, with greyish white felted hairs. Usually grown for its foliage, the whorls of pale pink, 2-lipped flowers are also attractive. These are enclosed in large green calyces at the ends of the shoots in early summer. Grow in full sun and dry soil. Cut back in spring to encourage new growth and to keep the plant compact. Size: 45 × 60 cm (1½ × 2 ft.). Zone 8.

Berberidopsis (Flacourtiaceae)

coral plant

Berberidopsis corallina from Chile, the only species in this genus of evergreen climbers, is very rare in its native country. It is, however, cultivated as an unusual plant grown for its dark crimson-red flowers over 1 cm (½ in.) across, hanging on slender red flower stalks from the underside of the branches in late summer. The leaves are dark green and leathery with spines around the margins. Grow in a sheltered position against a wall in part shade in a moist, lime-free soil. It does not respond well to the overuse of fertilizer. Prune in spring if it becomes too large. Height: 4–6 m (12–18 ft.). Zone 8.

Berberis (Berberidaceae) barberry

This is an enormous genus of shrubs with spiny stems and often spiny leaf margins as well. Like *Mahonia*, the wood and roots are bright yellow. The yellow or orange flowers, up to 1 cm (½ in.) across in clusters or short racemes in spring, attract bees, and the red or black berries are eaten by birds. The evergreen species have leathery foliage while many of the deciduous ones display good autumn colour. A choice can be made from many species and hundreds of cultivars and hybrids which have been raised and named. Many will make effective hedges with spines which could deter intruders. Grow in most soils in sun or partial shade. Prune after flowering, unless fruits are required, and clip hedges in summer. A small selection has been included below to illustrate the wide range of characteristics of this very versatile shrub.

Berberis darwinii 🏆 from Chile and Argentina is a very popular evergreen species bearing drooping clusters of orange flowers over a long period from mid to late spring. The round autumn fruits are blue-black about 6 mm (¼ in.) across. Size: 3 × 3 m (10 × 10 ft.). Zone 7.

***Berberis* 'Goldilocks'** is a vigorous and upright evergreen with glossy leaves. It is magnificent in flower with freely borne clusters of golden-yellow flowers on red stalks in mid to late spring, followed by spherical blue-black fruits 6 mm (¼ in.) across. In smaller spaces, it tolerates regular hard pruning. Size: 4 × 3 m (12 × 10 ft.). Zone 7.

Berberis* ×*stenophylla 🏆 has proved to be a reliable evergreen with arching branches bearing clusters of bright yellow flowers in midspring and blue-black fruits in autumn. This is good for hedging reaching 2.5 m (8 ft.) in height, or for covering a bank. A number of cultivars have been named including 'Corallina Compacta' 🏆 with coral-red buds opening to yellow flowers, or 'Etna' with bright orange flowers barely reaching 30 cm (1 ft.) in height. Zone 5.

Berberis thunbergii 🏆 from Japan is one of the deciduous species usually grown for its brilliant orange and red autumn foliage and glossy red fruits 8 mm (1/4 in.) long. The unusual, pale yellow, red-tinged, spring flowers are less showy. This plant is very useful for hedging and many cultivars are grown. 'Atropurpurea Nana' ♕ (synonym 'Crimson Pygmy') is a dwarf plant to 60 × 75 cm (2 × 2 1/2 ft.) with dark reddish purple summer foliage turning red in autumn. 'Aurea' to about 1 m (3 ft.) tall has bright yellow foliage becoming green by late summer. 'Golden Ring' ♕ with reddish purple leaves narrowly margined with gold, turning red in autumn and 'Pink Queen' with reddish purple foliage flecked with pink and creamy white are similar in height, growing to about 1 m (3 ft.) tall. 'Green Carpet' to 1 m (3 ft.) tall is ideal as a fresh green ground cover shrub changing to red in autumn. Zone 4.

↑ *Berberis thunbergii* 'Golden Ring'

Betula (Betulaceae) birch

There are many birch species, mainly tall deciduous trees, often with coloured peeling bark providing winter interest. Many have good yellow autumn colour, the early pendulous male catkins are attractive and the seeds provide food for birds. Most are fast growing but are usually graceful with neither a wide nor a dense canopy allowing other plants to thrive underneath. Regular pruning is not necessary.

Betula pendula ♕ (synonym *B. verrucosa*; silver birch, European white birch) from Europe and northern Asia is a fast-growing tree with peeling white bark, but 'Laciniata' ♕ (synonym 'Dalecarlica'; Swedish birch) is a more narrow tree with graceful weeping branches and deeply cut leaves. Size: 15 × 8 m (50 × 25 ft.). Zone 2.

Betula utilis (Himalayan birch) from the Himalayas has bark which may be pinkish or coppery brown while var. *jacquemontii* (synonym *B. jacquemontii*) has white bark. In early spring, before the leaves unfold, the very long, yellow-brown catkins to 13 cm (5 in. long) are an added feature. 'Silver Shadow' ♕ has exceptionally white bark and slightly larger, darker green leaves. Size: 18 × 10 m (55 × 30 ft.). Zone 7.

Brachyglottis synonym *Senecio* (Asteraceae)

A large group of evergreen shrubs from New Zealand and Tasmania grown both for their foliage and daisy-like flowers. They prefer full sun and are useful plants for coastal situations as they are wind tolerant. The larger species

↑ *Brachyglottis* 'Sunshine'

can be used for informal hedges or windbreaks. Prune in spring after the last frost if the plants become straggly.

Brachyglottis monroi 🏆 (synonym *Senecio monroi*) is a small shrub with thick, dark green leaves to 4 cm (1 ½ in.) long felted white underneath and tightly undulate around the margins. In summer, the yellow flowers to 2 cm (¾ in.) across are borne in dense heads. Size: 1 × 2 m (3 × 6 ft.). Zone 8.

***Brachyglottis* 'Sunshine'** 🏆 is larger with bolder, silvery grey leaves to 7.5 cm (3 in.) long without an undulate margin, and in summer, it is covered with larger yellow daisies to 3 cm (1 ½ in.) across. This plant has been grown incorrectly in gardens as *Senecio greyi*. Size: 1.5 × 2 m (5 × 6 ft.). Zone 8.

Buddleja synonym *Buddleia*
(Buddlejaceae) butterfly bush

This is a large genus and many species are popular free-flowering shrubs cultivated for their masses of tiny, colourful, usually fragrant flowers grouped into large clusters or dense conical panicles, which are especially attractive to butterflies and other insects. Most are not fussy in their requirements growing quickly in sunny positions in most soils, although a fertile soil is preferable. Some species are more tender and require very sheltered positions or even greenhouse conditions. The species listed below are all quite hardy. Prune *Buddleja davidii*, *B. globosa* and *B.* ×*weyeriana* hard in early spring but other species mentioned after flowering, only if necessary.

Buddleja alternifolia 🏆 from China is a very graceful, hardy, deciduous shrub with pendulous branches wreathed in early summer with round clusters of lilac flowers. It is very effective and easily trained into a small pendulous tree by removing the lower branches to create a single stem. Size: 4 × 4 m (12 × 12 ft.). Zone 5.

Buddleja davidii from China and Japan is probably the best known and popular species. The fragrant pale purple flowers with a tiny orange eye are borne in spectacular, dense, conical inflorescences reaching 30 cm (1 ft.) long. The species itself seeds with ease and has become naturalised in many wasteland areas. The cultivars are fast growing but can be grown in a border and pruned hard each year with the new growth reaching 2 m (6 ft.) again in a season. A selection can be made from over 50 different cultivars with a range of colours. 'Black Knight' 🏆 has deep purple flowers, while 'Empire Blue' 🏆 has violet-blue and 'Nanho Blue' 🏆 pale blue flowers. 'Dartmoor' 🏆 has reddish purple flowers unusually in a large branched inflorescence. 'Royal Red' 🏆 has dark purplish red flowers and 'Harlequin' is similar but with cream-margined leaves. *Buddleja* 'Pink Delight' 🏆 has pink flowers while *B. davidii* 'White Profusion' 🏆 has white flowers. Size: 3 × 5 m (10 × 15 ft.) if unpruned. Zone 5.

Buddleja globosa 🏆 (orange ball tree) from the South American Andes has dense balls to 2 cm (¾ in.) across of golden-orange flowers in early summer. It is vigorous and needs to be kept cut back in smaller spaces. Size: 5 × 5 m (15 × 15 ft.). Zone 7.

Buddleja lindleyana from China is less common in cultivation. It has dark green leaves and slender, curved heads to 20 cm (8 in.) long of dark violet flowers in summer. Size: 2 × 2 m (6 × 6 ft.). Zone 8.

Buddleja ×weyeriana has flowers tinged with mauve in loose clusters over a long period and is one of the most attractive to butterflies. 'Sungold' 🏆 has deep orange-yellow flowers whereas those of 'Moonlight' are creamy yellow. Size: 4 × 3 m (12 × 10 ft.). Zone 6.

Bupleurum (Apiaceae)

From this genus of herbaceous and woody plants, ***Bupleurum fruticosum*** (shrubby hare's ear) from southern Europe is a hardy, dense, evergreen shrub especially useful for difficult or coastal situations in any soil. The narrow, blue-green leaves to about 7.5 cm (3 in.) long contrast with the purplish brown young shoots and yellow flowers in umbels about 7.5 cm (3 in.) across produced through the summer. Grow in sun. Prune if required in late spring. Size: 2 × 2.5 m (6 × 8 ft.). Zone 8.

Buxus (Buxaceae) box, boxwood

Numerous species of these evergreen trees and shrubs grow in many parts of the world but only two are commonly found in temperate gardens. These are slow growing succeeding in sun or shade. As they adapt very well to clipping they are frequently used for hedging or

← *Buddleja globosa*

↑ *Callicarpa bodinieri* var. *giraldii* 'Profusion'

topiary as well as specimen plants. The dense, small, glossy, leathery leaves make box a very good choice for dwarf hedges in formal gardens and parterres. The small, yellowish green spring flowers, while not showy, do attract bees. Clip hedges in summer.

Buxus microphylla (small-leaved box), a dwarf, slow-growing, dense, rounded shrub of uncertain origin but introduced into western gardens from Japan, is seen less frequently than *B. sempervirens* ♕, but some of the smallest cultivars, such as *B. microphylla* 'Compacta' with tiny leaves, barely reach 30 cm (1 ft.) tall and can be used in a container. Size: not exceeding 1 × 1.5 m (3 × 5 ft.). Zone 6.

Buxus sempervirens ♕ (common box) grows wild in Europe, North Africa and western Asia. Naturally it is a shrub or small tree to about 5 × 5 m (15 × 15 ft.) but can be clipped to almost any shape or size required. The leaves of the typical plants are dark green to 3 cm (1½ in.) long but a large number of cultivars are available differing in their leaf size, shape and colour. 'Elegantissima' ♕ reaching 1.5 m (5 ft.) tall has narrow leaves to 2 cm (¾ in.) long, margined with white. 'Handsworthiensis' is a more vigorous shrub used for tall hedges with dark green leaves to 4 cm (1½ in.). 'Latifolia Maculata' ♕ has broad, bright yellow leaves which turn green blotched with yellow. Zone 5.

Callicarpa (Verbenaceae) beauty berry

A large genus of mainly tropical, evergreen and deciduous, woodland trees and shrubs, a very few of which are grown for their flowers and spherical berries. Grow in a border in sun or partial shade. Prune in early spring as required.

Callicarpa bodinieri* var. *giraldii from China is usually seen in gardens as the cultivar 'Profusion' ♕. This is a deciduous shrub with clusters to 3 cm (1½ in.) across of small pale pink flowers in summer followed by striking, long-lasting, deep violet fruits to 4 mm (1/8 in.) across. The young leaves are bronze. Size: 2.5 × 2 m (8 × 6 ft.). Zone 6.

Callistemon (Myrtaceae) bottlebrush

A genus of evergreen trees and shrubs from Australia grown for their flowers. The leaves are stiff and leathery, often lanceolate and the bottlebrush-like heads of flowers are composed of numerous long colourful stamens produced from late spring to summer. Several are hardy enough to grow in temperate gardens. Grow in a lime-free soil in sun. Trim after flowering and cut back hard if shrubs become too large.

***Callistemon citrinus* 'Splendens'** 🏆 (crimson bottle brush) has loose, somewhat pendulous branches with slightly lemon-scented leaves tinged pink as they unfold. The flowers are crimson. Size: 2 × 2 m (6 × 6 ft.). Zones 8–9.

Callistemon salignus 🏆 (white bottle brush) has pale yellow flowers. Size: 2.5 × 2.5 m (8 × 8 ft.). Zones 8–9.

Callistemon viminalis is similar to *C. citrinus* 'Splendens' but with a more weeping habit.

Calluna (Ericaceae) heather, ling

Calluna vulgaris, which grows across Europe to Siberia, is the only species in this genus. This dwarf evergreen shrub is usually grown for its flowers from midsummer to early winter, attracting both insects and butterflies. The leaves, coloured in some cultivars, are very small and scalelike, overlapping and pressed against the stems. The bell-shaped, red, pink, purple or white flowers with sepals and petals of a similar colour are borne in racemes to about 10 cm (4 in.) tall. Hundreds of cultivars vary in leaf and flower colour, size and time of flowering, a few of which are mentioned here. A specialist heather nursery will have a wide selection. Heathers may be grown singly but are more effective planted in groups. Grow in a lime-free soil in sun. Trim old flowering shoots after flowering. Size (depending on the cultivar): about 40 × 20 cm (16 × 8 in.). Zone 4.

'Beoley Gold' 🏆 with yellow foliage, has white flowers in midseason. 'County Wicklow' 🏆 is low-growing with double, clear pink flowers. 'Dark Star' 🏆 has late, double, crimson flowers with dark green foliage. 'Firefly' 🏆 has orange to red foliage in winter and deep pinkish purple flowers in midseason. 'Sir John Charrington' 🏆 has early pale pink flowers with red-tinged winter foliage.

Camellia (Theaceae)

A very large genus of evergreen shrubs grown for their large, thick-petalled and saucer- or bowl-shaped flowers. The leaves are leathery and glossy. Tea is produced from the tips of the shoots of *Camellia sinensis* but this species is not cultivated as an ornamental. Although most of the species are hardy, late frost can damage early flowers, so in frost-prone areas, plants are best sited facing west or north so that the morning sun does not catch them while still frosted. If the plants become too dry in summer, the developing flower buds may drop before opening. Smaller cultivars will adapt to growing in a

↑ *Camellia × williamsii* 'J. C. Williams'

container. Grow in a lime-free soil, preferably in dappled shade, or in sun as long as the roots do not dry out. Prune after flowering if necessary, dead head if practical and prune hard if the shrubs become too large. Many cultivars and hybrids have been raised from the relatively few species which have been cultivated over the years in the Far East and Europe. The flowers range in colour through white and all shades of pink to red and may be single, semi-double or double, sometimes with a very regular and formal pattern of overlapping petals. Thousands of cultivars have been named, some of which are barely distinguishable, but a specialist or local nursery will be able to advise on suitable cultivars for the area.

Camellia japonica from Japan and China is perhaps the most common species and the origin of many cultivars. 'Adolphe Audusson' 🏆 has scarlet-red, semi-double flowers to 10 cm (4 in.) across with showy central stamens. 'Nobilissima' has very early, double white flowers 9 cm (3½ in.) across. 'Tricolor' 🏆 has semi-double pink, white and red streaked flowers to 9 cm (3½ in.) across. Size: eventually to 4 × 3 m (12 × 10 ft.). Zone 8.

Camellia × williamsii has resulted in numerous free-flowering cultivars, the first flowering in early winter and others right up until late spring. 'Donation' 🏆, very reliable and one of the most popular cultivars, has large semi-double flowers to 10 cm (4 in.) or more across coloured a brilliant pink. 'Francis Hanger' has single white flowers to 9 cm (3½ in.) across. 'J. C. Williams'

♀, the first hybrid, named for its raiser, has single delicate pink flowers to 9 cm (3 ½ in.) across. Size: 4 × 3 m (12 × 10 ft.). Zone 8.

Campsis (Bignoniaceae) trumpet creeper, trumpet vine

A genus of deciduous woody plants which climb by aerial roots and are grown on a trellis, fence or wall for their impressive coloured flowers. The flowers in large panicles, have a narrow tube to 7.5 cm (3 in.) long, flaring at the mouth, from late summer into autumn. The leaves are pinnate with up to 11 leaflets. Keep under control as they are very vigorous. Tie up the stems initially until the plant is established. Grow in a sunny position. Prune hard in early spring.

↓ *Campsis radicans*

Campsis radicans from southeastern USA has orange and scarlet flowers. The hybrid *C.* ×*tagliabuana* 'Madame Galen' ♀ has salmon-red flowers. Height: 10 m (30 ft.). Zone 8.

Cantua (Polemoniaceae)

A small genus mainly of evergreen shrubs of which ***Cantua buxifolia*** (sacred flower of the Incas) from the Andes is grown for its flowers. It is a small, semi-evergreen shrub with arching branches which have pendulous, tubular, deep rose-pink flowers to 5 cm (2 in.) long in spring. The leaves are small to about 5 cm (2 in.) long. Grow in sun, trained against a warm wall, and support any scandent branches. Trim after flowering if necessary. Size: 2 × 1.5 m (6 × 5 ft.). Zone 9.

Carpenteria (Hydrangeaceae) tree anemone

Carpenteria californica ♀ from California is the only species in this genus. It is an evergreen shrub with large, white, open, poppy-like flowers to 8 cm (3 in.) across with a central mass of yellow stamens, covering the shrub in midsummer. The narrow, leathery, dark green leaves reach 13 cm (5 in.) long. Grow in a soil which is not too dry, in sun, preferably against a warm wall. Trim after flowering if needed. Size: 2 × 2 m (6 × 6 ft.). Zone 8.

Carpinus (Betulaceae) hornbeam

The majority of the species in this genus are very large deciduous trees but ***Carpinus betulus*** from Europe and western Asia is often used as a hedge with good yellow autumn foliage. The weeping form 'Pendula' makes a small tree which can be as little as 2.5 m (8 ft.) tall. The leader should be trained up a cane until it reaches the required height and then allowed to weep. The fruits are in pendulous clusters somewhat like hop. Grow in sun or partial shade. Prune hedges in late summer. Zone 5.

Caryopteris (Verbenaceae)

A genus of small deciduous shrubs and perennial plants from eastern Asia grown for their mainly blue flowers which are especially attractive to bees and butterflies. The leaves are aromatic and the small flowers formed in late summer are 2-lipped with a fringed lower lip to 8 mm (¼ in.) across and borne in clusters. Grow in a sunny position. Cut back the old flowering branches in early spring. If the plant becomes straggly, prune back quite near to the base.

Caryopteris* ×*clandonensis is the source of the majority of cultivars grown in gardens. The leaves are bluish green, whiter on the underside, to 5 cm (2 in.) long and irregularly toothed. The mid-blue flowers are in clusters towards the top of the stems. 'First Choice' 🏆 is one of the darkest blue-flowered cultivars. 'Heavenly Baby' 🏆 is a new and rare cultivar with a dwarf habit, mid blue flowers and very silvery foliage. 'Summer Sorbet' 🏆 has mid blue flowers and striking gold-margined leaves. 'Worcester Gold' 🏆 has mid blue flowers and yellow foliage becoming greener as the summer progresses. Size: 90 × 90 cm (3 × 3 ft.). Zone 7.

↑ *Caryopteris* ×*clandonensis* 'First Choice'

Caryopteris incana from China and Japan, useful as a cut flower, has mid-blue flowers in many dense whorls towards the tops of the stems. The leaves are broader with regular blunt teeth. Some clones are hardier than others and white- and pink-flowered forms are gradually becoming available. 'Blue Cascade' has a weeping habit and is hardier. Size: 90 × 90 cm (3 × 3 ft.). Zones 6–8.

Catalpa (Bignoniaceae)

A small genus of deciduous trees grown for their flowers which attract bees, their bold foliage as well as for their very long pendulous seed pods. Most are large and wide spreading trees, and, although the foxglove-like white flowers are very striking, the trees would quickly become overpowering in a small garden. However, the yellow-leaved form ***Catalpa bignonioides* 'Aurea'** ♀ (Indian bean tree) from eastern USA has large, soft, velvety, yellow leaves and can be coppiced each year to create a striking foliage shrub for a border, even though it will not flower. The leaves are heart-shaped and may reach 25 cm (10 in.) long. *Catalpa* ×*erubescens* 'Purpurea' ♀ with dark purple leaves can be treated in the same way. Grow in sun but protect young growth from wind and late frosts. Coppice by cutting almost to the ground in early spring. Size: 15 × 15 m (50 × 50 ft.) or more unless coppiced. Zone 5.

↑ *Ceanothus* 'Dark Star'

Ceanothus (Rhamnaceae)

Californian lilac

A genus of evergreen and deciduous shrubs from western North America grown for their mainly blue flowers which encourage bees. They are useful in a border and maritime conditions, and in colder areas could be grown against a warm wall. Some are more prostrate and suitable as ground cover, perhaps over a bank. All have tiny flowers to about 4 mm (1/8 in.) across, borne in tightly packed clusters from late spring to summer. There are many species and cultivars from which to choose, in different shades of blue and a few with pink or white flowers. Grow in a sunny position on all but very alkaline soils. Prune evergreen species after flowering if required and deciduous species in early spring.

***Ceanothus* 'Concha'** ♀ has arching branches and dark green leaves to 2 cm (3/4 in.) long. The flower buds are dark reddish in colour and open to dark blue flowers in rounded clusters to 3 cm (1 1/2 in.) across. Size: 3 × 3 m (10 × 10 ft.). Zone 8.

Ceanothus 'Dark Star' 🏆 is similar but slightly smaller, flowering earlier with purplish blue flowers.

***Ceanothus ×delileanus* 'Gloire de Versailles'** 🏆 is a deciduous shrub with large panicles of pale blue flowers to 10 cm (4 in.) long from summer to early autumn. The leaves are ovate to 7 cm (3 in.) long. *Ceanothus ×pallidus* 'Perle Rose' is similar but with bright pink flowers. Size: 2.5 × 2.5 m (8 × 8 ft.) but should be cut back each year. Zone 7.

***Ceanothus* 'Puget Blue'** 🏆 is a dense evergreen shrub with small leaves to 2 cm (¾ in.) long and quite dark blue flowers in rounded clusters to 2.5 cm (1 in.) across, from late spring. Size: 3 × 3 m (10 × 10 ft.). Zone 8.

Ceanothus thyrsiflorus* var. *repens 🏆 is a low-growing evergreen shrub forming a mound which is covered with large clusters to 7.5 cm (3 in.) across of bright blue flowers in early summer. Size: 1 × 2 m (3 × 6 ft.). Zone 8.

Celastrus (Celastraceae)

A genus of mainly deciduous shrubs and climbers grown for their colourful fruits.
Grow in full sun. Prune in late winter to keep within the allocated space.

Celastrus orbiculatus (oriental bittersweet) from eastern Asia is a vigorous, twining climber with rounded leaves to 10 cm (4 in.) long turning yellow in autumn. The insignificant greenish yellow flowers may be male or female but to ensure fruiting grow the more reliable hermaphrodite form *C. orbiculatus* Hermaphrodite Group 🏆. In autumn, the orange-brown fruits split to expose scarlet seeds which last well into the winter. Height: 10 m (30 ft.). Zone 4.

Ceratostigma (Plumbaginaceae)

A small genus of evergreen and deciduous shrubs and herbaceous plants grown for their long-lasting flowers. The blue flowers have long tubes which open out into flat, 5-petalled flowers. Grow in a light, well-drained soil in sun. Trim the old flowering shoots in spring.

Ceratostigma willmottianum 🏆 from China is a deciduous spreading shrub with lanceolate leaves becoming red in autumn. The flowers, bright blue to about 2.5 cm (1 in.) across, cluster at the ends of the stems from summer to autumn. DESERT SKIES 'Palmgold' has bright yellow leaves. FOREST BLUE 'Lice' is a free-flowering, compact shrub. Size: 1 × 1.5 m (3 × 5 ft.). Zone 7.

Cercidiphyllum (Cercidiphyllaceae)

katsura tree

A genus of deciduous woodland trees grown for their spring and autumn foliage. The flowers are small, red and insignificant. Although quite hardy, late frosts may damage young foliage. Grow in a lime-free soil in sun or partial shade. Prune in late winter if required.

Cercidiphyllum japonicum* f. *pendulum 🏆 from eastern Asia is a very elegant, weeping tree with long pendulous branches. The heart-shaped leaves about 10 cm (4 in.) across are bronze coloured as they unfold in spring. In autumn, they turn to yellow, orange and red, and when fallen and crushed, have a very distinctive smell of caramel or burnt sugar. The species itself is also attractive but becomes a much larger tree. Size: 10 × 10 m (30 × 30 ft.). Zone 5.

↑ *Cercis siliquastrum*

Cercis (Papilionaceae)

A small genus of deciduous trees grown for their flowers and foliage. The pea-like flowers, which attract bees, grow in stalkless clusters on both older and younger shoots before the leaves emerge in late spring. The leaves are heart-shaped. Grow in a good fertile soil in sun. Once planted avoid transplanting. Prune in late winter if necessary to remove weak or dead branches. **'Forest Pansy'** ♈, a cultivar of ***Cercis canadensis*** (eastern redbud) from North America, is grown for the dark reddish purple leaves to 10 cm (4 in.) long. The flowers are less conspicuous. Once established, this cultivar can be pruned back near to the ground each spring to encourage large new foliage each season while keeping the plant as a relatively small shrub. 'Appalachian Red' is a new cultivar with glistening pink flowers and may be treated in the same way. Size: 5 × 5 m (15 × 15 ft.) unless coppiced. Zone 4.

Cercis siliquastrum ♈ (Judas tree) from southern Europe has deep rose-pink flowers to 2 cm (¾ in.) across. Size: 10 × 10 m (30 × 30 ft.). Zone 7.

Cestrum (Solanaceae)

A large genus of evergreen and deciduous shrubs grown for their flowers. The foliage is not always pleasantly scented but the colourful, tubular or funnel-shaped flowers are often fragrant. None are reliably hardy but several grow in sheltered areas or against a warm wall and others may be kept outside in a container and given protection in winter. Grow in sun or partial shade. Cut back old flowering shoots to the base in early spring.

Cestrum parqui ♈ (willow-leaved jessamine) from Chile is an erect deciduous shrub which has greenish yellow, tubular, night-scented flowers to 2.5 cm (1 in.) long with 5 spreading petals at the mouth flowering from summer into autumn. The narrow leaves reach 13 cm (5 in.) long. In colder areas, it may behave as a herbaceous perennial dying down in winter and re-emerging the following spring. Size: 2 × 2 m (6 × 6 ft.). Zones 8–9.

↑ *Cestrum parqui*

Chaenomeles (Rosaceae) flowering quince, Japanese quince, japonica

A small genus of deciduous, usually spiny shrubs, grown for their flowers formed before the leaves unfold in spring. The flowers resemble large apple blossoms to 5 cm (2 in.) across. The rounded, aromatic, green to yellow fruits, to 6 cm (2 ½ in.) across, are sometimes produced in abundance and may be used in preserves in the same way as quinces. Although they will tolerate partial shade, grow in sun for the most prolific flowering and fruiting. Prune after flowering. Size (depending on the cultivar): 1 × 2 m (3 × 6 ft.). Zone 5.

Chaenomeles speciosa from China has cultivars including 'Moerloosei' 🏆 (synonym 'Apple Blossom') with pale pink and white flowers. 'Geisha Girl' 🏆 is a smaller plant with double, peach-pink flowers and 'Phylis Moore' has semi-double pink flowers. 'Simonii' has double, deep red flowers with prominent golden anthers.

Chaenomeles ×superba is a hybrid which includes several important cultivars. 'Jet Trail' has pure white flowers and a spreading habit while *C.* 'Toyo-nishiki' is a new and unusual Japanese cultivar with reddish pink, pink and white flowers on the same plant.

Chimonanthus (Calycanthaceae) wintersweet

A small genus of deciduous shrubs grown for their sweetly scented flowers in late winter and early spring of which ***Chimonanthus praecox*** (synonym *C. fragrans*) from China is the only cultivated species. The flowers to 2.5 cm (1 in.) across are bowl-shaped with many waxy, almost translucent, narrow, pale yellow petals produced in hanging pairs on very short stalks before the leaves open. This shrub flowers well if trained against a south-facing wall. Prune immediately after flowering, removing any long vegetative shoots. Size: 4 × 3 m (12 × 10 ft.) unless trained against a wall. Zone 7.

Choisya (Rutaceae)

A genus of evergreen shrubs grown for their sweetly scented flowers and aromatic foliage. It has palmate leaves with 3–5 leaflets and clusters of star-like, 5-petalled flowers. Grow in a sunny position. Lightly prune after flowering if needed.

↑ *Choisya* GOLDFINGERS 'Limo'

***Choisya* 'Aztec Pearl'** ♕ has leaves with 3–5 very narrow leaflets and the buds and flowers to 3 cm (1 ½ in.) across are slightly flushed with pink. GOLDFINGERS 'Limo' is a recent cultivar similar to 'Aztec Pearl' but with yellow leaves. There are several other new cultivars to look out for which should be reaching the market in a few years. Size: 2 × 2 m (6 × 6 ft.). Zone 7.

Choisya ternata ♕ (Mexican orange blossom) from Mexico and southern USA has dark green leaves with 3 broad leaflets. The white flowers to 2.5 cm (1 in.) across appear in late spring and early summer with a second flush in late summer and early autumn. SUNDANCE 'Lich' ♕ has bright golden-yellow leaves when grown in full sun and greenish yellow leaves in partial shade. It does not flower freely and is slightly smaller. Size: 2.5 × 2.5 m (8 × 8 ft.). Zone 7.

Cistus (Cistaceae) sun rose

A genus of evergreen shrubs from southern Europe grown for their flowers and aromatic foliage. The individual 5-petalled flowers open to reveal a central mass of showy yellow stamens. Each is short lived but new ones unfold each day through the summer. Grow in light, very well-drained soil in full sun. Do not prune hard but pinch out the growing shoots after flowering to encourage bushier plants.

↑ *Cistus ladanifer*

Cistus ladanifer ♕ is an erect shrub with very viscid dark green leaves to 10 cm (4 in.) long. The large flowers to 10 cm (4 in.) across are pure white and have a deep red blotch at the base of the petals. 'Blanche' has pure white flowers. Size: 1.5 × 1.5 m (5 × 5 ft.). Zone 7.

***Cistus* ×*pulverulentus* 'Sunset'** is a low-growing shrub with grey-green leaves and bright magenta-pink flowers to 5 cm (2 in.) across. Size: 50 × 90 cm (1 ½ × 3 ft.). Zone 8.

Cistus ×purpureus ♀ is an upright shrub with sticky red shoots and oblong undulate-margined leaves to 5 cm (2 in.) long. The flowers are large to 7 cm (3 in.) across, pinkish crimson with a dark maroon blotch at the base of each slightly crumpled petal. *Cistus salviifolius* is similar in size and habit to *C. ×pulverulentus* 'Sunset' but with yellow-centred white flowers. Size: 1 × 1 m (3 × 3 ft.). Zone 7.

Clematis (Ranunculaceae)

A genus of more than 20 species of mainly deciduous climbers, found growing wild in almost all parts of the world: plants climb by twining the leaf stalks around a support. There are also a few herbaceous perennial and some evergreen climbing species. Clematis are cultivated for their flowers which vary in shape from saucer-, bell- and star-shaped to tubular. There are species flowering in every season of the year in colours including white, blue, purple, yellow and red. A few are scented and almost all have attractive feathery seed heads. Most are hardy but some need more protection. A lot of breeding is being undertaken to create clematis for a wide range of situations and it is worth looking for these newer cultivars of different sizes and vigour, created for containers and growing in smaller spaces, on patios or even as house plants.

For clematis flowering in all seasons, these are a few examples. In winter, *Clematis cirrhosa* var. *balearica* bears creamy white bell-shaped flowers, some spotted with deep purplish red, to 4 cm (1½ in.) or more across. In early spring, *C. armandii*, one of the evergreen and slightly more tender species, has sprays of white or very pale pink, scented, star-shaped flowers to 5 cm (2 in.) across. Later in spring, *C. alpina* and *C. macropetala* and their many cultivars open with large sepals and many with smaller petal-like stamens, sometimes in a different colour, in the centre of the flower giving it a double appearance; flowers are 5 cm (2 in.) or more across, in white, pink and shades of blue and bluish purple. Early in summer, the very vigorous *C. montana* and its cultivars are covered with single flowers to 8 cm (3 in.) across in shades of

↑ *Clematis cirrhosa* var. *balearica*

pink and white. Later, the larger-flowered hybrids with flowers as much as 15 cm (6 in.) or more in diameter, in a whole range of colours, some striped, both single and double begin to open. In late summer, *C. viticella* and its cultivars have deeper purple and purplish red open bell-shaped flowers. Also in late summer and early autumn, *C. tibetana* subsp. *vernayi* (synonym *C. orientalis*) and its relatives bear hanging bell-shaped flowers with 4 thick yellow sepals to 4 cm (1 ½ in.) long which are followed by exceptionally silvery seed heads lasting for many weeks.

Grow in fertile, well-drained soil but one which is neither heavy and wet nor too dry, in sun or partial shade. Winter- and spring-flowering plants which produce their flowers on the older shoots generally need pruning after flowering, simply to restrict their growth. Prune the later summer- and autumn-flowering plants, which flower on the current season's growth and tend to be more vigorous, harder in late winter.

Clerodendrum (Verbenaceae)

A very large and variable but mainly tropical genus of evergreen and deciduous trees, shrubs and climbers of which one or two hardy species are grown for their flowers and fruits in a border. Grow in fertile soil in sun. Prune in late winter or early spring.

Clerodendrum bungei (synonym *C. foetidum*) from China is a deciduous suckering shrub with deep, strongly scented, purplish pink flowers in large clusters to 15 cm (6 in.) across in late summer and early autumn. The leaves have an unpleasant smell if crushed. It can be pruned back almost to ground level in spring to allow the new, deep reddish black stems to regrow. Size: 2 × 2 m (6 × 6 ft.) if regularly cut back. Zone 8.

Clethra (Clethraceae)

A genus of evergreen and deciduous woodland trees and shrubs grown for their flowers. The scented, white, bell-shaped flowers are borne in racemes at the end of the branches. Grow in a lime-free soil in partial shade. Prune in late winter or early spring.

Clethra alnifolia (sweet pepper bush) from the USA is a deciduous shrub with white, bell-shaped flowers about 1 cm (½ in.) across in erect racemes to 15 cm (6 in.) long appearing in late summer. While 'Hummingbird' is a smaller plant, 'Paniculata' 🏆 is more floriferous. 'Ruby Spice' is a more recent cultivar with rich pink flowers. Size: 2 × 2 m (6 × 6 ft.). Zone 3.

Clianthus (Papilionaceae)

A small genus of two evergreen, scrambling shrubs grown for their curious and brightly coloured flowers. The leaves are pinnate and the large showy flowers can be best described as clawlike. Grow in sun in a sheltered position. Trim if required after flowering.

Clianthus puniceus 🏆 (glory pea, lobster claw, parrot's bill) from New Zealand is the hardier species and if cut down by frost will often grow again in the spring. It is a scrambling plant best trained against a warm wall. The leaves to 15 cm (6 in.) long have up to 25 leaflets. From spring to early summer, the brilliant scarlet flowers to 7.5

↑ *Clianthus puniceus*

↑ *Colletia paradoxa*

cm (3 in.) long are borne in pendulous racemes to 15 cm (6 in.) long. Size: 4 × 3 m (12 × 10 ft.) if trained against a wall. Zones 8–9.

Colletia (Rhamnaceae)

A genus of deciduous shrubs grown for their flowers and as a curiosity. The green branches are modified and cylindrical or flattened but the leaves are minute or absent. They are, however, very spiny plants which would make a good deterrent to intruders. The small, white, scented flowers develop on the adapted stems in late summer and early autumn. Grow in a sunny position. Prune in late winter or early spring as necessary.

Colletia paradoxa (synonym *C. cruciata*) from Brazil and Uruguay is a rather slow-growing but strange plant in which the stems are flattened into blue-green, opposite, triangular structures to 4 cm (1½ in.) ending in strong spines. The bell-shaped flowers, about 4 mm (⅛ in.) across, are borne just below the spines and attract autumn flying insects. Size: 3 × 3 m (10 × 10 ft.). Zone 8.

Colquhounia (Lamiaceae)

Colquhounia coccinea from western China and the Himalayas is the only commonly cultivated species of this small genus of evergreen shrubs grown for their impressive, tubular, 2-lipped flowers. The scarlet to orange flowers to 2.5 cm (1 in.) long are arranged in whorls in spikes to 15 cm (6 in.) in late summer or early autumn. The ovate leaves are aromatic and hairy to 15 cm (6 in.) long. Even if it dies back after a cold winter, it will usually grow up again the following spring. A mulch will help to protect the plant. Grow in poor soils as long as it is in full sun and protected from cold winds. Cut back in early spring to the previous year's growth. Size: 2.5 × 2.5 m (8 × 8 ft.). Zone 8.

Convolvulus **(Convolvulaceae)**

A large genus of mainly evergreen and deciduous herbaceous plants and climbers, several of which can become invasive weeds. However, ***Convolvulus cneorum*** ♈ from southern Europe is one of the few small shrubs and is grown for its silvery foliage and beautiful large flowers which appear over a long period from late spring to summer. The narrow leaves reach 6 cm (2½ in.) long and the pink coloured buds open to pure white funnel-shaped flowers to 4 cm (1½ in.) across. This plant can be grown in a container and protected over winter in cooler areas. Grow in a sunny position. Trim after flowering. Size: 60 × 90 cm (2 × 3 ft.). Zone 8.

↓ *Cornus sanguinea* 'Midwinter Fire'

Cornus **(Cornaceae)** dogwood

A genus of mainly deciduous trees and shrubs grown for their flowers, fruits and autumn foliage. Some species also have coloured stems and are coppiced for their winter effect, especially if grown in a group. The individual flowers are small and often insignificant but are clustered in tight heads which in the flowering dogwoods are surrounded by large and showy bracts. Grow in sun or partial shade. The flowering dogwoods prefer a richer lime-free soil and those grown for their stem effect are best in full sun. Prune in late winter if necessary and coppice those with coloured stems by cutting to within 15 cm (6 in.) of the ground in early spring annually or every other year.

The flowering dogwoods are large shrubs and include ***Cornus*** **'Eddie's White Wonder'** ♈, a very floriferous example with 4–6 long-lasting, large, white, petal-like bracts to 7.5 cm (3 in.) long surrounding the tight head of tiny flowers in spring. In autumn, the leaves turn to dazzling shades of orange and red. 'Satomi' ♈ with rich pink bracts is a cultivar of *Cornus kousa* from Japan and Korea, while *C.* STELLAR PINK 'Rutgan' with pink bracts is a newer hardier hybrid which is resistant to the disease which can affect several dogwoods. Size: to 5 × 4 m (15 × 12 ft.). Zone 6.

Cornus mas (Cornelian cherry), a shrub or small tree from western Asia, has clusters to 2 cm (¾ in.) across of yellow flowers in late spring before the leaves unfold, followed by ovoid, fleshy, red fruits to 2 cm (¾ in.) long. Size: 5 × 5 m (15 × 15 ft.). Zone 5.

↑ *Corokia × virgata*

Cornus sanguinea from Europe is a shrub with reddish stems and dull white flowers in heads to 5 cm (2 in.) across followed by bluish black fruits, but it is more often grown for the winter stem effect. 'Midwinter Fire' has bright orange-red stems in winter. *Cornus alba* from eastern Asia is somewhat similar with red winter stems. 'Sibirica' 🏆 has especially bright red stems and red autumn foliage while 'Spaethii' has, in addition, leaves margined with yellow during the summer. Size: 3 × 2.5 m (10 × 8 ft.) unless coppiced. Zone 5.

Corokia (Escalloniaceae)

A small genus of unusual evergreen shrubs from New Zealand grown for their 5-petalled, star-like, yellow flowers and orange to red berry-like fruits. Grow in a sunny position. Trim after flowering and if necessary cut back hard to reduce size.

Corokia × virgata is one of the more frequently grown plants. It has rather sparse dark green leaves to 5 cm (2 in.) long which have a white underside. In late spring, it is covered with fragrant flowers to 1 cm (½ in.) across borne in clusters of 3 and followed by orange fruits to 5 mm (⅛ in.) across. Size: 2.5 × 2.5 m (8 × 8 ft.). Zone 8.

Coronilla (Papilionaceae)

A genus of evergreen and deciduous shrubs and herbaceous plants grown for their flowers. ***Coronilla valentina* subsp. *glauca*** 🏆 from the Mediterranean is one of the few woody examples of the genus. It forms a small evergreen shrub with blue-green pinnate leaves to 5 cm (2 in.) of up to 7 leaflets. The bright yellow, pea-like, fragrant flowers to 1 cm (½ in.) are borne in clusters of about 10 in spring but also intermittently throughout most of the summer. Grow in a sunny position. Trim if necessary in late winter and cut back straggly plants to encourage new branches. 'Variegata' has leaves edged with creamy white. Size: 75 × 75 cm (2½ × 2½ ft.). Zone 8.

Correa (Rutaceae)

A genus of small evergreen trees and shrubs grown for their flowers. The leaves are aromatic when crushed and the pendulous flowers are usually tubular with 4 spreading lobes at the mouth. In cooler areas, they may be grown in a container and moved into a conservatory or cool greenhouse to avoid severe frosts. If grown indoors, these shrubs may flower though the winter but later if outdoors. Grow in a lime-free soil in sun. Trim after flowering if required.

Correa backhouseana 🏆 from Tasmania has clusters of greenish yellow flowers to 2.5 cm (1 in.) long and oval leaves on reddish stems. Size: 1.5 × 1.5 m (5 × 5 ft.). Zones 8–9.

***Correa* 'Mannii'** ♀ (synonym 'Harrisii') has rosy red flowers to 2.5 cm (1 ½ in.) long and heart-shaped leaves to 3 cm (1 ½ in.) long. Size: 2 × 2 m (6 × 6 ft.). Zones 8–9.

Corylopsis (Hamamelidaceae)

A small genus of deciduous shrubs grown for their fragrant, yellow, bell-shaped flowers borne in pendulous racemes in early spring before the leaves emerge. Grow in moist but well-drained soil in partial shade or under other shrubs to help protect from late frosts. Prune after flowering if needed.

Corylopsis pauciflora ♀ from Japan and Taiwan is a spreading shrub with few flowered racemes to 3 cm (1 ½ in.) long of delicate pale yellow flowers. It prefers a lime-free soil. Size: 1.5 × 2 m (5 × 6 ft.). Zone 6.

Corylopsis sinensis ♀ from China is a large, more erect shrub with long racemes to 7.5 cm (3 in.) of lemon-yellow flowers. The leaves are broad and bluish green while those of 'Spring Purple' are purple when young. Size: 2 × 3 m (6 × 10 ft.). Zone 6.

Corylus (Corylaceae) hazel

A genus of deciduous shrubs or small trees usually grown for their edible nuts and early catkins which attract insects. The male flowers are produced in dangling yellow catkins in late winter and early spring, but the minute, red, female flowers are less visible. Grow in any reasonable soil in sun or partial shade, although coloured-leaved cultivars perform better in full sun.

↑ *Corylopsis sinensis*

Prune in late winter, but the species described can also be coppiced, cutting the stems down almost to the base to allow the regeneration of the shoots.

Corylus avellana (hazel) from Europe is a very large shrub which can be used as a hedge. The rounded leaves are about 10 cm (4 in.) across and the catkins to 6 cm (2 ½ in.) long. The curious cultivar 'Contorta' ♀ (corkscrew hazel, Harry Lauder's walking stick) is much slower growing and has twisted and curled stems which are very useful in flower arrangements as well as making a feature in winter. 'Red Majestic' has similar contorted branches but purple foliage through the summer and purple catkins in late winter. 'Aurea' has soft yellow leaves. If grown for their nuts, choose a named free fruiting cultivar from a reliable specialist nursery. Size: 4 × 4 m (12 × 12 ft.). Zone 4.

↑ *Cotinus coggygria* SMOKEY JOE 'Lisjo'

Cotinus (Anacardiaceae) smoke bush

A genus of two deciduous trees and shrubs grown for their autumn foliage and feathery flowers and fruits, which may be grown in a border or as specimen plants. The tiny flowers are borne in a huge feathery inflorescence which becomes a fluffy head of silvery seeds. The leaves are usually a marvellous autumn colour. Grow in sun or partial shade. Prune in late winter, cutting back hard if the plants become too large. Several very good cultivars with exceptional foliage are available.

Cotinus coggygria ♀ from southern Europe is a large shrub but can be kept small by pruning. The leaves are broad to 7.5 cm (3 in.) long and turn orange and red in autumn. The flower heads reach 15 cm (6 in.) across. GOLDEN SPIRIT 'Ancot' has golden foliage and 'Royal Purple' ♀ has dark reddish purple foliage during the growing season turning scarlet in autumn. SMOKEY JOE 'Lisjo' is a new, still uncommon, cultivar with a more compact habit and large clouds of smoky pink flowers. Size: 5 × 5 m (15 × 15 ft.). Zone 5.

Cotoneaster (Rosaceae)

A genus of evergreen and deciduous shrubs grown for their flowers, fruit and foliage which are important food sources for both birds, bees and other insects. The small saucer-shaped flowers in spring or early summer are white or pink, single or in clusters. These are followed by very attractive, small, usually red, occasionally black fruits which are mildly poisonous if eaten. Larger species can be trained as a standard, prostrate ones as ground cover or over a wall and others as hedges or in a border. Grow in almost all soils in sun or partial shade. Prune if required in winter or early spring.

Cotoneaster horizontalis ♀ from China grows in a distinct herringbone fashion and is useful for covering walls or banks with pink-tinged flowers 1 cm (½ in.) across, tiny leaves which turn a good red in autumn and bright red spherical fruits to 6 mm (¼ in.) across. Size: 1 × 1.5 m (3 × 5 ft.). Zone 4.

Cotoneaster integrifolius ♀ (synonym *C. microphyllus*) from the Himalayas is somewhat similar but is evergreen without the strict herringbone pattern of branching. Size: 1 × 1.5 m (3 × 5 ft.). Zone 5.

Cotoneaster salicifolius is a very variable evergreen species from China with white flowers

↑ *Crataegus laevigata* 'Paul's Scarlet'

in large many-flowered clusters followed by glossy bright red berries. The species itself is vigorous reaching to 5 m (15 ft.) tall but there are several smaller cultivars such as 'Gnom', a dwarf shrub with arching branches and lanceolate leaves to 3 cm (1½ in.) long. Size: 0.3 × 2 m (1 × 6 ft.). Zone 6.

Crataegus (Rosaceae) thorn

A genus of mainly deciduous, thorny trees and shrubs grown for their flowers, fruits and often autumn colour as well. They are very tolerant plants attracting bees and butterflies to the flowers and providing winter food for birds. The white 5-petalled flowers are borne in flattened clusters in late spring and early summer on the ends of short side shoots. The fruits, usually red, are spherical or ovoid. Grow in sun or partial shade. Trim hedges after flowering or fruiting, and prune specimen trees in late winter if needed.

Crataegus laevigata (synonym *C. oxyacantha*; may, Midland thorn) from Europe is a thorny tree with clusters of white flowers about 1 cm (½ in.) across in late spring. The red fruits are ovoid 1.5 cm (½ in.) long. It is frequently planted as a hedge. Several cultivars are popular small trees. 'Pauls' Scarlet' 🏆 has double scarlet flowers. 'Pink Corkscrew' has slightly twisted stems and bright pink flowers, 'Plena' has double white flowers, while *C. monogyna* 'Compacta' is closely related, forming a very small shrub with single flowers. Size: 8 × 8 m (25 × 25 ft.). Zone 5.

Crataegus ×persimilis 'Prunifolia' 🏆 (synonym *C. prunifolia*) is a popular small tree with very stout thorns. The glossy, dark green, oval leaves become red and orange in autumn and the spherical red fruits to 1.5 cm (½ in.) are very persistent. Size: 8 × 8 m (25 × 25 ft.). Zone 5.

Crataegus tanacetifolia from western Asia is a slow-growing tree with few thorns, but has attractive grey hairy leaves, white flowers with red anthers and orange to yellow spherical fruits to 2.5 cm (1 in.) across. Size: 8 × 8 m (25 × 25 ft.). Zone 6.

Crinodendron synonym *Tricuspidaria* (Elaeocarpaceae)

A genus of two evergreen trees and shrubs from Chile, both of which are grown for their bell-shaped flowers. Grow in a moist but well-drained, lime-free soil in partial shade, or in sun as long as the roots can be kept cool. Trim after flowering.

Crinodendron hookerianum 🏆 (synonym *Tricuspidaria lanceolata*; lantern tree) is a large shrub, fantastic in flower, with narrow dark green leaves to 10 cm (4 in.) long. The pendulous, crimson flowers are like small Chinese lanterns to about 2.5 cm (1 in.) long hanging on long stalks from the branches in late spring to early summer. 'Ada Hoffmann' is a rare cultivar with pink flowers. Size: 6 × 5 m (18 × 15 ft.). Zone 8.

Crinodendron patagua (synonym *Tricuspidaria dependens*) is a rarer shrub with white flowers to 2.5 cm (1 in.) long in late summer and dark green, ovate leaves about 5 cm (2 in.) long. Size: 6 × 5 m (18 × 15 ft.). Zone 8.

↑ *Crinodendron hookerianum*

Cytisus (Papilionaceae) broom

A genus of deciduous or evergreen shrubs grown for their pea-shaped, often scented flowers in late spring which encourage bees. The flowers are in small clusters or racemes and the small leaves are usually trifoliate while the stems are often green. The larger species may be grown in borders and the smaller or prostrate ones over a wall or as ground cover. Grow in a sunny position preferably not in extremely acid or alkaline soils. Prune immediately after flowering to avoid larger shrubs becoming leggy but do not cut back too hard as the shrubs will not easily regenerate from old wood.

↑ *Cytisus battandieri*

Cytisus battandieri 🏆 (pineapple broom) from Morocco is an upright deciduous treelike shrub with silvery grey leaves to 10 cm (4 in.) long. The pineapple-scented flowers, to 2 cm (¾ in.) long, bloom later than many other brooms, in midsummer in dense upright cone-shaped racemes to 15 cm (6 in.) long at the ends of the branches. Size: 5 × 5 m (15 × 15 ft.). Zone 7.

Cytisus* ×*kewensis 🏆 is a low-growing, almost prostrate plant covered with cream coloured flowers to 1.5 cm (½ in.) long. Size: 0.3 × 1.5 m (1 × 5 ft.). Zone 6.

Cytisus* ×*praecox 🏆 is a dense deciduous shrub with arching branches and pale yellow flowers to 2 cm (¾ in.) long. 'Allgold' has dark yellow flowers. Size: 1.2 × 1.5 m (4 × 5 ft.). Zone 5.

There are many other good broom cultivars in a range of colours including *Cytisus* 'Boskoop Ruby' 🏆 with deep red flowers, 'Hollandia' 🏆 with cream and deep pink flowers and *C. scoparius* 'Cornish Cream' with creamy yellow and white flowers. Size: 1.5 × 1.5 m (5 × 5 ft.). Zone 5.

Daboecia (Ericaceae) St Dabeoc's heath

A very small genus of heather-like shrubs useful for ground cover, with bell-shaped flowers and dark green leaves. They must be grown in a lime-free soil in sun or partial shade. Prune back flowering shoots in early spring.

Daboecia cantabrica from Western Europe has leaves to 1 cm (½ in.) long which are silvery white on the underside. The pinkish purple flowers about 1 cm (½ in.) long are in upright racemes to about 10 cm (4 in.) tall from early summer to autumn. A number of selected cultivars differ in size and flower colour. 'Silverwells' 🏆 is a slightly shorter plant with white flowers and lighter green leaves. 'Waley's Red' 🏆 is taller with deep crimson-red flowers. Size: to 30 × 30 cm (1 × 1 ft.). Zone 6.

Danae (Ruscaceae) Alexandrian laurel

Danae racemosa (synonym *Ruscus racemosus*; Alexandrian laurel) from southwestern Asia is the only species of this genus somewhat resembling a small bamboo in appearance with arching sprays of glossy "leaves". However, the

scarlet berries reach 1.5 mm (½ in.) across. It is commonly used in flower arrangements, often dried or coloured. Male and female plants are required for the production of fruits.

↑ *Danae racemosa*

↑ *Daphne cneorum* 'Eximia'

leaves are in fact flattened lanceolate stems to 10 cm (4 in.) long, which are good for cutting and for use in flower arrangements. The red spherical fruits to 8 mm (¼ in.) across produced in hot summers, are more interesting than the insignificant greenish yellow flowers. It prefers moist but well-drained soil in sun or shade. It does not require regular pruning but benefits if the old shoots are cut back to ground level in spring. Size: 1 × 1 m (3 × 3 ft.). Zone 7.

Ruscus aculeatus (butcher's broom) from Europe is somewhat similar but the phyllodes are stiff and spine-tipped, and the long-lasting,

Daphne (Thymelaeaceae)

A genus of small deciduous and evergreen shrubs almost all of which are valuable garden plants grown for their scented flowers early in the year. The flowers formed in small clusters are usually in shades of pink or white and attract bees, while the fruits feed birds. All parts of these plants are poisonous if eaten and the sap is a skin irritant to some people. Grow in sun or partial shade. Pruning is best avoided but if necessary carry out in late winter.

Daphne bholua from the Himalayas is an upright, deciduous or semi-evergreen shrub with very sweetly scented, late winter, white flowers 1.5 cm (½ in.) long tinged reddish pink on the outside. The berries are black. 'Jacqueline Postill' ♀ is an especially reliable, hardy and fragrant cultivar usually with evergreen leaves. Size: 2 × 1.5 m (6 × 5 ft.). Zone 7.

Daphne ×burkwoodii ♀ is a semi-evergreen shrub which has resulted in a number of different cultivars. 'Somerset' has pale pink flowers, purplish pink on the outside, to 1 cm (½ in.) across. 'Carol Mackie' also has pink flowers but the leaves are edged with creamy yellow. BRIGGS MOONLIGHT 'Brimoon', a new and still rare cultivar, is similar but with creamy white leaves edged with green. Size: variable to 1.5 × 1.5 m (5 × 5 ft.). Zone 5.

Daphne cneorum from Europe, a dwarf evergreen, spreading shrub has dark green leaves and pink flowers to 1 cm (½ in.) across. 'Eximia' ♀ with crimson buds and deep pink flowers is slightly taller. Size: 20 × 100 cm (8 × 36 in.). Zone 4.

Daphne jezoensis from Japan is an unusual, small, slow-growing species which loses its leaves in summer. It bears golden-yellow flowers from late winter to early spring and has red fruits. Size: 45 × 60 cm (1½ × 2 ft.). Zone 6.

Daphne laureola (spurge laurel) from Europe is a spreading evergreen with glossy foliage and clusters of slightly scented, green or yellow-green flowers in late winter. The berries are black. It tolerates shade under other shrubs. Size: 1 × 1 m (3 × 3 ft.). Zone 7.

↑ *Desfontainea spinosa*

Daphne mezereum (mezereon) from Europe to Siberia is a small, upright, twiggy, deciduous plant with clusters of reddish purple flowers in early spring before the leaves emerge, followed by attractive orange-red berries. The white-flowered forma *alba* is equally pretty. Size: 1.2 × 1 m (4 × 3 ft.). Zone 5.

Daphne odora from China is usually seen in gardens as the form 'Aureomarginata' ♀ with leaves margined with creamy yellow. This is a small evergreen shrub with highly scented reddish pink flowers which are white inside. Size: 1.5 × 1.5 m (5 × 5 ft.). Zone 7.

Davidia (Cornaceae) dove tree, ghost tree, handkerchief tree

Davidia involucrata ♀ from China is the only species of this genus and eventually makes a deciduous, rather elegant, conical tree with large, heart-shaped leaves to 15 cm (6 in.) long. The very tiny flowers in pendulous balls to 2.5 cm (1 in.) across are surrounded by two unequally sized, impressive, pure white, broadly ovate bracts, the larger to 20 cm (8 in.) long. These give the appearance of fluttering handkerchiefs and provide an astonishing show in late spring. Unfortunately, it will not flower as a young plant but a very new and still rare cultivar 'Sonoma' from the USA is slowly coming onto the market and flowers when less than about 3 m (10 ft.) tall. Grow as a specimen tree in sun or part shade. Prune only to remove dead or weak branches in winter. Size: 15 × 10 m (50 × 30 ft.). Zone 6.

↑ *Deutzia scabra* 'Candidissima'

Desfontainia (Loganiaceae)

Desfontainia spinosa 🏆 from Chile and Peru is the only species in this genus, which in leaf could be mistaken for a small holly. It is a slow-growing evergreen shrub with glossy, spiny leaves to about 5 cm (2 in.) long. It is grown for the nodding, narrow, tubular, orange-red flowers with a yellow throat to 4 cm (1½ in.) long produced through the summer to autumn. A moist lime-free soil in dappled shade protected from drying winds is important. Avoid allowing it to dry out and do not give any fertilizer. Prune in midspring to maintain shape and dead head if possible. Size: 2 × 2 m (6 × 6 ft.). Zones 8–9.

Deutzia (Hydrangeaceae)

A large genus of easy-to-grow, deciduous, summer-flowering shrubs, many of which are cultivated. The flowers are white or pink mostly with curious flattened or winged stamens. The species are very difficult to distinguish as their defining characters are based on quite small botanical differences in the flower or leaf structure. Many very attractive and popular hybrids and cultivars have been raised over the years especially in France. The simple leaves are often grey-green and the stems on older plants often have attractive peeling bark. Grow in sun or partial shade. Prune after flowering by cutting back old flowering shoots to allow new growth to emerge and to encourage bushiness, or to reduce size.

***Deutzia* ×*hybrida* 'Magicien'** 🏆 (synonym 'Strawberry Fields') has become very popular with large, open, deep rosy pink flowers edged white, to 2.5 cm (1 in.) across in early summer. Size: 1.5 × 1.5 m (5 × 5 ft.). Zone 6.

Deutzia ningpoensis 🏆 (synonym *D. chunii*) from China bears flowers to 1 cm (½ in.) across in clusters along the branches in midsummer. Size: 2 × 2 m (6 × 6 ft.). Zone 5.

***Deutzia* 'Rosea Plena'** (synonym 'Pink Pompom') has dense heads of fully double, pink flowers which fade to white in midsummer. Size: 2 × 2 m (6 × 6 ft.). Zone 6.

Deutzia scabra from Japan is tall with arching stems and pure white bell-shaped flowers in upright panicles to 15 cm (6 in.) in early to midsummer. 'Candidissima' has double pure white flowers, while in 'Plena', the double flowers are tinged pink. Size: 3 × 2 m (10 × 6 ft.). Zone 6.

Deutzia setchuenensis **var.** ***corymbiflora*** 🏆 from China is a very free-flowering upright shrub with pure white, star-shaped flowers in rounded clusters. Size: 2 × 1.5 m (6 × 5 ft.). Zone 7.

Disanthus (Hamamelidaceae)

Disanthus cercidifolius 🏆 from China and Japan is the only species of this genus and is grown for the breathtaking autumn colour in shades of bronze, copper, orange and red. It is a deciduous shrub with almost round, bluish green, heart-shaped leaves to about 7 cm (3 in.) across, on long leaf stalks. The tiny purplish red flowers produced in autumn are lost amongst the brilliant autumn foliage. Grow in moist, well-drained but lime-free soil in partial shade in a position where the young foliage is protected from late spring frosts or drying winds. Prune in winter if necessary. Size: 3 × 3 m (10 × 10 ft.). Zone 7.

Drimys (Winteraceae)

A small genus of evergreen trees and shrubs with bold aromatic leaves and many-petalled flowers. Grow in sun or partial shade. Prune in spring.

Drimys lanceolata (synonym *D. aromatica*; mountain pepper) from Australia is a large shrub with red-coloured shoots and narrow, glossy, dark green, aromatic leaves to 8 cm (3 in.) long which are bluish white on the underside. The star-shaped flowers are fragrant, creamy white with 7 or more petals and to 1.5 cm (½ in.) across in umbels of 15 or more in late spring followed by black spherical fruits. 'Suzette' is a very new cultivar with variegated leaves. Size: 4 × 2.5 m (12 × 8 ft.). Zone 8.

Drimys winteri **var.** ***andina*** (synonym *D. andina*) from Chile and Argentina is a similar but dwarf shrub often flowering when it is only 30 cm (1 ft.) tall.

Edgeworthia (Thymelaeaceae)

paper bush

A small genus of woodland shrubs with distinctive, thin, flaking bark used for making specialist papers in Japan. Only one species is commonly cultivated. Grow in moist but well-drained soil

↓ *Edgeworthia chrysantha*

↑ *Elaeagnus pungens* 'Maculata'

in sun or partial shade. Prune after flowering only if necessary.

Edgeworthia chrysantha (synonym *E. papyrifera*) from China is a small deciduous shrub with beautiful golden-yellow, tubular, fragrant flowers in late winter before the leaves unfold. The flowers, each to 1 cm (½ in.) long, are borne in nodding spherical clusters to 5 cm (2 in.) across at the ends of the branches. Size: to 1.5 × 1.5 m (5 × 5 ft.). Zone 8.

Elaeagnus (Elaeagnaceae) oleaster

A genus of fairly fast-growing deciduous and evergreen shrubs, which are useful for their foliage and as hedging plants, especially in seaside areas. The small white flowers are bell-shaped and the fruits are berries, some of which are edible. Grow in sun or partial shade. Prune evergreens in spring and deciduous species after flowering as long as fruits are not required. Large plants will tolerate hard pruning. Trim hedges in late summer.

Elaeagnus ×ebbingei has silvery scales on the underside of the leaves. It has resulted in several cultivars including 'Gilt Edge' 🏆 with a broad gold margin to the flat leaves and 'Limelight' with green leaves variegated in the centre with yellow and lime-green. Size: to 4 × 4 m (12 × 12 ft.). Zone 6.

Elaeagnus pungens from Japan is evergreen with ovate, dark green leaves, whitish with brown scales on the underside, to 10 cm (4 in.) long and with a wavy margin. The very sweetly scented, silvery flowers to 1 cm (½ in.) long in autumn, are succeeded by brownish red fruits. 'Hosuba-fukurin' is a new and still uncommon Japanese cultivar with white-edged leaves. 'Maculata' is grown for the large, central, rich yellow blotch on the leaves which are margined with green. Size: to 4 × 4 m (12 × 12 ft.). Zone 7.

Elaeagnus umbellata from Japan is deciduous with beautiful narrow, silvery leaves to 10 cm

(4 in.) long and stems often ending in spines. It bears tiny, pendulous, silvery white, fragrant flowers in late spring which are followed by ovoid, red, edible fruits to 8 mm (¼ in.) long covered with silvery scales. The hybrid *E.* 'Quicksilver' 🏆 is a very popular large shrub with especially silver leaves. Size: to 4 × 4 m (12 × 12 ft.). Zone 2.

↑ *Embothrium coccineum*

Embothrium (Proteaceae)

Chilean fire bush

A small genus of evergreen forest trees and shrubs which with their clusters of striking flowers are dramatic and take many years to reach their eventual size. Grow in a rich, moist, lime-free soil in sun or partial shade. Avoid the use of any fertilizer, especially one including phosphates. Plants tend to do better in areas with rainfall throughout the year. Prune after flowering or in spring if necessary.

Embothrium coccineum from Chile is a large suckering shrub or small tree with lance-shaped leaves to 8 cm (3 in.) long. The brilliant scarlet, narrow, tubular flowers to about 3 cm (1½ in.) long form loose clusters 10 cm (4 in.) across in late spring. Plants can be seen in Chile with yellow flowers and it would be exciting if these eventually became available in cultivation. Plants with very narrow leaves such as 'Ñorquinco' 🏆 tend to be hardier. Size: to 10 × 5 m (30 × 15 ft.). Zone 8.

Enkianthus (Ericaceae)

A small genus of deciduous woodland shrubs with umbels of nodding, bell-shaped flowers and bright autumn colours. Grow in a humus-rich, lime-free soil in sun or partial shade. Prune in late winter.

Enkianthus campanulatus 🏆 from Japan is a spreading shrub with several branches arranged in whorls growing from a single point. Similarly, the ovate leaves are produced in clusters at the ends of the stems. The flowers are

↑ *Enkianthus campanulatus*

very variable in colour which has resulted in a number of named cultivars such as 'Red Bells' with redder flowers. In a typical plant up to 15 creamy yellow flowers, veined with red, nearly 1 cm (½ in.) long on flowers stalks to 2 cm (¾ in.) are produced in late spring. The autumn leaves turn to fiery yellow, orange and red. *Enkianthus campanulatus* var. *sikokianus* has deep maroon flower buds opening to dark red with pink streaks. Size: to 3 × 3 m (10 × 10 ft.). Zone 5.

Enkianthus perulatus 🏆 from Japan, far less common in gardens, is a smaller, slower-growing shrub. The flowers are pure white without coloured veins and the lobes at the top of the corolla roll back. The autumn foliage is a vivid red. Size: to 2 × 2 m (6 × 6 ft.). Zone 6.

Erica (Ericaceae) heather, heath

A large genus of small evergreen shrubs with needle-like leaves grown for their flowers. The vast majority are tender species from South Africa, some of which are grown in greenhouses in cooler climates. A few hardy European species have resulted in hundreds of cultivars which are very popular, small garden shrubs. The numerous bell- or urn-shaped flowers in racemes or clusters, usually in shades of pink, red or white are very attractive to bees. Heathers are useful massed to create a coloured carpeting effect or in association with other shrubs or small conifers. All year interest can be achieved by choosing cultivars with coloured foliage which flower at different seasons. Many cultivars are quite similar and a very small selection has been listed below but it may be necessary to go to a specialist heather nursery to obtain specific cultivars. Grow in a well-drained, lime-free soil in sun. Trim after flowering to avoid the plants becoming straggly.

Erica carnea from central Europe is a spreading shrub with short needle-like leaves and urn-shaped flowers nearly 1 cm (½ in.) long in short racemes to 7.5 cm (3 in.). Cultivars flower from early winter to midspring with the majority in midwinter. 'Foxhollow' 🏆 has yellow foliage turning more orange in winter and pale pink flowers. 'Myretoun Ruby' is late flowering with dark rose-pink flowers. 'Springwood White' 🏆, an old and popular, strong-growing favourite, is white-flowered. 'Vivellii' 🏆 has deep purplish red flowers. 'Winter Beauty' flowers early with deep pink flowers. Size (depending on the cultivar): around 25 × 50 cm (10 × 20 in.). Zone 5.

Erica cinerea (bell heather) from Western Europe has bell-shaped flowers to 7 mm (1/4 in.) long in racemes to 5 cm (2 in.) from summer to midautumn. 'Fiddler's Gold' 🏆 is quite a new cultivar with mauve flowers and golden-yellow foliage flushed red. 'Hookstone White' 🏆 has large white flowers and bright green foliage. 'Lime Soda' 🏆, also new, has lime green foliage and pale purplish pink flowers. 'Pink Ice' 🏆 has clear pink flowers and dark green foliage. Size (depending on the cultivar): 30 × 50 cm (1 × 1 1/2 ft.). Zone 5.

Erica ×darleyensis flowers through the winter with longer racemes to 10 cm (4 in.) of pink flowers. 'Jenny Porter' 🏆 is a taller cultivar with soft pale pinkish white flowers. 'Kramer's Rote' 🏆 has magenta flowers and bronzy coloured leaves. Size: to 30 × 60 cm (1 × 2 ft.). Zone 6.

Erica lusitanica (Portugal heath) from southwestern Europe is a tall shrub with white tubular flowers to 5 mm (1/8 in.) long in branched racemes to 25 cm (10 in.) tall from late winter to early spring. 'George Hunt' has yellow foliage but is best sited out of the full sun. Size: to 2.5 × 1 m (8 × 3 ft.). Zone 8.

Erinacea (Papilionaceae)

hedgehog broom

Erinacea anthyllis 🏆 (synonym *E. pungens*) from the Mediterranean areas is the only species in this genus. It is evergreen forming a rounded, dwarf, flowering shrub with spine-tipped branches, especially suitable for small troughs. The trifoliate leaves reach 1 cm (1/2 in.) long. In mid to late spring, the pea-like violet-blue flowers to 2 cm (3/4 in.) are formed in small clusters of 2 to 4 all over the hummock. Grow in very well-drained soils in sun. Pruning is rarely necessary except to tidy up any dead stems. Size: to 30 × 90 cm (1 × 3 ft.). Zone 7.

Eriobotrya (Rosaceae)

A genus of large evergreen shrubs or trees with bold foliage producing edible fruits in warm climates. Grow in a sunny position. Prune in late winter.

Eriobotrya japonica 🏆 (loquat) from China and Japan is a large shrub or, in good conditions, a small tree, which is grown commercially for its fruit in many warmer countries of the world. After hot summers, it bears erect panicles of fragrant, white, 5-petalled, open flowers to 2 cm (3/4 in.) across from autumn to early winter; these may be followed by rounded yellow fruits to 5 cm (2 in.) across. However, the foliage is striking, attractive in its own right even if flowers and fruits are not produced. The bold leaves are glossy, leathery and dark green to 30 cm (1 ft.) long with deeply impressed regular veins, a sharply toothed margin and covered on the undersurface with a pale brown woolly tomentum. This plant could be grown for foliage in a large container in a sheltered sunny position and pruned to a reasonable size. Size: to 8 × 8 m (25 × 25 ft.). Zone 8.

Escallonia (Escalloniaceae)

A genus of evergreen shrubs and small trees from the mountain woodlands of South America. They have small colourful flowers in showy clusters and tend to bloom through the summer. All have neat, dark green, usually glossy leaves. Many of the most popular ones in gardens are cultivars in shades of pink, red and white. They make lovely flowering hedges which should be trimmed after flowering in midsummer and are very good in maritime situations. Grow in a sunny position. Prune after flowering or in spring.

***Escallonia* 'Apple Blossom'** ♕ has leaves to 4 cm (1½ in.) long and small pink flowers under 1 cm (½ in.) across. The flowers with a white centre, are in short upright racemes in early to midsummer. Size: to 2 × 2 m (6 × 6 ft.). Zone 7.

***Escallonia* 'Iveyi'** ♕ has large, glossy, green leaves to 5 cm (2 in.) or more with midsummer, fragrant white flowers to 1 cm (½ in.) in conical heads to 15 cm (6 in.). Size: to 3 × 3 m (10 × 10 ft.). Zone 7.

Escallonia rubra from Chile has tubular red flowers about 1 cm (½ in.) long and slightly sticky aromatic stems and leaves. It is the parent of many cultivars and 'Crimson Spire' ♕ with very glossy foliage and deep crimson flowers is popular for hedging. Size: to 3 × 3 m (10 × 10 ft.) or more if untrimmed. Zone 7.

Eucalyptus (Myrtaceae) gum tree

A large genus of evergreen trees and shrubs from Australia with attractive, leathery, aromatic, often blue-green foliage. The first formed leaves are frequently different in shape to those produced on more mature plants and both are often used in floral decoration. The flowers are only produced once the plant is mature and has developed the adult foliage after several years. Though they have no petals, the showy flowers are formed of masses of coloured stamens. Eucalyptus are not suitable for small gardens, because they can grow several metres in one season to become exceedingly tall. However, one or two of the hardier species can be grown in a border for their foliage by coppicing. This involves cutting the stems more or less to the ground in late winter every year or two and making use of the new stems which emerge. In this way, the foliage remains in its juvenile state but the plants will not flower. They grow in all well-drained soils unless very alkaline.

Eucalyptus globulus (Tasmanian blue gum) is less hardy but can be used as a summer bedding plant for its large, ovate, bluish green leaves which clasp the stems. It can be grown from seed for this purpose. Size: 30 × 15 m (100 × 50 ft.) unless grown from seed for bedding. Zones 8–9.

Species suitable for coppicing include ***Eucalyptus gunnii*** ♕ (cider gum) with rounded, blue-green, juvenile leaves. Size: 20 × 12 m (60 × 35 ft.) or more unless coppiced. Zone 8.

Eucryphia (Eucryphiaceae)

A genus of evergreen or deciduous, woodland trees and shrubs grown for their flowers and foliage. The leaves are either pinnate or undivided, dark green and leathery and the large, shallow, cup-shaped, white, usually 4-petalled flowers have a mass of showy stamens in the centre. All those in cultivation are good garden plants. Grow in lime-free soils. Prune in late winter or spring if necessary.

Eucryphia glutinosa (synonym *E. pinnatifolia*) 🏆 from Chile is usually deciduous in cultivation and has pinnate leaves with 3 or 5 leaflets which turn a good orange-brown in autumn. The flowers reach 6 cm (2 ½ in.) across with a central boss of stamens bearing red anthers in mid to late summer. Size: to 10 × 6 m (30 × 18 ft.). Zone 7.

Eucryphia milliganii from Tasmania is a smaller evergreen shrub than *E. glutinosa*. It has leaves under 5 cm (2 in.) long, bluish white underneath and has small, saucer-shaped flowers to 2.5 cm (1 in.) across in summer. Size: to 5 × 1 m (15 × 3 ft.). Zone 8.

Eucryphia ×nymansensis is an upright evergreen shrub with both undivided and trifoliate leaflets on the same plant. The flowers to 6 cm (2 ½ in.) across appear in late summer and early autumn. This hybrid is a little more tolerant of alkaline soils. 'Nymansay' 🏆 is the best known cultivar with an even more columnar habit. The rare 'Nymans Silver' has silver-edged leaves. Size: to 15 × 5 m (50 × 15 ft.). Zone 7.

Euonymus (Celastraceae) spindle

A variable genus of evergreen and deciduous climbers, trees and shrubs. The flowers are quite small and insignificant but the fruits have coloured seeds surrounded by a colourful fleshy coating with an interesting lobed or winged shape. The foliage of the deciduous species is often brightly coloured in autumn and some of the evergreen species can be used for hedging or ground cover. All parts, especially the fruits, are poisonous if eaten. Grow in sun or partial shade. Prune deciduous plants if necessary in late winter or early spring and evergreens, including hedges, in late spring.

Euonymus alatus 🏆 (winged spindle) from Japan is a fairly slow-growing deciduous shrub with unusual corky wings on the stems. In autumn, it bears bright crimson-red leaves and red barely lobed fruits with bright orange seeds. Size: to 2 × 3 m (6 × 10 ft.). Zone 3.

Euonymus europaeus from Europe is similar to *E. alatus* but does not have a winged stem and is more tolerant of chalky soils. 'Red Cascade' 🏆 is an exceptionally good cultivar with freely produced 4-lobed red fruits to 2 cm (¾ in.) across. Size: to 3 × 3 m (10 × 10 ft.). Zone 3.

Euonymus fortunei from Japan is a prostrate or scrambling evergreen which is usually seen in gardens as named cultivars grown for their glossy evergreen foliage rather than the fruits. Some of the taller ones can make low hedges including 'Emerald 'n' Gold' 🏆 reaching 1 m (3 ft.) tall with ovate green leaves margined with bright golden-yellow to 2.5 cm (1 in.) long. 'Emerald Gaiety' 🏆 differs in its white-margined leaves which become pink tinged in winter. 'Kewensis' is a prostrate plant barely 10 cm (4 in.) tall with tiny, neat, dark green leaves 1 cm (½ in.) long. Although *E. fortunei* is usually very hardy, severe late spring frosts can damage the young emerging foliage. Zone 5.

Euonymus japonicus from Japan is an upright, dense, evergreen shrub with narrow, glossy, dark green leaves to 7.5 cm (3 in.) long. It is a very useful town or seaside plant making a

↑ *Euonymus alatus*

good dense hedge. 'Chollipo' 𝕋 from Korea is an interesting cultivar with a very upright habit and leaves with a broad, brilliant gold margin. Size: to 4 × 2 m (12 × 6 ft.). Zone 7.

Euphorbia (Euphorbiaceae) spurge

A very large and extremely variable genus of evergreen and deciduous herbaceous plants, succulents and shrubs including the popular Christmas house plant, the poinsettia (*Euphorbia pulcherrima*). All have a very characteristic flower structure consisting of tiny greenish coloured flowers surrounded by showy, conspicuous bracts and nectar-producing glands to attract pollinating insects. The whole plant contains a milky sap which exudes if the stems or leaves are cut. This is an irritant. Avoid contact with the skin and especially the eyes. Grow in a sunny position. Cut back old flowering stems after flowering.

Euphorbia characias from southern Europe is one of the evergreen shrubby species which makes a showy and unusual flowering plant from early spring to early summer, the heads

↓ *Euphorbia characias*

lasting even longer if not cut back. It has upright unbranched stems with narrow grey-green leaves to 10 cm (4 in.) long. In the second year these produce club-shaped flower heads to 30 cm (1 ft.) tall by 10 cm (4 in.) across composed of numerous green flowers with yellowish green bracts contrasting with purplish brown coloured glands. After flowering, the stems die and should be cut back. SILVER SWAN 'Wilcott' has silver-variegated leaves. The subspecies *wulfenii* ♡ has yellowish green glands and several named cultivars such as 'John Tomlinson' ♡ are grown for the bright yellow colour of the flower heads. Size: to 1.2 × 1.2 m (4 × 4 ft.). Zone 7.

Euphorbia mellifera ♡ (honey spurge) from Madeira is less common. It has orangey brown, honey-scented flower heads to 10 cm (4 in.) across in late spring and narrow leaves with a pale midrib. Size: to 1.5 × 1.5 m (5 × 5 ft.). Zones 8–9.

Euryops (Asteraceae)

A large genus of shrubs and herbaceous plants mainly from South Africa with masses of bright yellow, daisy-like flowers. Grow in full sun. Prune lightly after flowering to maintain shape.

Euryops acraeus ♡ (synonym *E. evansii*) is a low mounded shrub for very well-drained soils. The narrow silvery leaves reach 3 cm (1½ in.) long and bright yellow flower heads to 2.5 cm (1 in.) across are held well above the plant on stems to 4 cm (1½ in.) tall in late spring and early summer. Size: to 30 × 30 cm (1 × 1 ft.). Zone 9.

↑ *Euryops chrysanthemoides*

Euryops pectinatus ♡ is a larger shrub with grey hairy leaves to 7.5 cm (3 in.) long divided into very narrow lobes and flowers to 4 cm (1½ in.) across over a long season from summer to autumn and even later in milder areas. *E. chrysanthemoides* is similar but with greener, less divided leaves. Size: to 1 × 1 m (3 × 3 ft.). Zone 8.

↓ *Exochorda* × *macrantha* 'The Bride'

Exochorda (Rosaceae) pearlbush

A small genus of woodland shrubs from China often with a graceful arching habit and showy, white, cup-shaped, 5-petalled flowers in late spring and early summer. Grow in good garden soils, unless very alkaline, in sun or partial shade. Prune after flowering cutting back old branches to allow new growth to emerge.

Exochorda* ×*macrantha, a mounded shrub, is most frequently represented in gardens by the cultivar 'The Bride' 🏆 with clusters of up to 10 flowers each over 2.5 cm (1 in.) across. *Exochorda serratifolia* 'Snow White' is very free-flowering, tolerates alkaline soils and is less affected by late frosts though less common in cultivation. Size: to 2 × 3 m (6 × 10 ft.). Zone 5.

Fabiana (Solanaceae)

A genus of small evergreen shrubs with very small needle-shaped leaves somewhat similar in appearance to heathers. They grow better in neutral or acid soils in full sun. Prune if necessary in spring.

Fabiana imbricata from Chile has branching, rather erect stems and leaves to 5 mm (1/8 in.) long. White tubular flowers 1.5 cm (½ in.) long cover the upper parts of the stems in early summer except in the more commonly grown f. *violacea* 🏆 which has pale lilac coloured flowers. Size: 2 × 2 m (6 × 6 ft.). Zone 8.

Fabiana imbricata f. *violacea* →

Fagus (Fagaceae) beech

In general, species of this genus are large deciduous forest trees, far too imposing for a small garden. However, the European beech is often used for hedging and a few cultivars might be considered as specimen trees. Grow in both sun or partial shade, although the purple-leaved cultivars colour best in sun. Prune if necessary in winter. Cut hedges in midsummer.

Fagus sylvatica 🏆 from Europe makes a good hedge and repeated clipping ensures that the plant retains its juvenility, retaining the dried, brown autumn leaves through most of the winter, whereas mature specimen trees drop all their leaves by late autumn. Beech hedges are favoured by nesting birds, but if birds do nest, avoid cutting until after the young have fledged. For something a little unusual, a hedge could be planted with a mixture of green and purple-leaved types. Small cultivars include

'Mercedes' with very narrow leaves deeply cut into fine lobes. This is a very slow-growing cultivar which reaches about 2 m (6 ft.) in 10 years. 'Franken', equally slow growing, is very rare with leaves variegated chalky white, best sited in the shade. Zone 5.

Fatsia (Araliaceae)

A small genus of evergreen spreading shrubs which do well in a wide range of conditions, in sun or shade, by the sea or in areas of high air pollution. They might also be grown in containers or conservatories. Prune if necessary in spring.

Fatsia japonica 🏆 from Japan and South Korea, although large, is a wonderfully architectural plant giving a subtropical flavour to a garden. The leathery, glossy, green leaves to as much as 40 cm (16 in.) across are deeply 7- to 11-lobed with slightly undulate margins. In autumn, creamy white flowers in large branching heads of spherical clusters to 4 cm (1½ in.) across attract insects followed by spherical black berries eaten by birds. Size: to a maximum of 4 × 4 m (12 × 12 ft.). Zone 8.

↓ *Fatsia japonica*

Forsythia (Oleaceae)

Members of this popular genus of deciduous shrubs are a very common sight in spring with their profusion of bright golden-yellow flowers. The 4-petalled, open bell-shaped, nodding flowers about 2.5–4 cm (1–1½ in.) across

↓ *Forsythia ×intermedia* WEEKEND 'Courtalyn'

are produced singly or in few-flowered clusters along the branches, opening on bare stems before the leaves. Although there are several species, it is the hybrids and cultivars with their showier flowers which are more commonly grown. These plants are very tolerant of trimming and, except for those with a more arching open habit, can be used as informal flowering hedges or cut to geometrical shapes. Trim immediately after flowering. Grow in sun or partial shade. After flowering, thin out and cut back the older flowering shoots almost to the old wood. Zone 5.

Forsythia giraldiana from China is a graceful and arching shrub with delicate, pale yellow flowers appearing in late winter. Size: 4 × 4 m (12 × 12 ft.).

Forsythia ×intermedia, a hybrid first raised in the late nineteenth century, has resulted in the many flowering cultivars grown today. 'Arnold Giant' has enormous deep yellow flowers. 'Lynwood Variety' 🏆 is commonly encountered with rich yellow flowers to 3 cm (1½ in.) across. 'Spectabilis', one of the older cultivars, is always smothered with slightly smaller, deep yellow flowers. WEEKEND 'Courtalyn' 🏆 is very floriferous with similar flowers but a more compact habit. Size: 1.5 × 1.5 m (5 × 5 ft.).

Other cultivars include *Forsythia* BOUCLE D'OR 'Courtacour' (synonym GOLD CURL), a dwarf shrub to 0.5 × 1 m (1½ × 3 ft.), which could be grown in a container. 'Golden Nugget' has golden-yellow flowers up to 4 cm (1½ in.) across and reaches to 1.5 m (5 ft.) in height. MARÉE D'OR (synonym GOLD TIDE) 'Courtasol' 🏆 is suitable as ground cover, barely reaching 60 cm (2 ft.) tall but spreading to twice this and bears early lemon-yellow flowers.

↑ *Fothergilla major*

Fothergilla (Hamamelidaceae)

A small genus of deciduous shrubs with fragrant flowers in spring before or just as the leaves unfold. Without petals, they have long white stamens resembling a bottlebrush. Grow in sun or partial shade and in a humus-rich, lime-free soil. Prune only if necessary after flowering.

Fothergilla major 🏆 (synonym *F. monticola*) from southeastern North America is fairly slow growing with erect flower spikes to 5 cm (2 in.) long. The broad leaves become a spectacular red, orange and yellow in autumn. *Fothergilla gardenii* is half the size. Size: 2.5 × 2 m (8 × 6 ft.). Zone 5.

← *Fremontodendron* 'California Glory'

Fremontodendron synonym *Fremontia* (Sterculiaceae) flannel bush

The large bright golden-yellow flowers of the shrubs in this small, evergreen genus from southwestern North America and Mexico have no true petals but 5 large, petal-like sepals. The leaves are dark green and covered with hairs which may irritate the eyes and skin. When grown against a warm wall they can exceed 5 m (15 ft.). For profuse flowering, grow in full sun and in soil which is not too acid. Prune if necessary in summer after flowering.

Fremontodendron californicum has dark green, 3-lobed leaves to 7 cm (3 in.) and flowers to 6 cm (2½ in.) across from early summer to autumn. *Fremontodendron* 'California Glory' 🏆 is a vigorous and very free-flowering hybrid. Size (if unpruned): 6 × 4 m (18 × 12 ft.). Zones 8–9.

Fuchsia (Onagraceae)

This is a genus of about 100 evergreen and deciduous species of trees and shrubs, many of which are cultivated by specialists in warm greenhouses. From a small number of these, thousands of cultivars have been raised and named but most are grown as show, indoor or bedding plants. Some are suitable for growing in gardens where they make attractive, small, summer-flowering shrubs, though few can be considered fully hardy. Many of those mentioned below will survive in drier climates and some can be protected from cold by planting them slightly deeper than usual in the soil. A protective mulch in winter can be used as long as it does not hold water, causing the stem base to rot. The flowers, which encourage bees, are usually pendulous with 4 short petals forming a tube surrounded by 4 large, spreading, colourful sepals often with long protruding, coloured stamens. Outdoors, grow in sun or partial shade but sheltered from cold winds. In frost prone areas, grow in containers, feed and water regularly during the growing season but keep much drier during winter or maintain as cuttings. Prune in early spring as the first new growth reappears, removing older flowering branches.

A small selection of the newer and well-known hardier cultivars are listed here. Some will die back in colder winters, behaving as herbaceous perennials and growing back in spring.

Fuchsia magellanica from Chile and Argentina is the hardiest species and is involved in the

↑ *Fuchsia magellanica* 'Aurea'

parentage of the majority of the hardier cultivars; *Fuchsia magellanica* var. *gracilis* ♈ is the form most commonly seen. The flowers to about 2.5 cm (1 in.) long have a long, narrow red tube, bright red sepals and purple petals. This is the plant often seen as a hedge in the milder parts of Great Britain and should be trimmed in spring. 'Aurea' ♈ has golden-yellow foliage but is best grown in partial shade, while 'Variegata' ♈ has grey-green leaves variegated with creamy white often tinged pink. *Fuchsia magellanica* var. *molinae* (synonym 'Alba') has white flowers. Size (in mild areas and unpruned): 3 × 2.5 m (10 × 8 ft.). Zone: 7.

Cultivars with a more complex parentage include *Fuchsia* 'Alice Hoffman' ♈ which reaches to 60 cm (2 ft.) and has semi-double flowers with white petals veined red and rose pink sepals. 'David' ♈ is a neat plant to about 90 cm (3 ft.) with very small, single flowers, with red sepals and purple petals, smothering the bush. 'Heidi Ann' ♈ reaching to 60 cm (2 ft.), is fully double with red sepals and lilac-pink petals. 'Madame Cornélissen' ♈, a trusted old favourite, has single flowers with scarlet-red sepals and bright white petals. 'Margaret Brown' ♈, a taller plant to 1 m (3 ft.) in height, has rose-pink sepals and purplish pink petals. 'Rose of Castile Improved' ♈ with a spreading habit has white sepals and violet, pink-veined petals. 'Rufus' ♈ to 60 cm (2 ft.) tall has red sepals and dusky red petals. 'Tom Thumb' ♈ is a dwarf compact shrub to 30 cm (1 ft.) with scarlet sepals and violet-purple petals while 'Lady Thumb' ♈ is similar in habit but with semi-double red and white flowers.

↑ *Garrya elliptica*

Garrya (Garryaceae) silk tassel bush

A small genus of evergreen shrubs or small trees with leathery leaves and long pendulous catkins in late winter and early spring. Plants are either male or female but as the male catkins are more impressive, select a male cultivar. Grow in sun or partial shade and protect from cold winds which might damage the foliage. Plants can be trained against a wall where the catkins are shown off to advantage. Dead head if practical and trim back after flowering if necessary.

Garrya elliptica from western North America is a shrub with greyish green leaves with undulate margins. In late winter, it bears unusually coloured, grey-green catkins to 15 cm (6 in.) or more. 'James Roof' 🏆 is a male plant selected for the spectacular catkins usually exceeding 20 cm (8 in.) long. Size: 4 × 4 m (12 × 12 ft.). Zone 8.

Gaultheria (Ericaceae)

This genus of evergreen shrubs, which often spread by underground shoots, have white urn-shaped flowers in late spring or early summer followed by coloured fruits which are mildly poisonous if eaten. They are tough, hardy plants needing little attention as long as they are grown in a lime-free, preferably peaty soil and a fairly shaded position. Many make useful ground cover. Prune after flowering if necessary.

Gaultheria cuneata 🏆 from China is a dwarf compact shrub with small neat leaves which are slightly aromatic when crushed. The sprays of white flowers on reddish coloured stems are followed by spherical white fruits to 6 mm (¼ in.) across. 'Pinkie' has pink fruits. Size: 30 × 100 cm (1 × 3 ft.). Zone 6.

Gaultheria mucronata (synonym *Pernettya mucronata*) from South America has the showiest fruits of this genus. These reach 1.5 cm (½ in.) across in shades of red, purple, pink or white depending on the cultivar selected and it is worth finding a supplier who can provide named cultivars. These shrubs fruit best when planted in small groups with at least one guaranteed male plant as a pollinator, although 'Bell's Seedling' 🏆 is a hermaphrodite form which bears large dark red fruits without a male plant nearby. The fruits of 'Crimsonia' 🏆 are large and crimson. 'Mulberry Wine' 🏆 has purplish red berries turning deep purple. 'Pink Pearl' 🏆 has pale mauve-pink fruits and those

↑ *Gaultheria mucronata*

of 'Wintertime' ♕ are large and white. Size: 1 × 1 m (3 × 3 ft.). Zone 6.

Gaultheria procumbens ♕ (checkerberry, wintergreen) from eastern North America can be used as a low-growing, creeping ground cover which will carpet the ground in shade. The glossy leaves are aromatic as are the long-lasting bright red berries about 1 cm (½ in.) across. Wintergreen oil is extracted from this plant and the leaves are used for tea. Size: 15 × 100 cm (6 × 36 in.). Zone 4.

Genista (Papilionaceae) broom

A genus of deciduous broom-like shrubs, some with spines, almost all with racemes of yellow pea-like flowers and small leaves on green stems. They survive in poor dry soils but prefer to be in sun. Prune weak or dead branches after flowering but avoid cutting back too hard into the older wood.

Genista hispanica (Spanish gorse) from southwestern Europe is a dense, spiny, mounded bush smothered with bright golden-yellow flowers each to 1 cm (½ in.) long in late spring and early summer. Size: 0.75 × 1.5 m (2½ × 5 ft.). Zone 6.

Genista lydia ♕ from the east Balkans has arching, slightly prickly branches with grey-green leaves and yellow flowers 1.5 cm (½ in.) long in early summer. Size: 60 × 100 cm (2 × 3 ft.). Zone 7.

Genista sagittalis (synonym *Chamaespartium sagittale*) from central and southern Europe has short, erect, green-winged stems which in early summer terminate in short spikes of deep yellow flowers 1 cm (½ in.) long. Size: 15 × 100 cm (6 × 36 in.). Zone 5.

↑ *Genista hispanica*

Genista tinctoria (dyers greenwood) from Europe is very variable in its growth and size but always non-spiny with dark green leaves and rich yellow flowers in erect racemes to 6 cm (2½ in.) long through the summer. 'Flore Pleno' 🏆 is almost prostrate reaching only 40 cm (16 in.) tall with double flowers and 'Royal Gold' 🏆 is low-growing to about 80 cm (2½ ft.). Size: to about 1 × 1 m (3 × 3 ft.). Zone 3.

Ginkgo **(Ginkgoaceae)** maidenhair tree

Ginkgo biloba 🏆 is a very unique deciduous conifer which, although known from cultivation in Chinese gardens and as a fossil, has only recently been found in a few remote places in the wild. The typical plant is a rather narrow, erect tree with flat, fan-shaped leaves to 10 cm (4 in.) across on long leaf stalks, turning a beautiful clear yellow in autumn. Male and female flowers are formed on separate trees. Although the yellowish green plum-shaped fruits are edible and widely prized in China, they have a very unpleasant smell, so for an ornamental, select a male cultivar. Grow in sun or partial shade. Prune only to remove dead or weak branches in early spring. A number of cultivars have been raised such as the very new dwarf 'Troll', exceedingly slow growing and suitable for a container, reaching 2 m (6 ft.) in about 10 years. Size: 30 × 8 m (100 × 25 ft.). Zone 4.

Gleditsia **(Caesalpiniaceae)** locust tree

These large deciduous trees with strong thorns on their trunks and branches are usually grown as specimen trees for their elegant pinnate or bipinnate leaves. The greenish white flowers are not striking. They are tolerant of industrial air pollution but prefer a sunny position. Prune to remove dead or weak branches in winter.

Gleditsia triacanthos (honey locust) from North America reaches to 30 m (100 ft.) in height and has attractive fern-like leaves to 20 cm (8 in.) long with up to 32 leaflets. There are a few shorter cultivars. 'Rubylace' has deep bronze-red young foliage but it is less commonly available at present. 'Sunburst' 🏆 has become a popular tree for smaller gardens with yellow-green leaves turning green as they mature before becoming bright yellow in the autumn. It is a smaller tree and has the enormous advantage of being spineless. Size: 10 × 8 m (30 × 25 ft.). Zone 3.

Grevillea **(Proteaceae)** spider flower

A genus of evergreen shrubs mainly from Australia which have unusual flowers produced over many weeks. The coloured lobes of the petal-like calyx are rolled back displaying long protruding styles giving them a very exotic appearance. They need a lime-free soil in full sun. It would be possible to grow these in containers or conservatories for protection in winter and moved outdoors in summer. Prune if required in early spring. A number of newer cultivars such as the Poorinda hybrids in a range of colours, some of which are slightly hardier, are becoming available in nurseries.

Grevillea rosmarinifolia 🏆 is a bushy shrub with narrow, sharply pointed leaves to 4 cm (1½ in.) long and clusters to 7.5 cm (3 in.) across

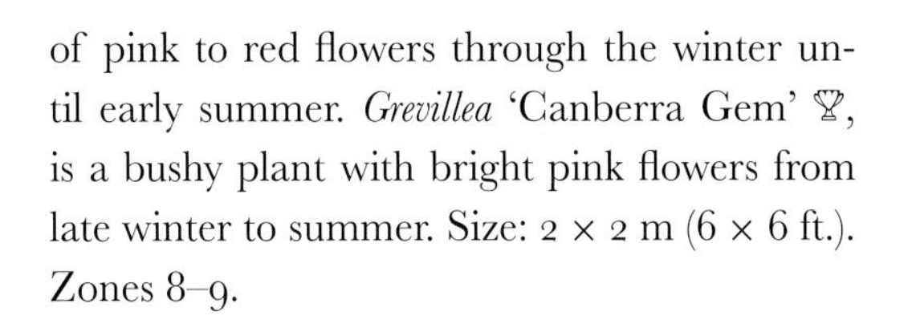

of pink to red flowers through the winter until early summer. *Grevillea* 'Canberra Gem' 🏆, is a bushy plant with bright pink flowers from late winter to summer. Size: 2 × 2 m (6 × 6 ft.). Zones 8–9.

Griselinia **(Griseliniaceae)**

A genus of evergreen shrubs or trees grown as individuals or hedges for their simple, glossy, leathery leaves rather than the inconspicuous yellowish green flowers. Grow in a sunny position and protect plants from cold winds in exposed areas. Prune hedges in summer.

Griselinia littoralis 🏆 from New Zealand, treelike in its native land, has attractive yellowish brown stems and fresh light green, broadly ovate leaves to 10 cm (4 in.) long. It is a useful

↓ *Grevillea rosmarinifolia*

↓ *Griselinia littoralis* 'Dixon's Cream'

informal hedge in coastal districts where it can also be used as a windbreak if allowed to grow a little taller. 'Dixon's Cream' has bright green leaves with central creamy yellow variegations, while 'Variegata' 🏆 has greyer-green leaves margined with creamy white. Size: 3 × 2 m (10 × 6 ft.). Zone 8.

↑ *Halesia tetraptera* var. *monticola* 'Vestita'

Halesia (Styracaceae) snowdrop tree

A genus of deciduous woodland trees, mostly from southeastern North America, grown for the wonderful spring display of pure white, snowdrop-like flowers, hanging on long flower stalks from the underside of the branches before the leaves are fully unfolded. The flowers are followed by unusual, 2- or 4-winged, pendulous fruits which are attractive through the winter. Grow in any good garden soil unless alkaline. Prune in winter if necessary.

Halesia diptera is a tree but often more shrublike in cultivation. It has more rounded leaves and 2-winged fruits. It is worth searching for the very rare var. *magniflora* with impressive, pure white flowers to 3 cm (1 ½ in.) across. Size: to 10 × 7 m (30 × 20 ft.). Zone 6.

***Halesia tetraptera* var. *monticola* 'Vestita'** 🏆 (synonym *H. monticola* var. *vestita*) is a very floriferous, upright tree with ovate leaves to 20 cm (8 in.) long turning yellow in autumn. The pendulous flowers, up to 3 cm (1 ½ in.) across in late spring, are in clusters of up to 5. Forma *rosea* has delicate pale pink flowers. Size: to 12 × 8 m (35 × 25 ft.). Zone 5.

×*Halimiocistus* (Cistaceae)

A genus of hybrids produced from crosses between *Cistus* and *Halimium* which are small, sun-loving, evergreen shrubs with shallow, cup-shaped, 5-petalled flowers. Grow in very well-drained, sandy soils in full sun, perhaps at the front of a border. Pruning is rarely needed.

×Halimiocistus sahucii 🏆 from southern France is a very hardy, low-growing, spreading shrub with narrow dark green leaves to 4 cm (1 ½ in.) long and pure white flowers with a yellow centre of numerous stamens to 3 cm (1 ½ in.) across, flowering through the summer. Size: to 45 × 90 cm (1 ½ × 3 ft.). Zone 8.

×Halimiocistus wintonensis 🏆 has grey-green, hairy, ovate leaves to 5 cm (2 in.) long and in late spring and early summer bears clusters of white flowers to 5 cm (2 in.) across which have a yellow base to each petal and a very

striking, broad, dark crimson band just above. A sport of this plant, 'Merrist Wood Cream' 🏆 differs only in its cream-yellow instead of white petals. Size: to 60 × 90 cm (2 × 3 ft.). Zone 8.

Halimium (Cistaceae)

A genus of low-growing evergreen shrubs with cup-shaped, 5-petalled flowers. Grow in a well-drained sandy soil in full sun in the front of a border or in containers. Pruning is rarely required.

Halimium calycinum from the western Mediterranean region is a dwarf, more or less erect shrub with very narrow, dark green leaves to 1 cm (½ in.) long and bright golden-yellow flowers to 2.5 cm (1 in.) across in early summer. Size: to 50 × 50 cm (20 × 20 in.). Zone 8.

Halimium lasianthum 🏆 from southwestern Europe is a small spreading shrub with grey-green ovate leaves to 4 cm (1½ in.) long and yellow flowers to 3 cm (1½ in.) across. Some, like

↑ *Halimium lasianthum*

'Sandling', have a maroon-red blotch on each petal. Size: to 1 × 1.5 m (3 × 5 ft.). Zone 8.

Hamamelis (Hamamelidaceae)

witch hazel

A genus of deciduous woodland shrubs grown for their autumn or winter flowers and broad, almost rounded leaves 10–15 cm (4–6 in.) long which give brilliant autumn displays of red, orange or yellow. The curious flowers 2–3 cm (1–1½ in.) across, often fragrant, are spider-like with 4 long, narrow petals, and formed in dense stalkless clusters along the branches. When buying a witch hazel, it is worth ensuring that the plant is a named cultivar or one which has been propagated vegetatively, because those grown from seed will not necessarily produce good flowering plants. Grow in moist but well-drained, fertile acid or neutral soil in sun or partial shade. Prune after flowering to remove weak or dead shoots. In a restricted space, cut back long shoots after flowering to keep the shrub within bounds.

Hamamelis ×intermedia has produced a number of the most commonly grown cultivars. 'Aurora' has very large and sweetly scented orange-yellow flowers. 'Barmstedt Gold' ♀ is an upright plant with large, deep yellow, slightly scented flowers. 'Diane' ♀ is one of the older red-flowered cultivars with good autumn colour but needs a lighter coloured background for the flowers to show well. 'Jelena' ♀ has yellow flowers suffused with coppery orange and orange-red autumn colour. 'Orange Peel' is one of the newer Dutch cultivars with an upright habit, scented, light orange flowers and red and orange autumn foliage. 'Pallida' ♀ has well-scented, sulphur-yellow flowers and its lighter yellow colour shows up well on a dark winter day. Size: to 4 × 4 m (12 × 12 ft.). Zone 6.

Hamamelis japonica (Japanese witch hazel) from Japan has yellow flowers, a slightly lemony scent and very twisted or crinkled petals in mid to late winter. Size: to 4 × 4 m (12 × 12 ft.). Zone 5.

Hamamelis mollis ♀ (Chinese witch hazel) from China has sweetly scented, golden-yellow flowers in mid to late winter. Size: to 4 × 4 m (12 × 12 ft.). Zone 6.

Hamamelis vernalis (Ozark witch hazel) from North America is sometimes grown for the autumn foliage, especially 'Sandra' ♀ with purple-tinged young leaves turning to all shades of yellow, orange and red in autumn. The yellow winter flowers are small. Size: to 5 × 5 m (15 × 15 ft.). Zone 5.

Hardenbergia (Papilionaceae)

coral pea

A small genus of twining climbers from Australia with pea-like flowers and usually pinnate leaves. Grow in sun or partial shade in a very sheltered position or in a container moving it into a conservatory for protection from winter frost. Prune after flowering to restrict size.

Hardenbergia violacea ♀ (purple coral pea) has violet flowers spotted with yellow at the base of the upper petals. The flowers to 1 cm (½ in.) across in pendulous racemes to 13 cm (5 in.) long, flower over a long season from late winter to early summer. This species has only one leathery leaflet to each leaf, to 10 cm (4 in.) long. Height: 2 m (6 ft.). Zone 9.

← *Hamamelis ×intermedia* 'Pallida'

Hebe 'Pink Paradise' →

Hebe **(Scrophulariaceae)**

This genus of evergreen shrubs, mostly from New Zealand, are tolerant plants grown for their flower and foliage. Variable in their habit, they make useful dwarf or small bushy shrubs attracting both bees and butterflies. As a general rule, the larger plants with larger leaves are less hardy but all grow well in coastal locations. The open flowers, white or in shades of pink or blue, reach about 5–10 mm (¼–½ in.) across with 4 petals, usually arranged in clusters or dense spikes from late spring to midautumn. The leaves are often arranged in 4 strict ranks giving an unusual cross-shaped appearance when viewed from above. Some species, known as whipcord hebes, have tiny scalelike leaves pressed tightly against the stem. Grow in any soils, unless strongly acid, in sun or partial shade. Prune rarely unless trimming to shape after flowering or to maintain bushiness.

Hebe macrantha 🏆 has large white flowers to 2 cm (¾ in.) or more across in small clusters in early summer. It is a branching, spreading shrub with leathery, bright green leaves reaching about 2.5 cm (1 in.). Size: to 60 × 90 cm (2 × 3 ft.). Zone 7.

Hebe ochracea **'James Stirling'** 🏆 is one of the small whipcord hebes with dull gold foliage especially attractive in winter. It initially has erect stems but later becomes a more spreading shrub. The white spring flowers are borne in few-flowered racemes to 2 cm (¾ in.). Size: to 45 × 60 cm (1½ × 2 ft.). Zone 6.

Hebe pinguifolia **'Pagei'** 🏆 is grown mainly for its grey-green leaves to 1.5 cm (½ in.) long contrasting with purplish red stems on a wide-spreading but dwarf shrub. The white flowers are borne in short, dense, erect spikes in early summer. The all-year-round foliage colour makes this a useful ground cover shrub. Size: to 30 × 90 cm (1 × 3 ft.). Zone 6.

Hebe **'Pink Paradise'** is a newer compact cultivar with small clusters of bright pink flowers from late spring through the summer. Size: to 60 × 60 cm (2 × 2 ft.). Zone 6.

Some of the larger-leaved, taller and less hardy cultivars include 'Autumn Glory' which is about 1 m (3 ft.) tall with dark violet-blue flowers in late summer to early autumn. 'Great Orme' ♕ has bright pink flowers which fade to almost white giving a two-tone effect to the dense spikes to 10 cm (4 in.) long. Flowering from midsummer to autumn, it reaches to about 1.2 m (4 ft.) tall. 'La Séduisante' has crimson-red flowers in racemes to 7.5 cm (3 in.) from late summer into the autumn. It forms a shrub to about 1 m (3 ft.) tall. 'Midsummer Beauty' ♕ to 2 m (6 ft.) tall has leaves flushed red underneath and long spikes of lilac-coloured flowers to 15 cm (6 in.) from midsummer to autumn. Zone 8.

Hedera (Araliaceae) ivy

A genus of evergreen shrubs which climb by attaching to a support using aerial roots. They are grown for their foliage and a large number of named cultivars with different leaf shapes and variegation can be obtained. Plants do not flower until reaching maturity, but then they become more shrublike, often change the leaf shape and produce clusters of greenish flowers in autumn which are very attractive to late flying insects. These are followed by black berries which are mildly poisonous but a useful winter food for birds. Many cultivars never reach this stage but all plants provide good shelter for birds and insects. Ivies adapt to a range of situations from covering trellis, fences or old stumps, creating arbours, growing in containers, serving as ground cover or even creating exotic shapes as topiary. Some cultivars are used as house plants in window boxes or hanging baskets. If grown against a wall with loose mortar, the roots may cause some damage, especially if removed carelessly. A few people find the hairs on the stems an irritant. Grow in any soils, unless extremely acid, and in most light conditions. The yellow-leaved cultivars give the best colour in a sunny position. Prune to shape at almost any time of year and remove any reverted green shoots which appear on variegated plants.

Hedera helix (common ivy or English ivy) from Europe has 3- to 5-lobed leaves to 5 cm (2 in.) or more across which become unlobed in maturity. Numerous cultivars have been selected which are grown in gardens. Height: 10 m (30 ft.) if unchecked. Zone 5.

'Adam' has small, 3-lobed, greyish green leaves with a creamy white margin. It is not vigorous and often used in containers. 'Buttercup' with rich yellow 5-lobed leaves, golden if grown in sun, does not normally exceed about 2–3 m (6–10 ft.). 'Congesta' ♕ is a curious dwarf shrub with erect, non-climbing branches to 45 cm (1½ ft.) bearing triangular leaves. 'Goldheart', an old and very popular cultivar which should correctly be called 'Oro di Bogliasco', has quite small leaves with a very striking gold central blotch. 'Maple Leaf' ♕ is an uncommon cultivar with green leaves deeply divided into 5 narrow lobes, the central lobe much longer than the rest. Forma *poetarum* (Italian ivy, poet's ivy) is an unusual and rare form with yellow berries and bright green leaves becoming bronze coloured in winter.

Helianthemum (Cistaceae) rock rose, sun rose

A genus of low-growing evergreen shrubs grown for their flowers, especially useful in the front of borders, in troughs, on a wall or

bank. The 5-petalled flowers, about 2.5 cm (1 in.) across, open in succession from early to midsummer and attract bees. Grow in any very well-drained soils, unless extremely acid, in full sun. Prune after flowering, cutting old flowered stems back to allow new growth to take over. A number of species are grown but the majority of plants seen in gardens are low-growing carpeting plants with narrow, grey-green leaves and a range of flower colours. All are hybrids of ***Helianthemum nummularium*** and one or two other related European species. Size: to about 30 × 45 cm (1 × 1½ ft.). Zone 5.

***Helianthemum* 'Fire Dragon'** 🏆 is an eye-catching orange-red. 'Raspberry Ripple' has bicoloured white flowers with a magenta coloured centre spreading into the petals. 'Rhodanthe Carneum' 🏆 has light pink flowers with a small orange eye. 'The Bride' 🏆 has white flowers. 'Wisley Primrose' 🏆 has primrose yellow flowers with a slightly darker yellow eye.

↑ *Helianthemum* 'The Bride'

Double-flowered cultivars include 'Jubilee' 🏆 with yellow flowers and green leaves and 'Mrs C. W. Earle' 🏆 with bright red flowers, a small yellow centre and dark green leaves.

Helichrysum (Asteraceae)

A very large and diverse genus of herbaceous and woody plants. Several are grown for their dried "everlasting" flowers or in hanging baskets but few are fully hardy. Grow in not too rich a soil in full sun. Prune in spring.

Helichrysum italicum* subsp. *serotinum (synonym *H. serotinum*; curry plant) from southern Europe has strongly curry-scented, linear, silvery leaves to 4 cm (1½ in.) long. In summer, flat heads to 8 cm (3 in.) across of tiny deep bright yellow flowers are formed. Size: to 60 × 60 cm (2 × 2 ft.). Zone 8.

↑ *Helichrysum italicum* subsp. *serotinum*

Helichrysum splendidum ♕ from South Africa is a small rounded shrub with erect, white, woolly stems covered with small grey leaves. In late summer, the bright yellow "everlasting" flower heads to 5 cm (2 in.) across are formed and will remain on the plant for many months. Size: to 1 × 1 m (3 × 3 ft.). Zone 7.

Heptacodium (Caprifoliaceae) seven son flower of Zhejiang

Heptacodium miconioides (synonym *H. jasminoides*) from China, the only species in this genus, is a vigorous deciduous shrub with attractive peeling bark and rather brittle stems. The ovate, dark green leaves with 3 prominent veins are almost folded along the midrib. The star-shaped, white, scented flowers form in branching 7-flowered clusters at the ends of the stems. In hot sunny conditions, the calyces turns a bright red as the flowers fade and remain on the plant for many weeks. Although large, it can be pruned regularly to keep it within bounds. It is a useful, but uncommon, shrub flowering later than most in late summer and early autumn. Grow in sun or partial shade. Prune in spring if necessary. Size: to 6 × 3 m (18 × 10 ft.). Zone 7.

Hibiscus (Malvaceae)

A genus of woody and herbaceous plants grown for their large and showy funnel-shaped flowers. Grow in any garden soil, unless strongly acid, in full sun. Prune if required in late spring.

Hibiscus syriacus from Asia has been cultivated in gardens for several hundred years and is the only truly hardy species, commonly grown for its late summer flowers. It is deciduous with a rather erect habit and dark green, ovate, usually toothed leaves unfolding late in spring. The large flowers to 6 cm (2 ½ in.) across are formed in succession, depending on the weather and the cultivar, from midsummer to midautumn but need warm weather to flower well. Numerous single and double-flowered cultivars have been named varying in flower colour from white through shades of pink, mauve and blue. It makes an effective flowering hedge. 'Diana' ♕ has very large, pure white, single flowers to 13 cm (5 in.) across. The white flowers of 'Red Heart' ♕ have a deep red eye. WHITE CHIFFON 'Notwoodtwo' ♕ has white, semi-double, rather flat flowers, while the similar LAVENDER CHIFFON 'Notwoodone' ♕ has lavender flowers with a red centre. 'Oiseau Bleu' ♕ (synonym 'Blue Bird') has single, violet-blue flowers with a small red eye, and 'Woodbridge' 🏆 has large, single, rose-pink flowers with a deeper reddish pink eye. 'Duc de Brabant' is double with purplish pink flowers. Size: to 2.5 × 1.5 m (8 × 5 ft.). Zone 5.

Hoheria **(Malvaceae)**

A small genus of evergreen and deciduous trees and shrubs from New Zealand grown for their fragrant, white, summer flowers. Grow as a specimen plant in any soil, unless extremely acid, in sun or partial shade. Prune only if necessary to remove dead or weak stems in spring.

Hoheria sexstylosa (ribbonwood) is a tall shrub or small tree with evergreen, glossy, lance-shaped, sharply toothed leaves to 8 cm (3 in.) or more long. Pendulous branches bear star-shaped flowers to 2.5 cm (1 in.) across in clusters in midsummer. 'Stardust' 🏆 is more erect with slightly larger flowers. Size: to 6 × 4 m (18 × 12 ft.). Zone 8.

Hydrangea **(Hydrangeaceae)**

A genus of deciduous and evergreen shrubs, some climbing by aerial roots, grown for their flowers arranged in large, showy, flattened or conical heads. There are usually two sorts of flower. The tiny ones normally found in the centre of the head are fertile, but the others are sterile with large, conspicuous, coloured petal-like sepals which attract the pollinating insects. The flowers tend to stay on the plant for many weeks and often change colour over time. They are also effective in floral arrangements when dried. Many species have white flowers but

↑ *Hibiscus syriacus* WHITE CHIFFON 'Notwoodtwo'

↓ *Hydrangea quercifolia*

others such as the popular hortensias may have blue or pink flowers and the depth of colour is affected by the acidity and other nutrients in the soil. In general, the more acid the soil the bluer the flower colour, so naturally pink flowers become more mauve in acid soils, and alternatively blue flowers become more mauve in alkaline conditions. However, flower colour is the result of a combination of factors, so a simple generalisation is not possible. A blueing compound can be purchased and applied to influence the colour. Flower heads may be described as lacecaps or mop-heads. In the lacecap type, the flower head is flattened with tiny fertile flowers in the centre and showy sterile flowers around the outside. In mop-heads, all the flowers are sterile creating a spherical head. Grow in sun or partial shade. Pruning depends on the species being grown.

Hydrangea anomala* subsp. *petiolaris 🏆 (synonym *H. petiolaris*) from eastern Asia is a climbing, deciduous species with heart-shaped leaves to about 10 cm (4 in.). In summer, it bears slightly rounded heads to 20 cm (8 in.) across, of small creamy white flowers surrounded by showy sterile flowers. This shrub needs to be attached to a support to encourage it to climb for the first year. Prune after flowering to train into the available space. Height: 15 m (50 ft.). Zone 5.

Hydrangea macrophylla (common hydrangea) from Japan has many cultivars of both the mop-head and lacecap type. It makes a rounded deciduous shrub, especially effective in coastal conditions. The shoots can be cut back by about a quarter each spring. 'Mariesii Perfecta' 🏆 (synonym 'Blue Wave') is a blue lacecap with mauve flowers in alkaline soils. 'Möwe' 🏆 (synonym 'Geoffrey Chadbund') a lacecap, has mauve flowers in acid and red in alkaline soils. 'Générale Vicomtesse de Vibraye' 🏆 is a mop-head with pure blue flowers in acid or pink in alkaline soils. 'Ami Pasquier' 🏆 is a deep red-flowered mop-head which in alkaline conditions is more reddish purple. Also a few new cultivars are being introduced with double ray florets such as 'Jogasaki', a lacecap with bluer ray florets in acid soil. Size: to 2 × 2 m (6 × 6 ft.). Zone 5.

Hydrangea paniculata from eastern Asia has conical heads 20 cm (8 in.) or more tall, of white flowers in late summer and early autumn. The flower heads will be even larger, the plant smaller and the flowers later, if the shoots are cut back hard to about 25 cm (10 in.) in spring. Mulch after flowering. 'Burgundy Lace' has white flowers becoming pink as they age. 'Limelight' has lime-green flowers and 'Phantom' has possibly the largest white flower heads to 30 cm (12 in.). Size: to 3 × 3 m (10 × 10 ft.) if not cut back. Zone 3.

Hydrangea quercifolia 🏆 (oak-leaved hydrangea) from southern USA is a mounded, deciduous shrub with large, 5- to 7-lobed, oak-like leaves to 20 cm (8 in.) long which turn bronze-red in autumn. In midsummer, both the sterile and fertile flowers, in large conical inflorescences to 25 cm (10 in.) tall, are initially white, becoming flushed with pink as they age. It can be cut back hard in early spring. Size: to 2 × 2.5 m (6 × 8 ft.). Zone 5.

Hydrangea serrata from Korea and Japan is a small deciduous shrub with narrow leaves to about 15 cm (6 in.) bearing lacecap type flower heads 5–10 cm (2–4 in.) across from summer to autumn. Cut back to below the flower heads after flowering or in spring. Several good cultivars are available. 'Grayswood' ♈ has white sterile flowers becoming pink and then dark red as they age while the fertile flowers may be pink or blue. 'Tiara' ♈ has blue fertile and sterile flowers in acid soils which are pink in alkaline conditions. The leaves are purple-tinged in autumn. Size: to 1.2 × 1.2 m (4 × 4 ft.). Zone 6.

Hypericum (Clusiaceae) St John's wort

A very large genus of woody and herbaceous plants grown for their flowers. The cultivated woody species may be evergreen or deciduous but all have bright golden-yellow flowers with a mass of showy stamens in the centre usually in summer or autumn. In some, the fruits are also ornamental but mildly poisonous. Some are dwarf species best grown in a well-drained soil in sun. Grow others in sun or partial shade. Cut back older flowering stems after flowering or in early spring.

Hypericum coris from southern and central Europe is a dwarf evergreen with tiny needle-like leaves to 1.5 cm (½ in.) long. In summer, up to about 20 cup-shaped flowers to 2 cm (¾ in.) across are borne in branching flower heads. Size: to 20 × 30 cm (8 × 12 in.). Zone 7.

Hypericum 'Hidcote' ♈ is possibly one of the hypericums most commonly seen in gardens. It is a tall, bushy, semi-evergreen shrub with narrow, dark green leaves to 6 cm (2½ in.) and is covered from summer to early autumn with clusters of up to 6 large cup-shaped flowers each to 6 cm (2½ in.) across. Size: to 2 × 1.5 m (6 × 5 ft.). Zone 6.

Hypericum kouytchense ♈ from China is a small semi-evergreen shrub with arching branches and bluish green leaves to 6 cm (2½ in.) long. It bears flowers to 6 cm (2½ in.) across with petals, which tend to turn back, developing into attractive bright red conical capsules. As the plant flowers from summer into autumn, both capsule and flowers may be present at the same time. Size: to 1 × 1.5 m (3 × 5 ft.). Zone 6.

Hypericum ×moserianum ♈ is usually represented in gardens as the variegated cultivar 'Tricolor'. This is a semi-evergreen shrub with arching branches bearing ovate leaves to 6 cm (2½ in.) long which are coloured pink, cream and green. The cup-shaped flowers reach 5 cm (2 in.) across through the summer until autumn. Size: to 30 × 60 cm (1 × 2 ft.). Zone 7.

Hypericum olympicum ♈ from the eastern Mediterranean is a dwarf semi-evergreen shrub with arching branches and small, narrow, blue-green leaves to 4 cm (1½ in.) bearing clusters of star-shaped flowers 5 cm (2 in.) across in summer. Size: to 25 × 30 cm (10 × 12 in.). Zone 6.

Hyssopus (Lamiaceae)

Hyssopus officinalis (hyssop) from southern Europe is the only commonly cultivated species in the genus. It has been used as both a culinary and medicinal herb and also attracts bees and butterflies. It is a small shrub with erect shoots bearing narrow, aromatic leaves to 5 cm (2 in.) long. In summer, spikes to 10 cm (4 in.) or more tall of bright blue, 2-lipped flowers 1.5 cm (½ in.) long are formed at the tops of the shoots. Grow in any well-drained soil, unless extremely acid, in sun. Cut back in early spring or after flowering to prevent the plant becoming straggly. Size: to 60 × 60 cm (2 × 2 ft.). Zone 3.

Ilex (Aquifoliaceae) holly

This is a very large genus of deciduous and evergreen trees, shrubs and climbers from all over the world. It includes tender species from tropical regions and very hardy plants from cold areas. A number are grown in temperate gardens for their berries including the common English holly, which is part of Christmas rituals in several countries. Plants are either male or female and only those with female flowers will produce berries. At least one related plant with male flowers is needed in the vicinity to ensure that the female flowers are fertilised and produce the berries for which these plants are usually grown. The evergreen species are useful for topiary and hedges, and most can be trained as standard trees. By growing larger plants in containers, they may be kept small and accommodated in a restricted space. Several species have a wide range of cultivars with differing plant shapes, leaf shapes, spine number, variegation and fruit colour. All provide berries for birds and nectar for bees. The majority are tolerant of sun or shade, coastal conditions and air pollution, as well as almost any soil with the exception of the American species, including *Ilex verticillata*, which prefer lime-free conditions.

↑ *Ilex ×altaclerensis* 'Lawsoniana'

Cut hedges in late summer and trim topiary in summer.

Ilex ×altaclerensis (Highclere holly) is a handsome evergreen tree or shrub with large, spiny or spineless leaves and red berries. It is very suitable for large hedges and windbreaks. 'Belgica Aurea' 🏆 (female) has narrow leaves with a creamy yellow marginal variegation. 'Camelliifolia' 🏆 (female) has dark green spineless leaves on purple stems. 'Golden King' 🏆 (female) has leaves with broad gold margins, often spineless. 'Lawsoniana' 🏆 (female) has large leaves with yellow central variegation, usually without spines. Size: 20 × 15 m (60 × 50 ft.). Zone 6.

Ilex aquifolium 🏆 (common holly, English holly) from Europe, North Africa and western Asia has long been cultivated as a dense evergreen tree or shrub with spiny leaves with a wavy margin and usually red, but sometimes yellow, fruits. It makes a good hedge. 'Alaska' with small, narrow, spiny leaves is a shorter, narrowly conical female plant which fruits even when young. 'Amber' 🏆 (female) has orange-yellow fruits. 'Ferox' (male) hedgehog holly has curious leaves with spines in centre as well as on margins. 'Ferox Argentea' 🏆 (male) similar to 'Ferox' but with silver-margined leaves. 'Madame Briot' 🏆 (female) has spiny leaves with golden-yellow margins contrasting with purple stems. 'Silver Milkmaid' (female) has leaves with central white variegation. The leaves of 'Silver Queen' 🏆 (male) are margined creamy white against purple stems and those of 'Golden Milkboy' (male) have a good yellow central variegation. Size: 25 × 8 m (75 × 25 ft.). Zone 6.

Ilex crenata (Japanese holly, box holly) from Japan, Korea and Russia has small, spineless, evergreen, dark leaves 2–3 cm (¾–1½ in.) long and usually black fruits. It is slow growing and especially useful for dwarf hedges and topiary. 'Golden Gem' 🏆 (female) is a compact, dwarf plant with yellow leaves especially showy in winter. 'Shiro-fukurin' (female) has leaves edged with silver. Size: 5 × 4 m (15 × 12 ft.). Zone 6.

Ilex* ×*meserveae (blue holly) resulted from hybridization in the USA to try to breed a hardier, evergreen, red-berrying holly. The result is a bushy, evergreen shrub, smaller than the common holly, with blue-green, spiny leaves and shiny red fruits. BLUE PRINCESS 'Conapri' is a female cultivar and BLUE PRINCE 'Conablu' is a very good male pollinator. Size: 2 × 1.5 m (6 × 5 ft.). Zone 6.

Ilex verticillata (black alder, winterberry) from eastern North America is a deciduous shrub with long-lasting red fruits and yellow autumn colour. Size: 5 × 5 m (15 × 15 ft.). Zone 4.

Indigofera (Papilionaceae)

A large genus of herbaceous and woody plants of which a few deciduous shrubs are grown in temperate areas for their racemes of small pea-like flowers as well as their graceful pinnate leaves. Most flower over a long period through the summer. Grow in a fertile, rich soil in full sun. Trim back any dead or weak branches in early spring and cut back any leggy plants hard. The genus *Lespedeza* differs slightly in the leaflets and fruits but can be treated in a similar way. *Lespedeza thunbergii* 🏆 (synonym *L. sieboldii*, *Desmodium penduliflorum*) with large branched inflorescences of pinkish purple flowers and

↓ *Indigofera heterantha*

the much less common white-flowered form, 'White Fountain', are useful autumn-flowering shrubs.

Indigofera amblyantha ♀ from China has bright green leaves with up to 11 leaflets and long upright racemes to 11 cm (4½ in.) of pink flowers through the summer. Size: 2 × 2.5 m (6 × 8 ft.). Zone 5.

Indigofera heterantha ♀ (synonym *I. gerardiana*) comes from the Himalayas. The leaves have up to 21 grey-green leaflets and the erect racemes of bright purplish pink flowers reach about 15 cm (6 in.) in length. Size: 2.5 × 2.5 m (8 × 8 ft.). Zone 7.

Itea (Escalloniaceae)

A small genus of evergreen and deciduous shrubs grown for their green or white, summer flowers. Grow in partial shade. Prune to maintain the shape after flowering for deciduous species and in midspring for evergreens.

Itea ilicifolia ♀ from China is an evergreen with glossy, dark green, spiny, holly-like leaves. In late summer and early autumn, it is laden with 30 cm (1 ft.) long pendulous catkins of tiny, fragrant, greenish white flowers. This species will also grow in sun and it does well against a warm wall where it is protected from wind and less likely to become waterlogged. In warmer parts of the country, it could be grown as a free standing plant. Size: to 3 × 3 m (10 × 10 ft.). Zone 7.

Itea virginica from eastern North America is a deciduous species with scented, creamy white flowers in racemes to 15 cm (6 in.) long in summer. The leaves colour well in autumn. Size: 2 × 1.5 m (6 × 5 ft.). Zone 5.

Jasminum (Oleaceae) jasmine, jessamine

This is a large genus of mainly evergreens, the majority of which are tropical twining climbers with highly scented white flowers. However, several species can be grown outdoors in temperate climates for their often scented flowers which are followed by black berries. Grow in sun or partial shade and train the climbing species against a wall, fence or trellis. Prune after flowering.

Jasminum beesianum from China is unique within the genus because of the colour of the fragrant, pinkish red flowers to 8 mm (¼ in.) across. It is a climber and, although naturally evergreen, may behave as a deciduous plant in colder areas. Height: 4.5 m (15 ft.). Zone 7.

Jasminum fruticans from the Mediterranean region is the only species found wild in Europe. It forms an erect semi-evergreen shrub with green stems covered by small, slightly scented, yellow flowers to 1.5 cm (½ in.) across through the summer. Size: 1.5 × 1.5 m (5 × 5 ft.). Zone 8.

Jasminum mesnyi ♀ (synonym *J. primulinum*; primrose jasmine) from China is a scrambling evergreen which needs support to enable it to climb. It bears large, semi-double, golden-yellow flowers to 4 cm (1½ in.) across in spring and summer but needs a warm sunny wall to thrive. Height: 3 m (10 ft.). Zones 8–9.

Jasminum nudiflorum ♕ (winter jasmine) from China is a deciduous scrambling plant grown for the abundance of welcome yellow flowers to 2.5 cm (1 in.) across in midwinter contrasting with green stems. Height: 3 m (10 ft.). Zone 6.

Jasminum officinale ♕ (common jasmine, poet's jasmine) from the western Himalayas to China has masses of white, highly scented flowers to 2.5 cm (1 in.) across through the summer. It is a vigorous, usually deciduous, twining climber, which may need to be pruned hard if it gets out of control in a small space. FIONA SUNRISE 'Frojas' has yellow-flushed foliage and the new 'Clotted Cream' has green leaves and cream flowers. The more tender *J. polyanthum* ♕ is somewhat similar with attractive red buds. Height: 12 m (35 ft.). Zone 7.

Jasminum parkeri from the western Himalayas is quite distinct forming a creeping mat rarely over 30 cm (1 ft.) tall. In late spring, it is covered with yellow flowers to about 1.5 cm (½ in.) across. Size: 30 × 30 cm (1 × 1 ft.). Zone 7.

Jovellana (Scrophulariaceae)

A genus of mainly herbaceous plants related to *Calceolaria* which includes the semi-evergreen subshrub, ***Jovellana violacea*** ♕ from Chile. It has small toothed leaves and in summer bears panicles of delicate pale purple flowers with yellow throats spotted with deep purple. Each flower is 2-lipped and about 1.5 cm (½ in.) across. It is worth taking cuttings each year as the plant can be short-lived. In cooler areas, grow under glass but elsewhere it survives in a sheltered garden or against a wall in sun or partial shade. Size: 60 × 90 cm (2 × 3 ft.). Zone 9.

↑ *Jovellana violacea*

Kalmia (Ericaceae)

These are mainly evergreen shrubs from North America covered in early summer with large showy clusters of red, pink or white bowl-

↑ *Kalmia latifolia*

shaped flowers which have an unusual pleated or crimped appearance, especially in bud. They are related to rhododendrons and grow in similar conditions in a moist, lime-free soil, preferably in sun for profuse flowering, although they thrive in dappled shade. Trim to thin plants only if necessary. All parts of the plant are poisonous if eaten.

Kalmia latifolia 🏆 (calico bush, mountain laurel) has pink flowers to 2.5 cm (1 in.) wide in larger clusters to 10 cm (4 in.) across. A number of cultivars are available. 'Carousel' has white flowers with dark red-purple banding on the inside. 'Freckles' 🏆 has pink buds opening to very pale pink flowers spotted with purple. 'Minuet' is a dwarf plant with pink flowers banded with dark red inside. 'Ostbo Red' has bright red buds opening to pale pink flowers. 'Snowdrift' is a compact plant with white flowers. Size: 2.5 × 2.5 m (8 × 8 ft.). Zone 4.

↑ *Kerria japonica* 'Pleniflora'

Kerria **(Rosaceae)** Jew's mantle

Kerria japonica from China and Japan is the only species of this genus. It is a reliable, hardy, deciduous, suckering shrub with slender green stems attractive in winter and covered in spring with bright golden-yellow flowers to 4–5 cm (1½–2 in.) across. Grow in sun or partial shade. Remove older stems and thin out suckers after flowering as this shrub can spread if not controlled. 'Albescens' is a very rare form with single white flowers. 'Golden Guinea' 🏆 has very large, single, yellow flowers to over 5 cm (2 in.) across. 'Picta' has leaves, grey-green and variegated with a creamy white margin. 'Pleniflora' 🏆 is the vigorous double-flowered form most commonly seen in gardens. Size: 2.5 × 3 m (8 × 10 ft.). Zone 4.

↑ *Koelreuteria paniculata*

↑ *Kolkwitzia amabilis*

Koelreuteria **(Sapindaceae)** golden rain, pride of India

A small genus of deciduous trees of which ***Koelreuteria paniculata*** 🏆 from China is an attractive, small, spreading tree which makes a good specimen plant. The young leaves are bronze-tinged as they unfold to handsome pinnately divided leaves with up to 15 leaflets, reaching 45 cm (1½ ft.) in length. The good yellow autumn foliage is an added bonus. In summer, large panicles to 30 cm (1 ft.) long with numerous small, star-like yellow flowers attract bees. These are followed in hot, dry summers by inflated capsules to 5 cm (2 in.) long containing the seeds. It is very tolerant, thriving in any soil in sun, but prefers hot summers to flower and fruit well. Pruning is rarely necessary. 'Fastigiata' is a rare but very upright and narrow tree with coral-red young foliage turning orange in autumn. Height: 9 m (30 ft.). Zone 7.

Kolkwitzia **(Caprifoliaceae)** beauty bush

Kolkwitzia amabilis from western China is the only species in this genus. It forms a deciduous shrub with peeling brown bark and in late spring and early summer is covered with arching branches of bell-shaped pink flowers with yellow throats to 1.5 cm (½ in.) long. It grows best in sun. Remove older or weaker shoots from the base after flowering. 'Pink Cloud' 🏆 is an especially good form. Size: to 3 × 4 m (10 ×12 ft.). Zone 4.

Laburnum **(Papilionaceae)** golden rain

A genus of small deciduous trees grown for their pendulous racemes of bright yellow flowers in late spring and early summer. These plants are poisonous and the black pea-like seeds are especially so, but the hybrids are less likely to produce seed in any quantity. Grow in a sunny position. The trees may be used as specimen plants or trained on an arch or pergola so that the hanging racemes are well displayed. Prune in late summer to autumn if necessary.

Laburnum ×watereri is more often seen in gardens than either of its parents. The 3 leaflets are about 7.5 cm (3 in.) long and the numerous fragrant flowers 2 cm (¾ in.) long are in racemes reaching 50 cm (20 in.) long. 'Vossii' ♕ is the cultivar most commonly grown with golden-yellow flowers in even longer racemes to 60 cm (2 ft.). Size: 7 × 6 m (20 × 18 ft.). Zone 6.

+*Laburnocytisus* 'Adamii' arose in France and is the result of a graft hybrid formed from a union between *Laburnum* and *Chamaecytisus* created in 1825. As well as pendulous racemes of yellow flowers like *Laburnum*, some branches bear denser clusters of the purple flowers of *Chamaecytisus* and yet others produce unusual intermediate flowers of yellow diffused with purple. This plant is never as stunning as either of the parents in flower but may be grown as a curiosity. It can only be propagated by grafting. Size: 7 × 6 m (20 × 18 ft.). Zone 6.

Lagerstroemia (Lythraceae)

A genus of large deciduous or evergreen trees or shrubs grown for their colourful flowers with unusual crumpled petals. Grow in a sunny position. If the plant becomes leggy, prune hard in winter or early spring to encourage the regeneration of new growth or to keep to a reasonable size.

Lagerstroemia indica ♕ (crape myrtle) from China and Korea is a deciduous shrub with large, conical inflorescences of numerous lilac, pink or red flowers each about 2.5 cm (1 in.) across from midsummer to autumn. It needs a hot summer to perform well. 'Rosea' has deep pink flowers. Cultivars in a range of other co-

↓ *Lagerstroemia indica*

lours are available. Size: 3 × 3 m (10 × 10 ft.). Zones 8–9.

Laurus **(Lauraceae)** sweet bay, bay laurel

A small genus of evergreen trees or shrubs grown for their aromatic foliage. Grow in sun or partial shade. Prune in late winter or trim topiary in summer.

Laurus nobilis 🏆 from Mediterranean areas has been grown since ancient times for its foliage which was used to make the laurel crowns presented to sporting and other heroes and distinguished people such as poets. It can be used in a variety of ways; as a specimen tree or shrub, as a hedge, in a container or clipped for topiary. However, if allowed to grow freely, this plant will become large. The leaves used as a culinary herb, either fresh or dried, are ovate to 10 × 4 cm (4 × 1½ in.). In spring, the tiny yellowish green flowers are produced in clusters, attract bees, and are followed occasionally by black berries. Avoid placing where the foliage can be damaged by cold winds. 'Aurea' 🏆 has golden-yellow leaves. 'Angustifolia' is less common but very hardy with attractive, narrow leaves. Size: 12 × 10 m (35 × 30 ft.) unless clipped. Zone 8.

Lavandula **(Lamiaceae)** lavender

A genus of small shrubs grown for their flowers and aromatic foliage. The evergreen leaves are usually grey or grey-green, very narrow, often with the edges rolled under so appearing even narrower. The tiny, blue or purple flowers, produced in dense spikes held above the plant on long stems, will attract butterflies. Lavender has

↑ *Lavandula angustifolia* 'Imperial Gem'

been cultivated for hundreds of years for its medicinal properties, oil and perfume. Plants may be used as dwarf informal hedges, clipped immediately after flowering. If the flowers are to be used for drying, cut before the flower heads are fully open. Cultivars with long flower stems, such as those from *Lavandula ×intermedia*, are easier to bunch and tie for hanging up. Grow in almost any soil, unless wet or waterlogged, in sun. Dead head after flowering and trim in early spring. It is worth pruning regularly to avoid the plants becoming woody and straggly but plants will not regenerate if cut back too hard. Plants usually need to be replaced after about 10 years. This is a genus where almost all species and cultivars are worth growing, differing in their hardiness, flower colour and plant size.

Lavandula angustifolia from southern Europe is one of the smaller-growing species with lavender-blue flowers in spikes on stems to 7.5 cm (3 in.). 'Hidcote' ♡ has dark purple flowers and 'Imperial Gem' ♡ has even darker flowers with silvery leaves. 'Loddon Pink' ♡ has pale pink flowers. MISS MUFFETT 'Scholmis' ♡ is a recent cultivar with white flowers. Size: 75 × 75 cm (2 ½ × 2 ½ ft.). Zone 5.

Lavandula ×intermedia, a larger plant, has spikes of purple flowers on long flower stems to 20 cm (8 in.). 'Arabian Night' ♡ has deep purple flowers. WALBERTON'S SILVER EDGE 'Walvera' is newer with silver-edged leaves. Size: 1 ×1 m (3 × 3 ft.). Zone 5.

Lavandula lanata ♡ from Spain is slightly less hardy with exceptionally soft, hairy, silver-grey leaves to 5 × 1 cm (2 × ½ in.). The pale purple flowers in spikes on stems to 10 cm (4 in.) long last throughout the summer. Size: 75 × 75 cm (2 ½ × 2 ½ ft.). Zone 8.

Lavandula pedunculata ♡ (synonym *L. stoechas* subsp. *pedunculata*), sometimes sold as *L. stoechas* 'Papillon', from the Iberian Peninsula has unusual, narrow, violet-coloured bracts to 3 cm (1 ½ in.) long emerging at the top of the flower spikes to 5 cm (2 in.) long. Size: 60 × 60 cm (2 × 2 ft.). Zone 8.

Lavandula stoechas ♡ (French lavender) from regions around the Mediterranean is distinguished by the short stumpy flower spikes to 3 cm (1 ½ in.) long on fairly short stalks with dark purple flowers and showy coloured petal-like bracts formed at the top. 'Kew Red' has bright red flowers and paler pink bracts. *Lavandula* 'Pretty Polly', a hybrid, has violet-blue flowers and creamy white bracts. Size: 60 × 60 cm (2 × 2 ft.). Zone 8.

Lavatera (Malvaceae)

A genus of deciduous shrubs, annuals and perennials grown for their very numerous, showy, funnel-shaped, summer flowers. Shrubs tend to be short-lived so propagate regularly. These plants remain in flower for many weeks. They seed freely but the resulting seedlings will produce a wide range of flower colour and size not necessarily as good as the parent. Grow in a sunny position. Prune hard in early spring to encourage the growth of new shoots.

Lavatera ×clementii bears wide open pink flowers to 7.5 cm (3 in.) across throughout the summer. 'Barnsley' has white flowers with a deep pink centre fading to pink. Remove any branches which revert to pink flowers. 'Burgundy Wine' ♡ has deep purplish red flowers with darker veins and 'Candy Floss' ♡ has pale pink flowers. 'Kew Rose' has slightly larger clear pink flowers and is the plant grown for many years as *L. olbia* 'Rosea'. Size: 2× 2 m (6 × 6 ft.). Zone 8.

Lavatera maritima ♡ (synonym *L. maritima* var. *bicolor*) from southwestern Europe and North

↑ *Lavatera* ×*clementii* 'Kew Rose'

Africa is often grown in milder gardens or in a container. It has attractive, wide open, lilac-pink flowers with deep purplish red veins to 7.5 cm (3 in.) across from summer to midautumn. Size: 1.5 × 1.5 m (5 × 5 ft.). Zone 9.

Lavatera olbia from the western Mediterranean countries has smaller, pink, somewhat frilled flowers compared to *L.* ×*clementii*. It has pretty, silvery grey leaves but it is less hardy. Size: 2 × 2 m (6 × 6 ft.). Zone 8.

Leonotis (Lamiaceae)

A genus of herbaceous plants and small deciduous shrubs grown for their tall stems bearing dense whorls of long, tubular, 2-lipped, brightly coloured flowers. Grow in sun or partial shade. Prune in early spring, cutting back old flowering shoots.

Leonotis leonurus (lion's ear) from South Africa is an upright shrub with vivid orange downy flowers to 5 cm (2 in.) long in autumn. In cooler areas, this may be grown in a container in a conservatory. Size: 1.5 × 1.5 m (5 × 5 ft.). Zone 9.

Leptospermum (Myrtaceae) tea tree

A genus of evergreen shrubs grown for their flowers and often aromatic foliage. The leaves are usually small as are the 5-petalled, open flowers which smother the branches. Grow in any lime-free soil in sun. Prune in spring to avoid plants becoming leggy.

Leptospermum scoparium from New Zealand is a compact, rather twiggy shrub with tiny, narrow, green leaves to 1.5 cm (½ in.) long and white flowers about 2 cm (¾ in.) across in late spring and early summer. The species itself is rarely grown but the cultivars are very variable in size and flower colour ranging from red through pink to white with both double and single flowers. 'Kiwi' 🏆 is a dwarf plant barely 30 cm (1 ft.) tall with red flowers. 'Pink Cascade' has a weeping habit and pink flowers. 'Red Damask' 🏆 reaches about 2 m (6 ft.) in height with dark leaves and freely produced, red, long-lasting, double flowers. Size: 3 × 3 m (10 × 10 ft.). Zone 8.

***Leptospermum* 'Silver Sheen'** 🏆, one of the hardier shrubs of the genus, bears small white flowers but is grown more often for the narrow-ovate silvery white leaves to about 1.5 cm (½ in.) covered in silky hairs. Size: 3 × 3 m (10 × 10 ft.). Zone 8.

Leucothoe (Ericaceae)

A genus of mainly evergreen, suckering, sometimes short-lived shrubs grown for their foliage and white urn-shaped flowers. Grow in any light, moist, lime-free soil in shade or partial shade. Cut out older branches after flowering if necessary.

Leucothoe fontanesiana 🏆 from southeast USA is a small shrub useful as ground cover. It has arching branches which in late spring bear racemes to 6 cm (2½ in.) long of white flowers all along the stems. The deep green, leathery leaves are lanceolate to 15 cm (6 in.) long and turn red or bronzy red in autumn and winter. 'Rainbow' is a slightly smaller plant which has green leaves variegated with reddish pink, white and creamy yellow. Dappled shade is important to ensure good leaf colour. SCARLETTA 'Zeblid' has reddish purple young foliage which turns to dark green in summer and red in autumn and winter. Size: 1.5 × 1.5 m (5 × 5 ft.). Zone 5.

Leycesteria (Caprifoliaceae)

A small genus of deciduous, suckering shrubs grown for their flowers and unusual, short-lived, green, hollow, bamboo-like stems which are replaced by new growth in succession. The flowers are formed in drooping racemes with conspicuous coloured bracts partially enclosing the flowers. Grow in sun or partial shade. Cut stems back hard after flowering or in early spring. Remove any suckers which spread too far.

↓ *Leucothoe fontanesiana*

Leycesteria formosa ♕ (pheasant berry, Himalayan honeysuckle) from the Himalayas has erect bluish green stems and pendulous racemes about 10 cm (4 in.) long of white tubular flowers 2 cm (¾ in.) long which are partially hidden by large, persistent, dark purplish red bracts in summer and early autumn. These are followed by glossy reddish purple berries which attract birds. GOLDEN LANTERNS 'Notbruce' has yellow leaves. Size: 2 × 2 m (6 × 6 ft.). Zone 7.

Ligustrum (Oleaceae) privet

A genus of small, deciduous or evergreen trees and shrubs grown for their simple leaves and small, but numerous, scented, sometimes unpleasantly so, creamy white flowers in branched inflorescences attracting insects. The berries are glossy, usually black and provide food for birds. Many make useful hedging plants and can be clipped as topiary. All parts of the plant are somewhat poisonous. Grow in sun, partial shade or shade. Prune individual plants in spring or clip hedges and topiary in summer.

Ligustrum ovalifolium from Japan is very commonly used for hedging and is evergreen except in colder areas. The ovate leaves are about 6 cm (2½ in.) long and the flowers form in dense clusters to 10 cm (4 in.) in midsummer followed by black fruits. 'Argenteum' has leaves edged with white. 'Aureum' ♕ (golden privet) has yellow foliage. Size: 4 × 4 m (12 × 12 ft.) unless clipped. Zone 5.

Liquidambar styraciflua →

Linum (Linaceae) flax

A large genus of small, mainly herbaceous and woody plants grown for their flowers.

Linum arboreum ♕ (tree flax) from the eastern Mediterranean regions is a dwarf evergreen shrub. It has loose clusters of golden-yellow funnel-shaped flowers to 3 cm (1½ in.) across at the ends of the branches in late spring and summer and narrow, blue-green leaves to 4 cm (1½ in.) long. Grow in a sunny position. Pruning is rarely necessary. Size: 30 × 30 cm (1 × 1 ft.). Zone 8.

Liquidambar (Hamamelidaceae) sweet gum

A small genus of deciduous trees grown for their outstanding autumn foliage. Grow in almost

any moist but well-drained, acid soil, in sun for the best autumn colour, or partial shade. Prune any dead or weak branches in winter.

Liquidambar styraciflua from eastern North America is a conical tree with 5- or 7-lobed leaves, superficially like a maple, to 15 cm (6 in.) across. To ensure a clone which gives reliable autumn colour, buy a named cultivar. However, in favourable conditions all could eventually reach 20 m (60 ft.) tall, although in colder areas it will not reach great heights. 'Worplesdon' 🏆 is an older cultivar. The leaves have long narrow lobes which are orange and yellow in autumn. 'Slender Silhouette' is a new and rare, slender, columnar tree which even when it reaches 15 m (50 ft.) tall is barely 1.5 m (5 ft.) wide. Zone 5.

Liriodendron (Magnoliaceae) tulip tree

A genus of large deciduous trees from Asia and North America grown for their autumn foliage and unusual tulip-like flowers. Although the species are large trees, the cultivar ***Liriodendron tulipifera* 'Fastigiatum'** is a very narrow tree which may eventually reach to 6 m (18 ft.) in height but is barely 2 m (6 ft.) wide at the base. The unusual and very distinct leaves are almost square in shape with 2 pointed lobes at the top and 2 at the side, to 15 cm (6 in.) across turning a beautiful clear yellow in autumn. The flowers in early and midsummer are tulip-shaped, green outside and yellowish green inside banded with orange, to 5 cm (2 in.) or more across. Unusually, flowers are produced on quite young plants. Grow in a moist but well-drained soil in sun or partial shade. Prune if necessary in late winter. Zone 4.

↑ *Lonicera periclymenum* 'Serotina'

Lonicera (Caprifoliaceae) honeysuckle

A large and very variable genus of evergreen and deciduous shrubs and climbers which are cultivated for their flowers, many fragrant, encouraging bees. The climbers may be grown on pergolas, fences, trellis or up walls, and the shrubs in borders or as hedging. The flowers are 2-lipped or funnel-shaped and produced in dense or open heads or in small clusters from winter to late summer. These are followed by red, black or white fleshy berries which are mildly poisonous though eaten by birds. Grow in sun or partial shade. Prune shrubs by removing old flowering branches after flowering. Prune climbers after flowering or in late winter to restrict growth and remove weak branches. Clip hedges in summer.

A small selection of the many available species and cultivars are included below.

***Lonicera ×heckrottii* 'Gold Flame'** is a semi-evergreen climber with paired ovate leaves, blue-green underneath, to 6 cm (2 ½ in.) long. The leaves immediately below the flower heads are joined so that the stem appears to pass through the middle. The tubular, 2-lipped, fragrant, bright orange-yellow flowers 4 cm (1 ½ in.) long are formed in whorls through the summer. Height: 5 m (15 ft.). Zone 5.

Lonicera japonica from Japan has strongly 2-lipped, tubular, sweetly scented, white flowers, sometimes flushed with reddish purple, to 4 cm (1 ½ in.) long in summer which fade to yellow as they age. These are followed by blue-black berries. The species itself is not commonly grown but 'Halliana' 🏆 is useful for covering less attractive areas of the garden. Being very vigorous, it must be kept pruned back to keep under control. 'Aureoreticulata' has leaves conspicuously veined with golden-yellow. Height: 10 m (30 ft.). Zone 4.

Lonicera nitida from China is an evergreen shrub with tiny, ovate, dark green leaves to 1 cm (½ in.) long which is rarely seen in flower. Amenable to clipping and fast growing, it makes a very useful, dense, hedging plant. 'Baggesen's Gold' 🏆 has yellow leaves in summer which become slightly greener in autumn. Size: 1.5 × 1.5 m (5 × 5 ft.). Zone 7.

Lonicera periclymenum from much of Europe and North Africa is a deciduous climber potentially to about 18 m (55 ft.) tall with paired ovate leaves about 6 cm (2 ½ in.) long. The flowers, formed in whorls at the ends of the stems, are highly scented, 2-lipped, tubular, cream to yellow to about 5 cm (2 in.) long in mid to late summer and followed by red berries. A number of cultivars vary slightly in colour. *Lonicera* HONEY BABY 'Novso' is a dwarf, bushy hybrid shrub with highly scented, creamy flowers. It is suitable for a container, reaches about 1 m (3 ft.) in height and benefits from being cut back each year. *Lonicera periclymenum* 'Serotina' 🏆 (late Dutch honeysuckle) has creamy white flowers, bright reddish purple on the outside and in bud. Zone 4.

***Lonicera ×purpusii* 'Winter Beauty'** 🏆 is a free-flowering deciduous shrub which has fragrant, creamy white, funnel-shaped flowers to 2 cm (¾ in.) in winter and early spring. Size: 2 × 2 m (6 × 6 ft.). Zone 6.

Loropetalum (Hamamelidaceae)

A very small genus of evergreen shrubs grown for their flowers and foliage.

Loropetalum chinense from eastern Asia is a spreading shrub with small clusters of white spider-like flowers to 2.5 cm (1 in.) across of numerous very narrow petals in late winter and

↑ *Loropetalum chinense* f. *rubrum* 'Fire Dance'

↑ *Lotus hirsutus*

early spring. Grow in a lime-free soil in sun or partial shade. Prune after flowering if required to encourage bushiness. There are several red-leaved cultivars named f. *rubrum* such as 'Fire Dance' with broad, ovate, deep reddish purple leaves to 5 cm (2 in.) long and bright pink flowers. Size: 2 × 2 m (6 × 6 ft.). Zone 8–9.

Lotus (Papilionaceae)

A genus of small herbaceous plants and shrubs of which ***Lotus hirsutus*** ♕ (synonym *Dorycnium hirsutum*; hairy canary clover) from southwestern Europe is the only shrubby species commonly grown in gardens for its flowers and foliage. It is a dwarf evergreen or semi-evergreen with pinnate, grey-green, hairy leaves each with 5 leaflets to 2 cm (¾ in.) long. The clusters of cream, pea-like flowers flushed pink are formed at the ends of the branches though the summer. Grow in a well-drained soil in sun. Pruning is rarely necessary except to encourage bushiness. Size: 50 × 90 cm (1½ × 3 ft.). Zone 8.

Lupinus arboreus →

Lupinus (Papilionaceae) lupin

A large genus of herbaceous perennials and evergreen or semi-evergreen shrubs grown for their flowers. The majority have palmate leaves with many narrow leaflets and dense spikes of colourful pea-like flowers. The seeds are somewhat poisonous. Grow in a light soil preferably in sun. Pruning is rarely necessary.

Lupinus arboreus ♕ (tree lupin) from California is a fast-growing but often short-lived semi-evergreen or evergreen shrub with grey-green leaves 5 cm (2 in.) across of up to 11 leaflets. The flower spikes reach 25 cm (10 in.) in length with

↑ *Malus floribunda*

(2 ft.) long with as many as 21 leaflets. The flowers are borne in clusters of long racemes to 35 cm (14 in.) at the ends of the shoots from early winter to early spring. 'Charity', one of the first named cultivars, has rather upright racemes of darker yellow flowers. 'Buckland' 🏆 has spreading racemes and 'Winter Sun' 🏆 is a more compact shrub. Size: 5 × 4 m (15 × 12 ft.). Zone 6.

Malus (Rosaceae) apple, crabapple

A genus of deciduous trees grown for their mid to late spring flowers and autumn fruits. The open 5-petalled flowers about 1–2.5 cm (½ –1 in.) across, usually white or pink, are borne in clusters on short branches. These are followed by apple-like fruits, some of which are large and juicy enough to be used for preserves as well as feeding wild birds. Most of the species and cultivars available in the trade are attractive small trees ideal as specimen plants. Some may be grafted onto dwarf rooting stocks resulting in smaller trees. Grow in sun or partial shade, although purple-leaved cultivars colour best in sun. Prune from autumn to early spring if necessary to remove dead or weak branches. Those mentioned below reach about 8 × 5 m (25 × 15 ft.). Zone 4.

Malus floribunda 🏆 (Japanese crab) is a small tree with very attractive deep purplish pink buds which open to very pale pink flowers about 5 cm (2 in.) across in mid to late spring. The fruits are yellow and red about 2.5 cm (1 in.) across.

***Malus* 'John Downie'** 🏆 is possibly one of the best fruiting crab apples for jellies and preserves. The fruits are large, conical, an attractive red and yellow in colour and 4 cm (1 ½ in.) or more long. It has a rather narrow, upright habit and white flowers. 'Harry Baker' is a new and still rare cultivar, also excellent for jelly, with deep pink flowers and red fruits. 'Evereste' 🏆 has white flowers and smaller, spherical, red fruits.

***Malus* 'Royal Beauty'** 🏆, a small weeping tree, has flowers and young leaves of reddish purple followed by deep red fruits.

***Malus ×zumi* 'Golden Hornet'** 🏆 is a good ornamental fruiting tree with long-lasting, ovoid, golden-yellow fruits to 2.5 cm (1 in.) across and white flowers.

Medicago (Papilionaceae) medick

A genus of herbaceous plants and small shrubs grown for the clusters of pea-like flowers. Grow in a sunny position. Pruning is rarely required.

Medicago arborea (moon trefoil) from the Mediterranean regions makes a small, bushy, evergreen shrub with trifoliate leaves and yellow flowers to 2 cm (3/4 in.) long in dense clusters of 6, throughout the summer. These are followed by interesting brown, flattened, spiral seed pods. It thrives in coastal situations and elsewhere, and does best against a sunny wall. Size: 1.5 × 1.5 m (5 × 5 ft.). Zones 8–9.

Melianthus (Melianthaceae)

A genus of small evergreen shrubs grown for their striking pinnate foliage giving a tropical, exotic look to a garden. The stems are hollow emerging from the ground with few branches. Grow in moist, but not wet, fertile soil in sun. Prune in spring by cutting back old stems to within about 30 cm (1 ft.) from the ground.

Melianthus major 🏆 (honey bush) from South Africa has bold blue-green leaves to 50 cm (20 in.) long each with up to 17 large toothed leaflets. In favourable conditions, the plant may produce large spikes to 30 cm (1 ft.) of numerous brownish red, 5-petalled flowers each to 2.5 cm (1 in.) long. In cooler areas, this can be grown in a container in a cool conservatory and put outdoors once the danger of frost is past. Size: 2 × 1 m (6 × 3 ft.). Zone 9.

Mimulus synonym *Diplacus* (Scrophulariaceae) musk, monkey flower

A large genus of small herbaceous plants and evergreen shrubs grown for their brightly coloured flowers. Grow in a very moist soil in sun or partial shade. Prune in late spring. Cutting back after flowering will encourage a second flush.

Mimulus aurantiacus 🏆 from western North America is the only commonly grown shrub. The leaves, borne on sticky stems, are lanceolate, rich green to 7.5 cm (3 in.) long and the open funnel-shaped flowers, from midsummer to early autumn, are orange, yellow or red. It grows well in milder coastal areas. Size: 1 × 1 m (3 × 3 ft.). Zone 8.

Mitraria (Gesneriaceae)

Mitraria coccinea from Chile and Argentina, the only species in this genus, forms a low-growing, slightly sprawling, evergreen shrub grown for the pendulous, tubular, orange-scarlet flowers to 3 cm (1 1/2 in.) long from early summer to early autumn. The small, glossy, dark green, toothed, leathery leaves reach 2.5 cm (1 in.) long. A recently introduced cultivar from Lake Puyehue is said to be slightly hardier. Grow in humus-rich, lime-free soil in light shade. Trim after flowering if necessary. Size: 1.5 × 1.5 m (5 × 5 ft.). Zone 9.

Morus **(Moraceae)** mulberry

A genus of small deciduous trees grown for hundreds of years for their fruit (*Morus nigra*, black mulberry), or their foliage for silk worms (*M. alba*, white mulberry). The large, heart-shaped leaves reach 20 cm (8 in.) long. The flowers are insignificant but the edible fruits are fleshy, somewhat like a raspberry about 2.5 cm (1 in.) across. Grow in well-drained soil in sun or light shade. Prune in late autumn to winter if necessary.

Morus alba **'Pendula'**, a weeping form of the white mulberry from China, is an attractive pendulous tree for a smaller garden. The leaves turn clear yellow in autumn, but, although the red fruits are slightly insipid, they are still attractive to birds. Train the stem up a cane to the required height before allowing it to weep. Size: 3 × 5 m (10 × 15 ft.). Zone 4.

Mutisia **(Asteraceae)** climbing gazania

A genus of small evergreen climbers grown for their flowers. Although not often seen in gardens, this could be grown in a container or conservatory, against a wall or even scrambling through larger plants in a border. Grow in rich soil preferably in sun. Prune in spring.

Mutisia ilicifolia from Chile has winged stems and dark green, holly-like leaves which have a tendril at the end by which the plant climbs. The pale pink daisy-like flowers to 7.5 cm (3 in.) across with yellow centres are borne in summer to early autumn. Height: 3 m (10 ft.). Zone 8.

Myrtus **(Myrtaceae)** myrtle

Myrtus communis 🏆 from Mediterranean regions is the only species in this genus of evergreen shrubs grown for their aromatic foliage and white flowers. The glossy, dark green leaves reach 5 cm (2 in.) and the 5-petalled white flowers with numerous white, showy stamens are about 2 cm (¾ in.) across formed in late summer and early autumn. These are followed by purplish black berries about 1 cm (½ in.) long. Trimmed plants are suitable for growing in a container or may be used as an informal hedge in milder areas but will only flower and fruit after a hot summer. Grow in sun, sheltered from cold winds. Lightly prune in spring to maintain shape. Subspecies *tarentina* 🏆 (synonyms *M. communis* 'Jenny Reitenbach', 'Microphylla', 'Nana') has smaller narrow leaves, a compact habit and freely produced pink-tinged flowers. 'Variegata' has greyer-green leaves edged with silvery white. Size: 2.5 × 2.5 m (8 × 8 ft.). Zone 8.

Luma apiculata 🏆 (synonyms *Myrtus luma*, *M. apiculata*) from Chile and Argentina is very similar. The cultivar 'Glanleam Gold' 🏆 with dark green leaves edged yellow and tinged with pink when young, makes a useful container plant if fertilised regularly.

Nandina **(Berberidaceae)** sacred bamboo, heavenly bamboo

Nandina domestica 🏆 from China and Japan is the only species in this genus. It is an ever-

↑ *Nandina domestica*

green or semi-evergreen shrub of an elegant upright habit which is frequently associated with Japanese gardens. The compound leaves to 90 cm (3 ft.) are tinged red when young and turn red again at the end of the season. In midsummer, it has large panicles of white, star-shaped flowers each to 1 cm (½ in.) across which are followed, especially after hot summers, by clusters of spherical red berries 8 mm (¼ in.) across lasting well into the winter. Grow in sun but do not allow plants to get too dry. Prune in spring if necessary. 'Fire Power' 🏆 is a short, compact cultivar with good orange to red winter foliage. The fruits of 'Richmond' are produced more reliably. Size: to 2 × 1.5 m (6 × 5 ft.). Zone 8.

Neillia (Rosaceae)

These deciduous, often suckering, shrubs are easy to grow in sun or partial shade for their flowers and their graceful, slightly arching habit. Thin out after flowering by removing some of the older stems and remove any invasive suckers which might spread if not kept under control.

Neillia thibetica (synonym *N. longiracemosa*) from China bears racemes to 15 cm (6 in.) long of numerous, rose-pink, tubular flowers to 8 mm (¼ in.) long in early summer. Size: to 2 × 2 m (6 × 6 ft.). Zone 6.

Nerium (Apocynaceae)

Nerium oleander (oleander) has been long cultivated, especially in tropical and subtropical regions where it has frequently become naturalized. It is effective as a flowering hedge in warmer climates and is seen in all Mediterranean resorts with its clusters of large periwinkle-like, often scented, rose-pink flowers to 5 cm (2 in.) across throughout the summer and into autumn. All parts are, however, extremely poisonous if eaten. It makes a very effective container plant which can be kept over winter in frost free conditions and will grow in sun and in any soil, except in chalk. Cultivars are available in all shades of pink, red, cream and white with single, double or semi-double flowers. The leaves are long, narrow, dark green and leathery. Plants may be pruned hard in late summer to autumn to keep them small. 'Variegatum' 🏆 has leaves margined with creamy white. Size (depending on the cultivar): to about 3 × 2 m (10 × 6 ft.). Zones 8–9.

↑ *Nerium oleander*

leaves to 15 cm (6 in.). In 'Sheffield Park' the leaves tend to turn several weeks earlier in autumn. 'Autumn Cascades' is a rare, slow-growing cultivar with arching branches. Size: eventually to 20 × 10 m (60 × 30 ft.). Zone 3.

Nyssa (Cornaceae) tupelo

Deciduous trees grown for their habit and their stunning red and orange autumn colours which are especially vibrant after hot summers. Although eventually large trees, they are slow growing. Grow in fertile, moist, lime-free soil in sun or part shade. They do well near water and the reflection of the autumn colours in the water is an added bonus. They can be difficult to transplant so purchase as small plants grown in a container. Prune in late winter only if necessary.

Nyssa sylvatica 🏆 (black gum, sour gum) from eastern North America has ovate, dark green

Olea (Oleaceae) olive

A genus of evergreen trees and shrubs of which ***Olea europaea*** from the Mediterranean is the only one cultivated. For centuries, this species has been of enormous economic value for its wood, fruits and oil. They are very slow-growing trees eventually becoming old and gnarled specimens attractive for their shape and bark. In more northern regions, olives have become popular for growing in a sheltered position in a container and can be trained as a standard or clipped into different shapes. The narrow leaves are grey-green and tiny creamy white flowers are formed in summer. These are followed by the typical olive fruits but are not reliably produced away from the hot Mediterranean summers. There are numerous cultivars available from specialist sources. Grow in a sunny position. Prune in early spring to maintain the shape. Size: to 13 × 13 m (40 × 40 ft.) in ideal conditions and over a long period of time but can be clipped regularly. Zone 8.

Olearia (Asteraceae) tree daisy, daisy bush

A very large genus of mainly evergreen shrubs and small trees grown for their daisy-like flowers and often also for their attractive foliage. Some will make useful hedges especially in maritime locations and should be pruned after flowering. Most are tolerant of salt-laden wind and

↑ *Olearia ×haastii*

atmospheric pollution, and the flowers attract bees. The larger shrubs can be pruned to keep them under control. Grow in a fertile, well-drained soil in full sun. Prune in spring for those which flower in late summer and after flowering for others.

Olearia ×haastii is a natural hybrid from New Zealand with ovate, dark green, glossy leaves felted with white underneath to 2.5 cm (1 in.) long. The white flowers to 8 mm (¼ in.) across are in dense heads to 7.5 cm (3 in.) or more wide. This species is good for hedging. Size: to 2 × 3 m (6 × 10 ft.). Zone 7.

Olearia macrodonta 🏆 from New Zealand has green leaves with spiny margins to 10 cm (4 in.) long. It resembles a holly but is silvery white on the under side. In summer, it bears large heads to 15 cm (6 in.) across of fragrant white flowers with a brownish yellow centre. This species can be used for hedging. Size: to 3× 3 m (10 × 10 ft.). Zone 8.

Olearia nummularifolia from New Zealand is a dense, slow-growing shrub with small, almost round, leathery leaves to 1 cm (½ in.) long. The white star-like flowers are borne in small clusters. Size: to 2 × 2 m (6 × 6 ft.). Zone 7.

Olearia phlogopappa (synonym *O. gunniana*) from Australia and Tasmania is another useful hedging plant but with white, occasionally blue or pink, flowers in spring and early summer. The greyish green, aromatic leaves are narrow and toothed, some to about 4 cm (1½ in.) long. 'Combers Pink' has pink flowers. Size: to 2 × 2 m (6 × 6 ft.). Zone 8.

Osmanthus (Oleaceae) sweet olive, Chinese holly

A large genus of evergreen trees and shrubs with leathery leaves and scented white flowers. The fruits are usually small, blue-black and fleshy. Grow in sun or partial shade. Prune in spring for those which flower in late summer and after flowering for others. Clip hedges in summer.

↑ *Osmanthus delavayi*

Osmanthus delavayi 🏆 from China has small, dark green, almost round, glossy, leathery leaves to 2.5 cm (1 in.) long with sharply toothed margins. The white tubular flowers to about 1 cm (½ in.) long are beautifully scented in early to midspring. This species also makes an attractive, dense, scented-flowering hedge which can be clipped after flowering. Size: to about 3 × 3 m (10 × 10 ft.). Zone 7.

Osmanthus heterophyllus (synonym *O. ilicifolius*) from Japan is a dense shrub with leaves, which might be mistaken for holly because of its usually spiny margins, to 6 cm (2½ in.) long. From late summer to early autumn, it has small clusters of sweetly scented, white, tubular flowers to about 8 mm (¼ in.) long. It makes a dense spiny hedge and is used for topiary. A number of cultivars are available varying mainly in their leaf colouration. 'Goshiki' has young leaves speckled with pink and yellow, becoming blotched with green and gold later in the season. 'Gulftide' 🏆 is slower growing with a dense compact habit. 'Purple Shaft' is a less well-known cultivar with rich purple young leaves becoming greener as the season progresses. 'Variegatus' 🏆 has leaves margined with creamy white. Size: to 5 × 5 m (15 × 15 ft.). Zone 7.

Ozothamnus synonym *Helichrysum* (Asteraceae)

A genus of evergreen shrubs which have masses of white daisy-like flowers. Grow in a well-drained soil in full sun, protected from cold winds. Prune after flowering if required.

Ozothamnus ledifolius 🏆 (kerosene bush) from Tasmania is a compact bush with needle-like, dark green, aromatic leaves about 1 cm (½ in.) long which, like the shoots, are covered underneath with greenish yellow woolly hairs. The flowers about 5 mm (⅛ in.) across are massed into heads in early summer. The common name comes from the aromatic oils which are said to make the plant very flammable. Size: to 2.5 × 1.5 m (8 × 5 ft.). Zone 8.

Ozothamnus rosmarinifolius (synonym *Helichrysum rosmarinifolium*) from Australia is somewhat similar but has white woolly stems and the dark green leaves are longer to 4 cm (1½ in.). The masses of red flower buds are as attractive as the white scented flowers in early summer. 'Silver Jubilee' ♡ has exceptionally silver foliage but is a little less hardy. Size: to 2.5 × 1.5 m (8 × 5 ft.). Zone 8.

Paeonia (Paeoniaceae) peony

A genus of shrubs and herbaceous plants grown for their large and dramatic but often short-lived flowers. These flowers are usually bowl-shaped with a mass of showy stamens in the centre, borne on the tops of the stems. The woody species are long-lived but do not transplant easily, so plant in their final position. Grow in a well-drained soil in sun or partial shade but shelter from cold winds. Remove faded flowers and prune back old flowered shoots.

Paeonia ludlowii ♡ (synonym *P. delavayi* var. *ludlowii*) from Tibet is a deciduous shrub with stout, erect, unbranched stems and large, deeply divided leaves to about 25 cm (10 in.) long. The bright yellow, cup-shaped flowers can reach 10 cm (4 in.) across in late spring and early summer. Size: 2 × 2 m (6 × 6 ft.) or more. Zone 6.

Paeonia suffruticosa (tree peony) from China is rarely grown but it has resulted in numerous cultivars, many originating in Japan, with both double and single flowers in a range of colours and available from specialist nurseries. The plants are erect with few branches but produce very large flowers up to 30 cm (1 ft.) across in late spring and early summer. The plants grown under a number of names including *P.* 'Joseph Rock' and 'Rock's Variety' are similar in habit but have enormous white or very pale pink-tinged flowers marked with a prominent reddish purple blotch at the base of each petal and should be included under *P. rockii*. Size: 2 × 2 m (6 × 6 ft.). Zone 7.

Parahebe synonyms *Hebe, Veronica* (Scrophulariaceae)

A genus of small deciduous shrubs and subshrubs grown for their numerous but small flowers in summer. Some are dwarf spreading plants which may be used for ground cover or on walls. Grow in well-drained soil in sun. Cut back old stems and reduce size if necessary after flowering.

Parahebe catarractae from New Zealand is a low ground covering shrub with dark green leaves to 4 cm (1½ in.) long and short racemes of white, blue or pink flowers to 1 cm (½ in.) across veined with red and marked with a red ring around the centre of each flower. Size: 30 × 30 cm (1 × 1 ft.). Zone 7.

Parahebe lyallii from New Zealand is a prostrate shrub with small dark green leaves to 1 cm (½ in.) long. In early summer, it bears white flowers to 1 cm (½ in.) across veined with deep pink along with unusual blue coloured anthers. Size: 25 × 30 cm (10 × 12 in.). Zone 7.

Parahebe perfoliata ♡ (Digger's speedwell) from Australia is a subshrub and, although the older shoots may die back during the winter,

↑ *Parahebe catarractae*

new shoots reappear next spring. The slightly leathery, bluish green leaves about 5 cm (2 in.) long are formed in opposite pairs up the stems and overlap so that they appear joined. Tall branching racemes to about 15 cm (6 in.) in midsummer bear clear bright blue flowers each about 1 cm (½ in.) across. Size: to about 50 × 30 cm (1½ × 1 ft.). Zone 8.

Parrotia (Hamamelidaceae)

Parrotia persica 🏆 (Persian ironwood) from Caucasus and Iran is a large, wide-spreading, deciduous tree grown for its late winter flowers, red, yellow and orange autumn colours and attractive peeling bark. 'Jodrell Bank', however, is an uncommon but upright, less spreading and smaller tree reaching about 3 m (10 ft.) in 10 years with brilliant autumn colours and would be more suitable in a smaller space. The flowers are formed of clusters of crimson stamens about 1 cm (½ in.) across and the leaves reach 10 cm (4 in.) or more long. Zone 5.

Parthenocissus synonym *Vitis* (Vitaceae)

A genus of deciduous woody plants which climb using tendrils and suckers. They are grown for their foliage, especially fiery in autumn, and may be used for covering fences or walls. Most are very vigorous and root themselves readily, so need to be kept strictly under control. The inconspicuous flowers attract bees in summer and may be followed in hot seasons by small, spherical, fleshy fruits which are mildly poisonous, although relished by birds. Grow in sun or partial shade and give support or tie up shoots until the plants are well established. Prune in autumn or winter to reduce growth and again in summer if necessary.

Parthenocissus henryana 🏆 from China has palmate leaves to 13 cm (5 in.) long with 3–5 dark green leaflets each with a conspicuous white midvein and white side veins. They turn bright red in autumn. Height: 10 m (30 ft.). Zone 7.

Parthenocissus quinquefolia 🏆 (Virginia creeper) from eastern USA is very vigorous and needs to be regularly cut back. The palmate leaves to 10 cm (4 in.) have 5 leaflets which become a brilliant red in autumn. Height: 15 m (50 ft.) if unchecked. Zone 3.

Passiflora (Passifloraceae) passion flower

A large genus of evergreen, mainly tropical climbers with tendrils which are grown for their distinct, beautiful and exotic flowers. The saucer-shaped flowers usually have 10 colourful sepals and petals and in the centre is a corona composed of several whorls of coloured stamens and a curious looking column which bears the branching styles. The leaves are palmately lobed or divided and the leaf stalks often bear small glandular knobs. Some of the tropical species are cultivated for their edible fleshy fruit. Grow in sun or partial shade. Regularly feed any plants grown in containers. Prune to keep under control in early spring and again after flowering if necessary.

Passiflora caerulea 🏆 from South America is the hardiest species with white flowers to 10 cm (4 in.) across which continue from early summer into the early autumn. The corona is violet-blue and white, deepening to purple in the centre. The fleshy, ovoid, orange fruits over 5 cm (2 in.) long are not tasty, having little flesh and many seeds. In milder gardens it can become very vigorous, spreading quickly by rooting itself if not kept in check. 'Constance Elliott' has creamy white flowers with cream coloured stamens. Height: 10 m (30 ft.) if unchecked. Zone 8.

↑ *Perovskia* 'Blue Spire'

Penstemon (Scrophulariaceae)

A large genus of mainly herbaceous plants but a few small shrubs are grown for their flowers. Grow in a sunny position. Dead head if possible.

Penstemon pinifolius 🏆 from southern USA is a small, spreading, evergreen shrub. The leaves are needle-like to 2.5 cm (1 in.) long and in summer it produces narrow, tubular, bright red flowers to 2.5 cm (1 in.) long in a raceme. 'Mersea Yellow' has bright yellow flowers. Size: 40 × 25 cm (16 × 10 in.). Zone 8.

Perovskia (Lamiaceae)

A genus of small deciduous shrubs from Asia grown for their attractive, grey-green, aromatic foliage and large branching panicles of numerous, purplish blue, 2-lipped, tubular flowers in late summer and early autumn which attract bees. Grow preferably in a sunny position. Cut back in spring removing older shoots.

***Perovskia* 'Blue Spire'** ♕ is the cultivar usually seen in gardens. It is an erect shrub with greyish white stems and finely divided, feathery, silvery green leaves to 5 cm (2 in.) long. The flowers form a blue haze in panicles to 30 cm (1 ft.) tall. 'Filigran' has even more finely divided fern-like foliage. Size: 1.2 × 1 m (4 × 3 ft.). Zone 6.

Persicaria synonym *Polygonum* (Polygonaceae)

A genus mainly of herbaceous perennial plants but includes a few small woody plants grown for their cylindrical heads of tiny, usually pink, flowers. Grow in sun or partial shade. Cut back in early spring to maintain size.

Persicaria vacciniifolia ♕ (synonym *Polygonum vacciniifolium*) from the Himalayas is a creeping, semi-evergreen, subshrub which is useful as ground cover. The deep pink flowers to 5 mm (1/8 in.) long are tightly massed in erect narrow spikes to 8 cm (3 in.) tall from late summer to early autumn. These contrast with the red stems and glossy leaves to 2.5 cm (1 in.) long which turn red in autumn. Size: 20 × 50 cm (8 × 20 in.). Zone 7.

Philadelphus (Caprifoliaceae)

mock orange

A genus of deciduous shrubs grown for their white flowers which are usually highly scented, cup-shaped, double or single, solitary or in clusters. There are numerous good cultivars, many of which are complex hybrids raised at the beginning of the twentieth century in France. Grow in sun or partial shade. Prune after flowering by cutting back any flowering shoots.

***Philadelphus* 'Belle Etoile'** ♕ has large, single, white flowers to 5 cm (2 in.) across flushed with pale purplish red in the centre and reaches about 1.5 m (5 ft.) tall. 'Manteau d'Hermine' ♕ is smaller to 75 cm (2 ½ ft.) with creamy white, double flowers to 4 cm (1 ½ in.) across, while 'Virginal' is taller to 3 m (10 ft.) with pure white, double flowers to 4 cm (1 ½ in.) across. Zone 6.

Philadelphus coronarius from southern Europe, a very adaptable species, is often grown. It has single, strongly scented, creamy white flowers to 2.5 cm (1 in.) across in early summer. 'Aureus' is a slightly smaller shrub to 2 m (6 ft.) but chosen for its golden-yellow spring foliage becoming slightly more lime-yellow in summer. Place this out of the full midday sun for the best foliage effect. Size: to 3 × 2.5 m (10 × 8 ft.). Zone 5.

Philadelphus microphyllus from the USA is a smaller shrub than most other species in cultivation, with small leaves to 2 cm (¾ in.) long and highly scented, white flowers to 2.5 cm (1 in.) across. Size: 1 × 1 m (3 × 3 ft.). Zone 6.

↑ *Philesia magellanica*

↑ *Phlomis fruticosa*

Philesia (Philesiaceae)

Philesia magellanica (synonym *P. buxifolia*) from Chile, the only species in this genus, is a small, suckering, evergreen shrub grown for its showy, bright crimson-pink, tubular and rather waxy petalled, summer and early autumn flowers to about 5 cm (2 in.) long. The stiff, leathery, dark green leaves, whitish on the underside, reach 4 cm (1 ½ in.) long. Grow in a fertile and moisture-retentive, lime-free soil in partial shade. Prune lightly in spring to maintain shape. Size: 1 × 2 m (3 × 6 ft.). Zone 9.

Phlomis (Lamiaceae)

A genus of herbaceous perennials or evergreen shrubs grown for their flowers and foliage. The 2-lipped, hooded flowers are borne in a series of dense whorls around tall flowering stems. Most of the woody species in this genus make ornamental foliage shrubs. Grow in a well-drained soil in sun. Prune in spring to remove any frost damaged stems and lightly after flowering to maintain shape.

Phlomis fruticosa 🏆 (Jerusalem sage) from the eastern Mediterranean has greyish green leaves to 10 cm (4 in.) long which are grey woolly underneath. The flowers are a bright golden-yellow to 3 cm (1 ½ in.) long borne from early to midsummer. Size: 1 × 1.5 m (3 × 5 ft.). Zone 7.

Phlomis italica from the Balearic Islands has leaves covered with silvery white hairs to 5 cm (2 in.) long. The lilac-pink flowers in midsummer are 2 cm (¾ in.) long. Size: 45 × 60 cm (1 ½ × 2 ft.). Zone 8.

↑ *Phormium* 'Maori Sunrise'

Phormium (Phormiaceae)

A genus of large, evergreen, perennial plants from New Zealand which, although not strictly woody, are bold architectural plants grown for their shape and foliage rather than the tall panicles of summer flowers. The long strap-like leaves can reach 1.5 m (5 ft.) or even longer. They are useful in coastal conditions, in borders or as single specimen plants. Grow in a sunny position. Many cultivars are available, usually grown more frequently than the species from which they are derived.

***Phormium* 'Maori Sunrise'** has bronze leaves striped with pink. 'Sundowner' 🏆 has upright leaves edged with deep pinkish red. 'Yellow Wave' 🏆 has arching green and yellow striped leaves. Two smaller, hardier cultivars are *P. cookianum* 'Cream Delight' 🏆 with leaves striped with creamy yellow and *P. tenax* 'Nanum Purpureum' with reddish purple foliage. Size: can reach to 4 × 2 m (12 × 6 ft.). Zone 8.

Photinia synonym *Stranvaesia* (Rosaceae)

A genus of deciduous and evergreen trees and shrubs from the Himalayas to eastern Asia grown for their coloured spring foliage and white flowers followed by red fruits. Many are large shrubs but some evergreen species can be used to create good dense hedges useful for birds as shelter and food. Grow in sun or partial shade. Prune in spring and trim hedges again in summer if necessary.

***Photinia* ×*fraseri* 'Red Robin'** 🏆 is a useful evergreen which can be used as a hedge as well as a specimen shrub for a border. The leathery, dark green leaves reach 15 cm (6 in.) or more in length. On opening, they are a gleaming red which gradually fades to green as they mature. Size: 5 × 5 m (15 × 15 ft.) unless clipped as a hedge. Zone 8.

Phygelius (Scrophulariaceae)

A small genus of evergreen suckering shrubs from South Africa grown for their showy and long-lasting flowers through the summer into autumn. The flowers are pendulous, tubular, straight or curved and flaring at the mouth into 5 lobes. In colder areas, these plants may be treated as herbaceous perennials which die down during winter. Grow in a sunny position and prune in early spring. The species themselves are seen in gardens less often than the

↑ *Phygelius ×rectus* 'African Queen'

cultivars which can be found with a range of shades of flower colour.

Phygelius aequalis is the smaller and slightly less hardy species. The nodding, dusky pink flowers to 6 cm (2½ in.) long have a yellow throat and are borne on an inflorescence to 25 cm (10 in.) tall. SENSATION 'Sani Pass' is a newer cultivar with deep magenta pink flowers. 'Yellow Trumpet' 🏆 has creamy yellow flowers. Size: 1 × 1 m (3 × 3 ft.). Zone 8.

Phygelius capensis 🏆 is a larger species with tall, open panicles to 60 cm (2 ft.) of nodding, yellow-throated, orange-red flowers to 6 cm (2½ in.) long, which are held on longer flower stalks away from the stem and tend to turn backwards towards the stem once fully open. Size: 1.2 × 1.5 m (4 × 5 ft.). Zone 8.

Phygelius ×rectus is a hybrid of the two species and a number of cultivars have been raised in the last 30 years which are intermediate in their characteristics. The flowers of 'African Queen' 🏆 are red; of 'Moonraker', yellow; and of 'Salmon Leap' 🏆, orange-red. Size: 1.5 × 1.5 m (5 × 5 ft.). Zone 8.

Physocarpus (Caprifoliaceae)

A genus of suckering deciduous shrubs grown for their peeling bark, flowers and some for their coloured foliage. The small white flowers are formed in dense clusters at the ends of the shoots in early summer. Grow preferably in an acid soil, in sun or partial shade. Remove some of the older flowering branches to maintain size and shape.

Physocarpus opulifolius (ninebark) from eastern North America could become too large for a small garden, but the cultivars with coloured foliage tend to be smaller and make attractive features if pruned regularly. 'Diabolo' 🏆 has dark chocolate-purple coloured foliage during the summer which turns a startling red in autumn. 'Dart's Gold' 🏆 is shorter and has bright yellow summer foliage. Size: 3 × 4 m (10 × 12 ft.). Zone 2.

Pieris (Ericaceae)

This genus of evergreen shrubs is grown for the urn-shaped flowers borne in racemes in early to midspring contrasting with glossy, dark green leaves, often red as they unfold, although this young foliage may be damaged by late frosts in spring. Grow in a fertile, well-drained, lime-free

↑ *Pieris japonica* 'Flamingo'

soil in sun or partial shade. Prune lightly after flowering and dead head if possible.

Pieris floribunda from the USA, although less commonly cultivated than *P. japonica* and other cultivars, is a slower-growing dense shrub. The white flowers which open from greenish white buds are held in clusters of erect racemes to about 13 cm (5 in.) long. Size: 2× 3 m (6 × 10 ft.). Zone 7.

***Pieris* 'Forest Flame'** 🏆 is a large and popular shrub grown particularly for the exceptionally bright red young foliage changing to pink and white before it eventually turns green later in the spring. Size: 4 × 2 m (12 × 6 ft.). Zone 7.

Pieris japonica from Japan is a rounded shrub with narrow leaves to about 8 cm (3 in.) long and clusters of pendulous racemes to 15 cm (6 in.) long of white flowers at the ends of the shoots. 'Little Heath' 🏆 is a dwarf cultivar with white-edged leaves which barely reaches 60 cm (2 ft.) in height. 'Cavatine' 🏆 and 'Sarabande' 🏆 are two of a number of more rounded and compact cultivars reaching to about 1 m (3 ft.) tall which have been raised in Holland. 'Flamingo' is a large upright shrub with pink flowers opening from deep pink buds which are attractive for several months before the flowers open. 'Katsura' has scented pink flowers and dark burgundy red young foliage. Size: 4 × 3 m (12 × 10 ft.). Zone 6.

Pittosporum (Pittosporaceae)

A genus of evergreen shrubs and trees grown mainly for their foliage. The leaves are usually leathery, dark green and glossy and some such as *Pittosporum tenuifolium*, are cultivated commercially for floristry. The small flowers are not showy, though often scented. These shrubs are especially good for seaside locations and can be used for hedging. Grow in sun or partial shade. Prune in spring if required and hedges again in summer.

***Pittosporum* 'Garnettii'** 🏆 is a large shrub with grey-green leaves margined with white and usually spotted with pink. Size: 3 × 2 m (10 × 6 ft.). Zone 8.

Pittosporum tenuifolium 🏆 from New Zealand is the hardiest species. It often has black stems which contrast with the ovate, glossy green leaves to about 5 cm (2 in.) long frequently with undulate margins. The scented, late spring flowers are bell-shaped to 1 cm (½ in.) across but coloured deep maroon to black so not very conspicuous. 'Irene Paterson' ♕ has white speckled leaves, striking, although not to everyone's taste. 'James Stirling' is a less common cultivar with tiny silvery green leaves. 'Silver Queen' ♕ has grey-green leaves margined with white. 'Tom Thumb' ♕, a compact, small shrub to about 1 m (3 ft.) tall, has deep purplish red leaves, although they are green when they first unfold. 'Warnham Gold' ♕ has golden foliage which is especially effective in winter. Size: 10 × 5 m (30 × 15 ft.) but many of the cultivars are much smaller. Zone 8.

Poncirus (Rutaceae)

Japanese bitter orange

Poncirus trifoliata from China and Korea is the only species in this genus. It is a slow-growing deciduous shrub closely related to citrus plants and, although not edible, the fruits resemble small oranges to 4 cm (1½ in.) across. The orange-blossom scented, white, cup-shaped, spring flowers reach 5 cm (2 in.) across on stiff green stems with strong sharp spines and trifoliate leaves. It has been used as a very thorny hedge which could act as a good deterrent to intruders. Grow in a sunny position. Prune after flowering and fruiting only if necessary. Size: eventually 4 × 4 m (12 × 12 ft.) or more. Zone 5.

Potentilla (Rosaceae)

A genus of small deciduous shrubs and herbaceous plants grown for their flowers. The shrubs tolerate poor soils, in sun or some shade. Prune after flowering or in early spring, cutting back old flowering shoots.

Potentilla fruticosa comes from the temperate Northern Hemisphere. The species is usually

↓ *Potentilla fruticosa* 'Abbotswood'

represented in gardens by one of the many cultivars varying in habit, flower and leaf colour. The leaves to 4 cm (1½ in.) long are pinnate with 5–7 leaflets. The saucer-shaped, 5-petalled flowers, produced over a long period from late spring to early autumn, are about 4 cm (1½ in.) across. Those with pink, orange or red flowers, have a more intense colour when sited in dappled shade during the hottest and sunniest part of the day. 'Abbotswood' 🏆 has white flowers and darker green leaves. MARIAN RED ROBIN 'Marrob' 🏆 is a lower-growing shrub and one of the most reliable red-flowered cultivars. 'Hopleys Orange' 🏆 has orange flowers and the petals have a narrow yellow rim. The flowers of 'Limelight' 🏆 are pale yellow with a darker yellow centre. 'Pink Beauty' 🏆 has pink, semi-double flowers. 'Primrose Beauty' 🏆 is a smaller shrub with larger, pale yellow flowers and greyish green foliage. 'Medicine Wheel Mountain' 🏆 has a low-growing spreading habit with large bright yellow flowers. 'Sommerflor' 🏆 is a taller bushy shrub with very large golden-yellow flowers. Size (depending on the cultivar): about 1 × 1.5 m (3 × 5 ft.). Zone 4.

Prostanthera (Lamiaceae) mint bush

A genus of evergreen shrubs and small trees from Australia grown for their flowers and aromatic foliage. The flowers in large branching inflorescences are 2-lipped with a more or less hooded upper lip. Grow in well-drained, moist soil in sun. Prune after flowering.

Prostanthera cuneata 🏆 (alpine mint bush) from southeastern Australia is one of the hardier, smaller species and could be grown in a sheltered position. The tiny, dark green, leaves may be barely 8 mm (¼ in.) long but are very aromatic. The flowers are white-tinged with lilac, marked with yellow and purple, to 1.5 cm (½ in.) across and borne in racemes of about 15 cm (6 in.) long in late spring. Size: about 60 × 60 cm (2 × 2 ft.). Zones 8–9.

↑ *Prostanthera cuneata*

Prunus (Rosaceae)

A large genus of deciduous and evergreen trees and shrubs grown for their flowers, foliage and some, such as cherries, almonds and apricots, for their edible fruit. Some, especially evergreen species, are suitable for hedging or ground cover but most are ornamental, flowering trees or shrubs. The flowers are usually pink or white, saucer- or cup-shaped and with 5 petals or sometimes double. In fruit, they attract birds and in flower, butterflies and bees. Grow in sun or partial shade. Remove any weak or

↑ *Prunus* × *subhirtella* 'Autumnalis'

dead branches of trees and shrubs in late winter and trim deciduous hedges after flowering. Trim evergreen hedges in early spring.

Many flowering cherries raised in Japan over 1000 years ago have a complex parentage. Many are trees to about 6 m (18 ft.) in height suitable for the smaller garden, creating a wonderful spectacle in spring, often followed by colourful autumn foliage. Avoid planting too close to the house as their roots are quite robust, especially in a heavy soil. Zone 5.

Prunus 'Amanogawa' 🏆 is a columnar tree with upward pointing branches and dense clusters of pale pink, semi-double flowers in mid to late spring. It may become slightly more spreading with age. 'Kiku-shidare-zakura' 🏆 (synonym Cheal's Weeping) has early, very double, bright pink flowers and a slightly weeping habit to about 3 m (10 ft.) tall. 'Shirotae' 🏆 (synonym 'Mount Fuji') is a tree with spreading and pendulous branches and pendulous cup-shaped, single to semi-double, white flowers to 5 cm (2 in.) across. 'Shogetsu' 🏆 has clusters of up to 6 pendulous, double, very pale pink to white flowers with fringed petals. 'Ukon' 🏆 has yellowish green, semi-double flowers.

Prunus* ×*blireana 🏆 has early, double pink, scented flowers to 2.5 cm (1 in.) across and reddish purple young leaves. Size: 3 × 3 m (10 × 10 ft.). Zone 6.

Prunus incisa (Fuji cherry) from Japan, is a deciduous shrub and is used as a flowering hedge and by specialists for bonsai. The flowers are open, pale pink or white to 2 cm (¾ in.) across in clusters of 2–3 in early spring. The fruits are purplish black about 8 mm (¼ in.) across. Smaller cultivars may be grown in a container. 'Kojo-no-mai', a small, slow-growing cultivar, makes a twiggy shrub to about 2 m (6 ft.) with very pale pink flowers 1.5 cm (½ in.) across. 'Mikinori', a new, small, shrubby cultivar, has semi-double, white flowers and very good red autumn colour. Forma *yamadae* is a small tree with pure white flowers reaching 5 m (15 ft.) tall. Zone 6.

Prunus laurocerasus ♀ (common laurel, cherry laurel) from Eastern Europe is a vigorous evergreen, often used for screening, with large, oblong, glossy green leaves to 15 cm (6 in.) long. In spring, it bears erect racemes to 12 cm (5 in.) of white scented flowers which are followed by glossy, poisonous black fruits about 1 cm (½ in.) across. Although this is a very large shrub, it can be clipped as a hedge, and several much smaller cultivars could be used as ground cover in a limited space and are tolerant of shade under other shrubs or trees. 'Otto Luyken' ♀ is low spreading to about 1 m (3 ft.) tall with narrow leaves and sometimes has a second flush of flowers in autumn. Size: 8 × 10 m (25 × 30 ft.). Zone 7.

Prunus mume (Japanese apricot) from China and Korea is a spreading deciduous tree but the cultivar 'Beni-chidori' is a smaller upright shrub with deep pink scented flowers to about 2.5 cm (1 in.) across borne in late winter on green stems before the leaves unfold. Size: 2.5 × 2.5 m (8 × 8 ft.). Zone 6.

***Prunus pendula* 'Pendula Rosea'** ♀ (synonym *P.* ×*subhirtella* 'Pendula') has pink flowers in early spring. It is a small and graceful, weeping tree to about 8 m (25 ft.). Several other cultivars are equally attractive with different habit or flower colour from pink to white. Zone 5.

***Prunus* ×*subhirtella* 'Autumnalis'** ♀ is a small tree which flowers intermittently from early winter to early spring with semi-double, white flowers tinged with pink to 2 cm (¾ in.) across. Size: 8 × 8 m (25 × 25 ft.). Zone 5.

Prunus triloba from China is rarely grown but the cultivar 'Multiplex' has very double, pink flowers to 3 cm (1½ in.) across in early to mid-spring. It forms a densely branched shrub with small 3-lobed leaves to 7.5 cm (3 in.) long, and it can be kept small by cutting back the flowering branches after the flowers have faded. Size: 4 × 4 m (12 × 12 ft.). Zone 5.

Ptelea (Rutaceae)

A small genus of deciduous trees and shrubs from North America grown for their foliage. The flowers are inconspicuous, but the winged fruits provide winter interest. Grow in sun or partial shade. Prune in spring if necessary.

Ptelea trifoliata (hop tree) from eastern North America is often represented in gardens by the cultivar 'Aurea' ♀. This may be grown as a small specimen tree or in a border as a large shrub. It has very small but intensely honeysuckle-scented, greenish yellow flowers in early summer. However, it is usually grown for the soft butter-yellow spring foliage, greener in summer and becoming yellow again in autumn. Size: 5 × 3 m (15 × 10 ft.). Zone 5.

Pyracantha (Rosaceae) firethorn

This genus of thorny evergreen shrubs is grown mainly for their fruits, but they also bear white flowers in early summer. They may be trained against a wall and will thrive in more difficult, cold north or east facing aspects. Alternatively, firethorns will make a good hedge, colourful both in flower and fruit, and they are tolerant of atmospheric pollution. The spherical fleshy fruits about 8–10 mm (½ in.) across are not edible but attract birds, and the clusters of white flowers about 1 cm (½ in.) across attract many insects. Grow in sun or partial shade. Prune in spring and trim the long vegetative shoots of hedges after flowering but avoid the developing berries. Select the newer disease resistant cultivars rather than the species or older cultivars.

***Pyracantha* 'Golden Charmer'** 🏆 has early and quite large, orange-yellow berries. The bright orange-red berries of 'Orange Glow' 🏆 are long lasting. SAPHYR ROUGE 'Cadrou' 🏆 has bright red berries. 'Soleil d'Or' has very large golden-yellow berries while those of 'Knap Hill Lemon' are clear lemon-yellow. *Pyracantha coccinea* 'Red Column' is an erect shrub with early red berries. Size: about 3 × 3 m (10 × 10 ft.) for most cultivars but they can be cut back in a limited space. Zone 7.

Pyrus (Rosaceae) pear

A genus of deciduous trees and shrubs grown for their habit, flowers and fruit. The open saucer-shaped white flowers are produced in spring and followed by small pear-like fruits, although only those of the common pear, *Pyrus communis*, are edible. These trees are tolerant of cold and pollution and will grow in most conditions. Grow in sun or partial shade. Prune in late winter to remove any weak or dead branches only if necessary.

↑ *Pyrus salicifolia* 'Pendula'

***Pyrus salicifolia* 'Pendula'** 🏆 is a tree grown for its attractive weeping habit and the narrow, very silvery grey leaves to 8 cm (3 in.) long. The white flowers about 2 cm (¾ in.) across are borne in clusters and followed by small, green, pear-shaped fruits about 3 cm (1½ in.) across. Size: 4 × 4 m (12 × 12 ft.). Zone 4.

Quercus (Fagaceae) oak

Oaks would not normally be thought suitable for a garden, even a large one, but one species can be used as a hedge and one or two cultivars are slow growing or columnar and might be possible considerations. All species support a vast diversity of insect life and will therefore encourage birds to the garden. This genus includes both evergreen and deciduous plants. Grow in good fertile soil in sun or partial shade. Prune if required in late winter.

Quercus ilex ♈ (holm oak, evergreen oak) from southern Europe, normally a very large evergreen tree to 25 m (75 ft.) tall, can be used as a dense, dark green and, until it is well established, a slow-growing, hedge especially in maritime gardens where it will withstand exposure to wind and salt. The leathery, oblong leaves, sometimes toothed, are usually silvery grey underneath and the young foliage is bright green. Trim in spring. Zone 7.

***Quercus palustris* 'Green Dwarf'** is a very slow-growing, upright, bushy form of the pin oak from Canada which has glossy leaves and bright red autumn foliage. *Quercus robur* 'Compacta' is a slow-growing shrubby cultivar of the English oak. Neither is common as yet in cultivation. Size: about 2 m (6 ft.) in 10 years. Zone 6.

Rhamnus (Rhamnaceae) buckthorn

A large genus of deciduous and evergreen shrubs a few of which are grown for their foliage. The flowers are insignificant but the fleshy fruits, although eaten safely by birds, are poisonous to us. Grow in sun or partial shade. Prune in spring if necessary. Most members of this genus are probably not worth growing in a small garden but consider trying the variegated ***Rhamnus alaternus* 'Argenteovariegata'** ♈ (synonym 'Variegata') which is an evergreen grown for its exceptionally good grey-green foliage edged with white. The ovate, leathery leaves reach 7.5 cm (3 in.) in length. Cut out any shoots with leaves which lose their variegation. This shrub is slightly tender and needs a warm sunny position for the best foliage effect. Size: 5 ×4 m (15 × 12 ft.). Zone 8.

Rhodochiton (Scrophulariaceae)

A small genus of deciduous, twining climbing plants grown for their flowers. Except in the mildest areas they need to be planted in containers and protected indoors or in conservatories during winter. Grow in a fertile soil in sun (but in a greenhouse, protected from strong sunlight) or part shade. Prune in spring to reduce in size.

Rhodochiton atrosanguineus ♈ (synonym *R. volubilis*) from Mexico is the only commonly cultivated species and it may be short-lived. It has heart-shaped leaves to 8 cm (3 in.) long. Throughout the summer, the unusual pendant flowers hang from the stems with a purplish black, tubular corolla to 4.5 cm (2 in.) long protruding from a large, bell-like, deep rose-pink calyx. Height: 3 m (10 ft.). Zone 9.

Rhododendron (Ericaceae)

An enormous genus of evergreen and deciduous shrubs grown for their flowers and foliage. The majority are hardy but some need a greenhouse in cooler climates. There are about 800 distinct species and thousands of named hybrids and cultivars ranging from shrubs over 20 m (60 ft.) tall to prostrate dwarf species. The

↑ *Rhododendron yakushimanum* in leaf.

earliest ones start flowering in midwinter and some not until midsummer but the main season is from spring to early summer with colours covering the whole spectrum: spotted, blotched or plain. The flowers formed in dense or loose heads may be funnel-, bell- or saucer-shaped and several are sweetly scented. The leaves of many are attractive all year. Although simple and mainly ovate in shape, many are a glossy dark green or covered on the lower surface with a tomentum of matted hairs, in silver or shades of brown; others are hairless or blue-green.

Rhododendrons must be grown in a lime-free, humus-rich and moisture-retentive soil, preferring partial shade, although most tolerate sun as long as the roots do not dry out. The roots

are shallow and benefit from a mulch to maintain the moisture. In areas with an alkaline soil, it is possible to grow the smaller shrubs in containers with lime-free compost, always remembering to water with rain water rather than tap water which could contain lime. Removing the dead flowers will improve their flowering in the following year but pruning is rarely necessary.

A hugely popular garden shrub, many of the species are very variable in their native habitat and the ranges of colour have given rise to numerous named cultivars. Others have been used in hybridisation to create groups of cultivars suitable for different situations. Azaleas are often listed separately but they are in fact simply one section of rhododendrons. A specialist nursery will be able to give advice on the species or cultivars most suitable for the garden, and local nurseries will be familiar with the regional soil and climatic conditions. There are also many books on the subject.

Rhododendron yakushimanum from Japan has become a favourite as a parent of numerous reliable, small, compact, free-flowering shrubs which will grow in full sun. The species has rounded heads of pink buds which open in late spring to pale pink flowers, fading to white as they age. The leaves are equally attractive being covered on the upper surface when young with silvery white hairs and on the lower surface with a felt of ginger-brown. The "yak" hybrids are very successful garden plants. Size (depending on the cultivar): 2 × 2 m (6 × 6 ft.). Zone 5.

Some of the deciduous species such as *Rhododendron luteum* and *R. molle* have been used to create a range of deciduous azaleas with funnel-shaped flowers, some scented, in shades of orange and yellow as well as pinks and reds. The leaves of many turn good yellows and reds in autumn. An average height is about 2 m (6 ft.) and they are very hardy.

There are several series of evergreen azaleas, many raised in Japan, which are usually small shrubs to about 1 m (3 ft.) tall, some much shorter, forming dense mounds covered in small funnel-shaped flowers especially in red, pink, mauve and orange.

← *Rhododendron* 'Christopher Wren', one of the scented deciduous azaleas.

Rhus (Anacardiaceae)

A genus of deciduous shrubs and trees grown for their foliage. The sap of some species such as the extreme example, poison ivy (*Rhus radicans*), found wild in the USA, can cause severe blistering and are therefore not grown, but ***R. typhina*** 🏆 (stag's horn sumach) from North America is often cultivated. It is a wide spreading, deciduous shrub or small tree with stout hairy stems and very large pinnate leaves to 60 cm (2 ft.) with up to 31 lanceolate toothed leaflets turning brilliant orange and scarlet in autumn. The flowers are tiny but formed in dense, cone-like inflorescences in summer developing into large, crimson, hairy, conical heads which may be a slight skin irritant for sensitive people. This shrub suckers freely once it is established and new shoots can appear in the ground several feet away from the parent, so must be removed before they become established as young plants. Disturbance of the ground around the roots will encourage the suckers. Grow in sun for the best autumn colour. Prune in spring.

***Rhus typhina* 'Radiance'** is a very new cultivar with salmon pink foliage when young and scarlet and yellow in autumn. TIGER EYES 'Bailtiger' is a slightly smaller shrub with golden-yellow leaves through the summer becoming yellow and red in autumn. Size: 5 × 6 m (15 × 18 ft.). Zone 3.

Ribes (Grossulariaceae)

A large genus of deciduous and evergreen shrubs grown for their flowers or for their edible fruit (blackcurrants, gooseberries and red currants). Some become big plants but can be kept smaller by trimming. The 5-petalled flowers, usually formed in short pendulous racemes, are tubular, greenish yellow or more colourful in the ornamental types. The juicy berries are usually small except those cultivated for food, but all provide food for birds. Grow in sun or partial shade. Prune after flowering and remove older branches.

↓ *Ribes speciosum*

Ribes laurifolium from China is a small, spreading, evergreen shrub with ovate, leathery, green leaves to 10 cm (4 in.) long. Male and female flowers are found on separate plants. Both have somewhat stiff, pendant racemes of greenish yellow flowers in late winter and early spring followed by reddish black berries on female plants. However, the male has catkins almost twice as long to 5 cm (2 in.). Size: 1 × 1.5 m (3 × 5 ft.). Zone 8.

Ribes odoratum (often sold as *R. aureum*; buffalo currant) from central North America is a deciduous shrub with tubular, yellow, scented flowers in small clusters to 5 cm (2 in.) long in midspring followed by black berries. Size: 2 × 2 m (6 × 6 ft.). Zone 5.

Ribes sanguineum (flowering currant) from western North America is deciduous with deep pinkish red flowers in racemes to 10 cm (4 in.) long in spring. It is best to buy a named cultivar as the species and seedlings are usually inferior in colour. This shrub can be used as a flower-

ing hedge and is also good for forcing as floral decoration in early spring. 'King Edward VII' is a slightly smaller plant with very good red flowers. 'White Icicle' 🏆 has white flowers. Size: 2 × 2 m (6 × 6 ft.). Zone 6.

Ribes speciosum 🏆 (fuchsia-flowered currant) from California is a deciduous or semi-evergreen shrub with narrow, scarlet, pendulous flowers to 2.5 cm (1 in.) long with long protruding stamens hanging from the branches from mid to late spring and followed by small bristly berries. It does especially well if trained against a warm wall. Size: 2 × 2 m (6 × 6 ft.). Zone 7.

Robinia (Papilionaceae)

A genus of deciduous, bristly or thorny trees and shrubs grown for their pinnate leaves and pendulous racemes of pea-like flowers followed by long pods containing poisonous seeds. The branches tend to be rather brittle and damaged by strong winds. Grow in sun or partial shade. Prune to remove any weak or dead branches in late summer.

Robinia hispida (rose acacia) from south-eastern USA is a suckering shrub but can be trained against a wall to keep it under control. The stems are bristly and the leaves to 30 cm (1 ft.) long have up to 13 leaflets. From late spring to early summer, it bears pendulous clusters to 13 cm (5 in.) long of rose-pink flowers. Size: 2.5 × 3 m (8 × 10 ft.). Zone 5.

Robinia pseudoacacia (common acacia, false acacia, black locust tree) from eastern USA is large up to 25 m (75 ft.) tall, but the yellow-leaved cultivar 'Frisia' 🏆 is a smaller thorny tree and often seen in gardens. It is grown for the golden-yellow foliage from spring through the summer which turns to a more orange yellow in autumn. It can be cut right back as a coppiced shrub. The pendulous racemes of white flowers are less frequently produced. Size: up to 15 × 8 m (50 × 25 ft.). Zone 3.

***Robinia ×slavinii* 'Hillieri'** 🏆 is a small tree with very pale pink, fragrant flowers in late spring and delicate leaves with up to 19 leaflets. Size: 7 × 7 m (20 × 20 ft.). Zone 5.

Romneya (Papaveraceae) tree poppy

A very small genus of suckering subshrubs grown for their large and showy flowers. Grow in fertile, well-drained soil in sun and sheltered from cold winds. A mulch around the base in winter will help protect it in cold weather. Prune in spring by cutting out old flowering shoots to the ground.

Romneya coulteri 🏆 from California has white, poppy-like flowers to 12 cm (5 in.) across with a central mass of golden-yellow stamens over a long period of the summer. The blue green pinnate leaves to 15 cm (6 in.) long have 3–5 lanceolate leaflets. Size: 2 × 2 m (6 × 6 ft.). Zone 8.

Dendromecon rigida also from California is a little larger, differing only in its slightly smaller yellow flowers and narrow, less divided leaves. It can be treated in the same way.

↑ *Rosa banksiae* 'Lutea'

↓ *Rosa rugosa* is useful as a hedge in flower and fruit

← *Rosa* 'Nozomi' is a ground-cover rose

Rosa (Rosaceae) rose

A very large and popular genus of thorny shrubs and climbers grown for their flowers since Roman times. About 150 species grow wild in the Northern Hemisphere, many grown in their own right and some used in the hybridisation over hundreds of years to create the thousands of cultivars in nurseries today. The earlier roses known in the fifteenth and sixteenth centuries flowered once each season. The introduction of Chinese roses saw the start of the development of new types, such as the Hybrid Perpetuals of the nineteenth century, which flowered over a longer period, and the eventual development of the modern hybrid tea (large-flowered bush) and floribunda (cluster-flowered bush) roses. New cultivars are being developed continually to breed plants with more disease resistance, more fragrance, new colours and shapes, and of different types and size for cutting or the garden. There are roses for every situation from formal rose beds or mixed border, to standards, to climbers suitable for a trellis or wall, ground cover and hedging, in containers for patios or even as house plants. They range in size from almost unstoppable climbers like *Rosa multiflora* and its relatives to miniatures about 30 cm (1 ft.) tall. Many, but not all are fragrant and their colours span the spectrum, though true blue or black roses have yet to be created. Flowers may be single, semi-double or fully double with a regular, quartered or formal shape. The earliest roses such as *R. banksiae* start flowering in late spring and the colourful fruits of the species roses including *R. rugosa* provide interest through much of the early winter. There are many books on the subject of roses and a local specialist supplier will be in the best position to advise in detail on the type of rose for your soil and climate as well as its care. The majority of roses are quite hardy, growing in sun and in most fertile, well-drained soils, unless exceptionally acid or alkaline. Pruning depends on the type of rose, but one general point to remember is that many are grafted, so shoots emerging from below the graft need to be removed.

Rosmarinus officinalis →

Rosmarinus (Lamiaceae) rosemary

A small genus of evergreen shrubs grown for their aromatic foliage and early flowers. The very narrow leaves are dark, paler on the underside, and can be used both fresh and dried in cooking. The 2-lipped flowers are produced in

small clusters between the foliage mainly from midspring to early summer but intermittently through much of the year. This shrub can be grown as an individual, in a container or a border or as an informal flowering hedge. Grow in a sunny position. Prune in spring to reduce size or maintain the shape of the bush. Trim hedges after flowering.

Rosmarinus officinalis from southern Europe is an upright bushy plant with blue flowers about 1 cm (½ in.) long. There are many cultivars from which to choose, a few are listed below. 'Miss Jessopp's Upright' 🏆 has a more upright habit and pale blue flowers. 'Roseus' has pink flowers while 'Lady in White' has white flowers. Prostratus Group includes all the low-growing plants which can be used to tumble over a wall but which are slightly more tender than other cultivars. Size (depending on the cultivar): 1.5 × 1.5 m (5 × 5 ft.). Zone 7.

Rubus (Rosaceae)

A genus of evergreen and deciduous, prickly shrubs grown for their flowers and fruit. Most are very vigorous, suckering shrubs but blackberries and raspberries are grown for their edible fruits. ***Rubus cockburnianus*** and ***R. thibetanus*** 🏆 (often sold under the name 'Silver Fern') from China may be used at the back of borders so that their striking white stems can create interest in winter. 'Golden Vale' 🏆 is a yellow-leaved cultivar of *R. cockburnianus* with the added advantage of clear yellow foliage in spring and summer. Cut the old stems back to within a few inches of the base in spring allowing new growth to develop for winter effect. Remove unwanted suckers. Grow in sun. Size: 2.5 × 2.5 m (8 × 8 ft.) unless coppiced. Zone 6.

Ruta (Rutaceae) rue

A genus of shrubs from Mediterranean regions and southwestern Asia grown for their pinnate foliage and flowers. Rue has been used in the past as a culinary and medicinal herb but this genus should be considered with caution as the plants are mildly toxic if eaten. Contact with the foliage, especially in sun, can cause severe irritation or blistering, so use gloves when handling. Grow preferably in full sun or in partial shade. Prune in spring.

***Ruta graveolens* 'Jackman's Blue'** is often grown for its striking blue-green, deeply divided leaves to 10 cm (4 in.) long. It has a compact habit and the heads of rather dull, acid yellow, 4-petalled flowers 2 cm (¾ in.) across are formed in summer. Size: 60 × 40 cm (24 × 16 in.). Zone 5.

Salix (Salicaceae) willow

A large genus of deciduous trees and shrubs grown for their stout, erect catkins, coloured winter stems or foliage. Male and female catkins are formed in late winter or early spring on separate plants and it is the male plants which usually have the showier, larger catkins, often silvery in colour and covered with masses of bright yellow anthers bearing pollen. Many species are too large in a smaller garden, but several make very attractive plants for the shrub border and some of the dwarf species may be used in troughs. Some species may be coppiced allowing the new and young coloured stems to give an attractive display through the winter. Grow in almost any moist soil, unless excessively alkaline, in sun or partial shade. Avoid planting larger shrubs too near the house. Prune in late winter or early spring.

Salix alba (white willow) from Europe is one of the species with several cultivars suitable for coppicing for their winter stem effect, although if allowed to grow, will become very large trees. Subspecies *vitellina* 🏆 (golden willow), has yellow young stems while 'Britzensis' 🏆 (synonym *S. alba* 'Chermesina'; scarlet willow), has bright red stems. Size: approximately 2 × 2 m (6 × 6 ft.) if coppiced. Zone 2.

Salix caprea (goat willow) from Europe is large but the cultivar 'Kilmarnock' is an attractive, small weeping tree with rather stiff hanging branches covered with stout, silver, male catkins to 3 cm (1 ½ in.) long in spring before the leaves emerge. Size: to 3 × 2 m (10 × 6 ft.) but often a lot shorter. Zone 5.

***Salix hastata* 'Wehrhahnii'** 🏆 is a slow-growing, spreading shrub with dark purplish brown shoots against which the silvery catkins to 7.5 cm (3 in.) are well displayed in early spring. Size: 1 × 1 m (3 × 3 ft.). Zone 6.

Salvia (Lamiaceae) sage

This is a very large genus of evergreen and semi-evergreen shrubs and herbaceous plants grown for their flowers and also some for their scented foliage as well. Many of the cultivated species are herbaceous but several are sufficiently woody to be classified as shrubs. The flowers are usually brightly coloured and two-lipped with the upper lip forming a hood and the lower lobes spreading. Grow in a sunny position. Prune in spring to maintain the shape and bushiness.

Salvia ×jamensis is a hybrid which is found both in the wild in Mexico and created in gardens. An increasing number of named cultivars

↓ *Salvia officinalis* 'Tricolor'

are becoming available with a range of flower colour from red to pink, yellow and orange. All have aromatic leaves to 3 cm (1 ½ in.) or more long. The flowers up to 2.5 cm (1 in.) are formed in racemes throughout the summer to early autumn. Although not fully hardy, these shrubs are easily propagated by cuttings in late summer and maintained through the winter for the following season. The flowers are deep crimson-red in 'James Compton', cream to pale yellow in 'La Luna' and peach-coloured in 'Pat Vlasto'. Size: to about 75 × 50 cm (2 ½ × 1 ½ ft.). Zones 8–9.

Salvia microphylla (synonyms. *S. grahamii*, *S. neurepia*) from Mexico is a small evergreen with fruit-scented leaves to 5 cm (2 in.) long. The crimson to pink flowers to 2.5 cm (1 in.) are borne from summer to early autumn in short racemes. Several cultivars with different coloured flowers are cultivated including the quite recent and striking introduction, 'Hot Lips' which bears white flowers with a bright red lower lips. Size: 100 × 75 cm (3× 2 ½ ft.). Zones 8–9.

Salvia officinalis (common sage) from the Mediterranean regions and North Africa is semi-evergreen with hairy, aromatic, greyish green, oblong leaves to 8 cm (3 in.) long. In early to midsummer, racemes of bluish purple flowers each to 1.5 cm (½ in.) long are formed. This species has long been cultivated as a popular culinary herb, but several cultivars with coloured leaves are edible as well as ornamental. 'Icterina' 🏆 is low-growing with leaves splashed with yellow; 'Purpurascens' 🏆 has reddish purple coloured young foliage and 'Tricolor' is more compact with greyish green, pink and creamy yellow leaves. Size: 75 × 100 cm (2 ½ × 3 ft.). Zone 5.

Sambucus (Caprifoliaceae) elder

A genus of deciduous shrubs from Europe grown for their flower, fruit and some for their coloured foliage. The numerous tiny flowers are in large, flat or conical heads useful for insects and are followed by fleshy berries which attract birds. The leaves to 15 cm (6 in.) long are pinnately divided into up to 7 leaflets. These easy to grow shrubs tolerate sun, partial shade and atmospheric pollution. To keep the plants small enough, they may be cut back almost to the previous year's growth in late winter.

Sambucus nigra (common elder) has flattened heads to 20 cm (8 in.) across of fragrant, creamy white flowers in early summer, followed by glossy, black, fleshy berries about 8 mm (¼ in.) across. Wine may be made from both the flowers and the fruits, and the flowers may be used for a delicate culinary flavouring or in conserves. A number of cultivars are available. Some examples of these are BLACK BEAUTY 'Gerda' 🏆 and BLACK LACE 'Eva' with pink flowers contrasting with purplish black foliage. The leaves of BLACK LACE 'Eva' are more delicate and finely divided. 'Madonna' has yellow-edged leaves and 'Thundercloud' has reddish purple leaves. Size: 6 × 6 m (18 × 18 ft.). Zone 5.

Santolina (Asteraceae) lavender cotton

A genus of small, rounded, evergreen shrubs grown for their finely divided, aromatic foliage

↑ *Santolina pinnata* subsp. *neapolitana* 'Edward Bowles'

and summer flowers. The leaves are often silvery or greyish green, finely pinnately divided to 4 cm (1 ½ in.) long, densely covering the grey stems. The flowers are in dense, round, flattened heads 2 cm (¾ in.) across held on long stalks well above the leaves. These are drought-tolerant shrubs which could be used as low hedging. Grow in well-drained soil in sun. Prune in spring almost back to the old growth.

Santolina chamaecyparissus ♈ from southern France has very fine, narrow, silvery foliage with bright yellow flower heads. Size: 50 × 100 cm (1 ½ × 3 ft.). Zone 8.

Santolina pinnata from Italy has greener, slightly longer leaves and almost white flowers but is less commonly grown than subsp. *neapolitana* ♈ with bright lemon-yellow flowers and attractive greyish green leaves. 'Edward Bowles' has very pale creamy yellow flowers. Size: 75 × 100 cm (2 ½ × 3 ft.). Zone 8.

Sarcococca (Buxaceae) sweet box

A genus of small evergreen shrubs found wild in shaded woodlands and cultivated for their sweetly scented, winter flowers, spherical, black or red berries and foliage. The simple leaves are dark green and the highly fragrant, tiny, white flowers about 5 mm (⅛ in.) long are produced in small clusters in the axils of the leaves. They are easy to grow and make useful ground cover in shade. Grow in almost any moist, but not water-logged, soil in shade or partial shade. Prune after flowering to maintain the shape.

↑ *Sarcococca confusa*

Sarcococca confusa ♕ (Christmas box) from China has very glossy, often slightly undulate leaves to 6 cm (2½ in.) long and shiny, black berries about 5 mm (⅛ in.) across. *Sarcococca ruscifolia* var. *chinensis* ♕ also from China is similar but with dark red berries. Size: 1 × 1 m (3 × 3 ft.). Zone 6.

Sarcococca hookeriana* var. *digyna from China has narrower leaves to 7.5 cm (3 in.) long, creamy white flowers and black berries. Size: 1 × 1 m (3 ×3 ft.). Zone 6.

↑ *Schizophragma hydrangeoides*

Schizophragma (Hydrangeaceae)

A small genus of deciduous climbing shrubs related to *Hydrangea* and grown for their flowers. They climb by attaching themselves to their support, whether a wall, fence or up a large tree, with tiny aerial roots. The young shoots need only be tied on until the plants become established, after which time, they are self-supporting, although this may take a while. The tiny creamy white flowers are produced in large flattened heads which are surrounded by showy, petal-like bracts. Grow preferably in full sun. Prune after flowering if necessary.

Schizophragma hydrangeoides from Japan and Korea has dark green, toothed leaves to 15 cm (6 in.) long and in midsummer bears heads to 25 cm (10 in.) across with narrow, ovate, white bracts to 6 cm (2½ in.) or more long. 'Moonlight' has blue-green leaves with a silver sheen. 'Roseum' ♕ has pale pink-flushed bracts. Height: eventually to about 12 m (35 ft.). Zone 5.

Pileostegia viburnoides ♕ from India and China is somewhat similar but has glossy evergreen leaves and small, white, star-like flowers in late summer without the showy outer sterile bracts. Height: eventually to about 6 m (18 ft.). Zone 8.

Skimmia (Rutaceae)

A genus of evergreen shrubs grown for their clusters of small but highly scented, early spring flowers and long-lasting, usually red berries. These are not edible and are mildly poisonous. Berries are only produced from female flowers which have been pollinated by a male plant, the male flowers being more fragrant. A few cultivars are hermaphrodite and could be chosen

↑ *Skimmia japonica*

when space is limited. These shrubs are very tolerant of coastal conditions and atmospheric pollution except when grown in dry soil or in full sun. Grow in a lime-free soil in shade or partial shade. Prune in spring when necessary to maintain shape.

Skimmia ×confusa, has cultivars with either male or female flowers, but usually the male form, 'Kew Green' 🏆 is cultivated. This is a compact shrub with extremely fragrant, creamy white flowers in large conical inflorescences to 10 cm (4 in.) or more long in spring. Size: 2 × 2 m (6 × 6 ft.). Zone 7.

Skimmia japonica from China and Japan is a rounded shrub with dark green, leathery leaves to 10 cm (4 in.) long. The white, 4-petalled, star-like flowers are formed in rounded clusters to 5 cm (2 in.) across, followed on the female plants by bright scarlet-red, spherical berries about 1 cm (½ in.) across. A named cultivar should be chosen to ensure that the plant is male, female or hermaphrodite but there is quite a selection. There are cultivars with white berries but these tend to be slightly weaker plants. 'Fragrans' (often sold as 'Fragrant Cloud') 🏆 is an exceptionally good scented male cultivar. 'Nymans' 🏆 is a free fruiting female plant. 'Rubella' 🏆 is a male form with conspicuous red buds throughout the winter before the flowers open. Subspecies *reevesiana* (synonym *S. reevesiana*) is a reliable hermaphrodite and its cultivar 'Chilan Choice', although not yet common in nurseries, has very attractive leaves which are reddish on the undersurface. Size: 2 × 2 m (6 × 6 ft.). Zone 7.

Solanum (Solanaceae)

This large and cosmopolitan genus of deciduous and evergreen, climbing and erect shrubs and herbaceous plants includes the edible potato and aubergine (eggplant) as well as ornamentals grown for their flower. The fruits of many species are poisonous if eaten. Two of the hardier, climbing, woody species are very attractive plants for a wall or trellis in warmer gardens. Vigorous young shoots may need to be tied up. They thrive in sun and in almost any, except the most acid, soils. Prune back to strong

↑ *Solanum crispum*

growth and remove weaker shoots after flowering or in early spring.

Solanum crispum (Chilean potato vine) from Peru and Chile is a semi-evergreen, scrambling climber with dark green, ovate leaves to about 10 cm (4 in.) long, and during the summer, bears clusters to 15 cm (6 in.) across of star-shaped, 5-petalled, pale purplish blue flowers to 2.5 cm (1 in.) across with a prominent central cone of yellow stamens. The fruits are yellowish white to about 8 mm (¼ in.) across. 'Glasnevin' 🏆 (synonym 'Autumnale') has deeper coloured flowers over a longer period through the summer into autumn. Height: 6 m (18 ft.). Zone 8.

Solanum laxum (synonym *S. jasminoides*) from Brazil is similar and its white-flowered cultivar 'Album' is quite commonly grown.

Sollya (Pittosporaceae)

A very small genus of evergreen, twining climbers grown for their flowers. In cooler areas it should be protected in a sheltered garden or conservatory in winter. Grow in sun or partial shade and provide supports around which the stems can twine. Prune in late winter or early spring, cutting back to strong shoots and removing weaker shoots if necessary to maintain size.

Sollya heterophylla 🏆 (synonym *S. fusiformis*; bluebell creeper) from western Australia has numerous, nodding, beautiful sky-blue, 5-petalled, bell-shaped flowers to 1.5 cm (½ in.) across throughout the summer into early autumn. The dark blue sausage-shaped fruits reach 2.5 cm (1 in.). Height: 1.5 m (5 ft.). Zones 9–10.

Sophora (Papilionaceae)

A genus of evergreen and deciduous trees, shrubs and herbaceous plants. Several of the hardier woody species are grown for their fern-like foliage and their flowers. They thrive in full sun and grow best against a warm wall in cooler areas for profuse flowering. The seeds are poisonous. Prune after flowering in summer if necessary to maintain the shape.

Sophora microphylla from New Zealand and Chile is an evergreen shrub or small tree with elegant pinnate leaves to 15 cm (6 in.) long bearing up to 20 pairs of tiny leaflets. The yellow nodding flowers to 5 cm (2 in.) long, more bell-shaped than pea-like, are formed in small clusters in early spring. Size: 8 × 8 m (25 × 25 ft.). Zones 8–9.

↑ *Sophora* SUN KING 'Hilsop'

Sophora SUN KING 'Hilsop' ♀ is a hardier, smaller and bushier cultivar with bright yellow flowers flowering from late winter to spring.

Sorbus (Rosaceae)

↑ *Sorbus* 'Joseph Rock'

A genus of deciduous trees grown for their flowers, fruit, autumn foliage and habit. In one section (*Aucuparia*) the leaves are pinnate, divided into up to 21 or more leaflets and often exhibit striking autumn colour. Another section (*Aria*) has silvery grey undivided leaves. The flowers which attract bees are white (occasionally pink) to 2 cm (¾ in.) across in large, showy, often flattened clusters to 13 cm (5 in.) or more across in late spring and early summer. These are followed by berry-like fruits which may be red, white, yellow, orange or pink and useful as winter food for birds. Grow in almost any soil in sun or partial shade. Those with pinnate leaves thrive better on lime-free soils but others will tolerate more alkaline conditions. Prune in winter to remove dead or weak branches and maintain shape.

Sorbus aria (whitebeam) from Europe has broad undivided leaves to 10 cm (4 in.) long which are green above and white below so that when the wind blows, a beautiful silver haze is achieved. In autumn, they turn a golden-yellow contrasting with the red fruits. 'Lutescens' ♀ is an exceptional cultivar with leaves which are silvery grey on the upper surface and white beneath. Size: 10 × 8 m (30 × 25 ft.). Zone 5.

Sorbus aucuparia (rowan, mountain ash) from Europe and Asia is a very common species with bright red fruits about 8 mm (¼ in.) across. Size: 15 × 7 m (50 × 20 ft.). Zone 2.

Sorbus 'Chinese Lace' is closely related with similar bright red fruits but deeply cut and very feathery leaves to 20 cm (8 in.) long. Size: 6 × 5 m (18 × 15 ft.). Zone 4.

Sorbus cashmeriana 🏆 from Kashmir bears large white fruits to 1.5 cm (½ in.) across. It has pinnate leaves with up to 21 leaflets and very pale pink flowers. Size: 8 × 7 m (25 × 20 ft.). Zone 5.

Sorbus 'Joseph Rock' has pinnate leaves with 15–21 leaflets which turn coppery orange to red in autumn. The fruits are yellow becoming paler with age, about 1 cm (½ in.) across. Size: 9 × 6 m (30 × 18 ft.). Zone 6.

'Pink Pagoda', 'Pink Pearl' and 'Pink-Ness', all pink fruited cultivars with pinnate leaves, are also suitable small trees for the garden.

Spartium (Papilionaceae) Spanish broom

Spartium junceum 🏆 from southern Europe and North Africa is the only species in this genus of deciduous shrubs, grown for their flowers. It may be grown in a border or against a wall in cooler areas but it thrives in coastal situations and on chalky soils. It is an erect shrub with dark green stems but very few, small, narrow leaves. The large, golden-yellow, pea-like flowers to 2.5 cm (1 in.) long are produced in abundance in racemes to 45 cm (1½ ft.) long throughout the summer to early autumn. The seeds are poisonous. Grow in a sunny position. Prune in spring to maintain shape and keep small, cutting old straggly plants back hard but not right into the old wood. Dead head if practical. Size: 3 × 3 m (10 × 10 ft.). Zone 8.

Spiraea (Rosaceae)

A large and varied genus of mainly deciduous shrubs grown for their flower and foliage. Horticulturally, it is a very useful group, most species flowering profusely with showy clusters of tiny, pink or white flowers from early spring through the summer depending on the species chosen. Grow in a sunny position. Prune after flowering for those flowering in spring and in early spring for those which flower later in the summer. The individual flowers are small but massed in spectacular heads. Plants which become too large or straggly may be thinned out by cutting older shoots to the ground.

Spiraea 'Arguta' 🏆 (bridal wreath, foam of May) is a popular spring-flowering shrub with graceful, arching branches which are covered with clusters to 5 cm (2 in.) or more across of pure white flowers. The leaves are narrow, toothed to 4 cm (1½ in.) long. Size: 2 × 2 m (6 × 6 ft.). Zone 4.

Spiraea japonica from China and Japan is a small mounded shrub with lanceolate toothed leaves to about 7.5 cm (3 in.) long. The tiny

↑ *Spiraea japonica* 'White Gold'

purplish pink flowers are produced in flattened heads up to 20 cm (8 in.) across in midsummer. A variety of cultivars are grown, some for their coloured foliage rather than their flowers. 'Anthony Waterer' has brighter pink flowers and the leaves often have cream and pink variegation. 'Candlelight' 🏆 is grown for its soft yellow leaves which become a richer gold in summer while 'Firelight' has orange red leaves becoming red in autumn. MAGIC CARPET 'Walbuma' 🏆 is a lower-growing, compact plant with bright red young foliage turning yellow in the summer. A relatively new cultivar is 'White Gold' with golden spring and autumn foliage but white instead of pink flowers. Size (depending on the cultivar): 1.5 × 1.5 m (5 × 5 ft.). Zone 5.

***Spiraea nipponica* 'Snowmound'** 🏆 from Japan is a mounded shrub covered with clusters to 4 cm (1½ in.) across of white flowers in early summer. Size: 2 × 2 m (6 × 6 ft.). Zone 4.

Stachyurus (Stachyuraceae)

A small genus of deciduous or semi-evergreen shrubs grown for their winter flowers formed before the leaves emerge. They may be trained against a wall. Grow in almost any fertile soil in sun or partial shade. Prune in early spring to maintain the shape. Old flowering shoots may be cut to the base to allow new growth to develop. Several newer variations are beginning to be listed in catalogues.

Stachyurus praecox 🏆 from Japan is a spreading shrub with dark reddish coloured branches and large leaves to about 15 cm (6 in.) or more long. The pale yellow bell-shaped flowers to 8 mm (¼ in.) across are formed in stiff but hanging racemes to 10 cm (4 in.) long. *Stachyurus* 'Magpie', a slightly smaller shrub, is a very showy variegated plant with leaves broadly margined creamy white creating interest through the summer as well. Size: 3 × 2 m (10 × 6 ft.). Zone 7.

Styrax (Styracaceae)

A genus of deciduous and evergreen trees and shrubs grown for their summer flowers. Several somewhat similar species are suitable, although the following is the most commonly available in the trade. Grow in a fertile, moist but well-drained, lime-free soil in sun or partial shade. Protect from cold winds. Prune in winter or early spring if necessary.

Styrax japonicus ♕ (Japanese snowbell) from Japan and Korea is a graceful, deciduous, wide spreading tree with ovate, dark green leaves to 10 cm (4 in.) long which turn yellow in autumn. In early summer, it bears small clusters of white bell-shaped flowers to 1.5 cm (½ in.) long which hang from the undersides of the branches. 'Pink Chimes' is a less common cultivar with freely produced pale pink flowers. Size: 10 × 8 m (30 × 25 ft.). Zone 5.

Symphoricarpos (Caprifoliaceae)

A genus of deciduous woodland shrubs grown for their long-lasting fruits. The clusters of bell-shaped flowers are tiny but attractive to insects and followed by showy, coloured, spherical, fleshy fruits. The fruits are mildly poisonous and should not be eaten. These plants, which are very tolerant of atmospheric pollution and poor soils, may be used either in a border, for hedging or even as ground cover. If the shrubs become large and untidy, they may be cut back hard. Grow in sun, partial shade or even shade. Prune in early spring so that the fruits are retained through the winter.

↓ *Symphoricarpos* ×*doorenbosii* 'White Hedge'

Symphoricarpos ×doorenbosii, a hybrid raised in Holland, has resulted in a number of very useful cultivars with fruits to 1.5 cm (½ in.) across including 'Magic Berry' with bright pink fruits, 'Mother of Pearl' with white fruits flushed with pink and 'White Hedge' more erect, especially suitable for hedging, with pure white fruits. Size: 2 × 2 m (6 × 6 ft.). Zone 4.

Syringa (Oleaceae) lilac

A genus of deciduous shrubs and small trees grown for their flowers in a border or as specimen plants. There are a number of species but it is usually the cultivars of *Syringa vulgaris* which are the most popular. However, some of the less well-known species are equally attractive. Grow in sun or partial shade. Prune by removing old flowering branches as soon as the flowers fade; cut back if the shrub becomes too large.

***Syringa ×josiflexa* 'Bellicent'** ♕ is an upright shrub with narrow leaves to 15 cm (6 in.) long. The highly fragrant flowers are clear pink formed in late spring and early summer in heads to 20 cm (8 in.) long. Size: 4 × 4 m (12 × 12 ft.). Zone 5.

***Syringa meyeri* 'Palibin'** ♕ from China is a smaller, slower-growing shrub but has equally fragrant, lilac-pink flowers in dense heads to 10 cm (4 in.) long. Size: 1.5 × 1.5 m (5 × 5 ft.). Zone 5.

Syringa vulgaris from southern Europe is a vigorous shrub with heart-shaped leaves to 10 cm (4 in.) long and dense conical heads up to 20 cm (8 in.) long of fragrant 4-petalled flowers in late spring and early summer. Numerous cultivars have been developed. 'Firmament' ♕ has single, pale lilac-blue and 'Andenken an Ludwig Späth' ♕ single, reddish purple flowers. 'Vestale' ♕ has single and 'Madame Lemoine' ♕ double, pure white flowers. Other double-flowered cultivars include 'Charles Joly' ♕, very dark reddish purple, and 'Katherine Havemeyer' ♕, pale purple flowers, pinker as they fade. Size: 6 × 6 m (18 × 18 ft.). Zone 5.

Tamarix (Tamaricaceae) tamarisk

A small group of mainly deciduous trees and shrubs with tiny scalelike leaves about 4 mm (1/8 in.) long and masses of tiny flowers in large, showy, light and feathery inflorescences. They make excellent seaside plants resisting wind and salt spray and can also be useful as windbreaks or informal hedges as well as specimen plants. Grow in a sunny position in a well-drained soil. So that they do not become leggy, regularly prune hard immediately after flowering for *Tamarix tetrandra* or in early spring for *T. ramosissima*.

Tamarix ramosissima (synonym *T. pentandra*) from western to central Asia flowers from midsummer to early autumn. It has pink 5-petalled flowers and can either be trained to form a small tree or kept as a shrub by hard pruning. 'Pink Cascade' has richer pink flowers. *Tamarix tetrandra* ♕ from southeastern Europe is slightly smaller with 4-petalled flowers in late spring. Size (unless pruned hard): 5 × 5 m (15 × 15 ft.). Zone 3.

Teucrium (Lamiaceae) germander, wood sage

This is a large genus of herbaceous plants and shrubs with aromatic foliage. Grow in a neutral or alkaline soil in full sun.

Teucrium fruticans (shrubby germander) from the western Mediterranean is a bushy evergreen shrub with aromatic, grey-green leaves, white and woolly on the underside, to 2 cm

↓ *Teucrium fruticans*

(¾ in.) long. Throughout the summer, the pale blue flowers to 2.5 cm (1 in.) long with a long lower lip and prominently protruding stamens are formed in whorls up the stems. Prune by cutting back in early spring. 'Azureum' 🏆 has darker blue flowers but is slightly less hardy. Size: to 1.5 × 1.5 m (5 × 5 ft.). Zone 8.

Thymus **(Lamiaceae)** thyme

A genus of dwarf shrubs and herbaceous plants grown for their aromatic foliage, often used as a herb. The clusters of flowers are also attractive to butterflies and bees. The small leaves are usually about 1 cm (½ in.) long and tiny 2-lipped flowers about 5 mm (⅛ in.) long are borne in tight heads in summer. There is a wide selection of cultivars with a range of size, flower and leaf colour as well as differing scents. Grow in a sunny position, in all but very acid soils, in the front of a border or in the case of the prostrate species as carpeting plants among paving. Trim shrubby species after flowering to prevent them from becoming straggly.

Thymus vulgaris from the Mediterranean region is the most commonly grown culinary herb making a small shrub with pale purplish pink flowers. Size: to about 30 × 30 cm (1 × 1 ft.). Zone 7.

Tilia **(Tiliaceae)** lime

The majority of limes are far too large for a small garden but it might be worth considering the very rare ***Tilia henryana*** (Henry's lime) from China which is slow growing reaching about 3 m (10 ft.) in 10 years. The cream coloured flowers in early autumn are highly scented and the ovate leaves with bristly teeth around the margins, to 13 cm (5 in.) long are silvery pink as they unfold. Prune autumn to winter if required. Zone 7.

↑ *Trachelospermum jasminoides*

Trachelospermum **(Apocynaceae)**

These evergreen twining climbers from eastern Asia superficially resemble jasmine with highly scented, usually white, 5-petalled, open flowers from mid to late summer contrasting with dark, glossy, green leaves. The two species usually seen in cultivation need a warm, sunny position protected from severe frosts. They can be grown on a wall, trellis or pergola in a fertile, well-drained soil. Prune after flowering or in early winter to remove dead or weak branches and excessive growth.

Trachelospermum asiaticum 🏆 is slightly hardier with leaves to 5 cm (2 in.) long and the creamy white flowers to 2 cm (¾ in.) across deepen to pale yellow as they age. Height: 6 m (18 ft.). Zones 8–9.

Trachelospermum jasminoides 🏆 (star jasmine, Confederate jasmine) has slightly larger leaves and larger, pure white flowers aging pale cream. 'Variegatum' 🏆 has creamy white-variegated leaves. Height: 7 m (20 ft.). Zones 8–9.

Ulex (Papilionaceae) gorse, whin, furze

This is a genus of dense spiny shrubs in which the leaves do not remain on the plant for long and spiny, green stems take over their function. They seed freely and can become quite invasive and are seen in the British countryside growing on poor sandy soils in sun. Cut plants back after flowering nearly to the old wood.

***Ulex europaeus* 'Flore Pleno'** 🏆 is worth considering in a garden as it is more compact and slower growing than the species, flowers for longer and does not produce seed, nor become invasive. It grows in poor acid soil in sun but not on chalk. In mid to late spring, and intermittently at other times of the year, it produces masses of bright yellow, fragrant, semi-double, pea-like flowers to 2 cm (¾ in.) long. Size: to 1.5 × 1 m (5 × 3 ft.). Zone 6.

↑ *Ulex europaeus* 'Flore Pleno'

Ulmus (Ulmaceae) elm

Several species of elm have long been a characteristic of the British landscape, but since the devastation of Dutch elm disease, they have been lost in most counties. Younger trees are less likely to succumb until they reach a certain size. Some Asian species show more resistance. However, although the majority of elms are large trees and can rarely be considered garden plants, there are one or two more disease resistant, small cultivars of interest. Grow in sun or shade. Remove dead or weak shoots in early spring. Prune if necessary in late winter.

***Ulmus ×hollandica* 'Jacqueline Hillier'** (synonym *U. ×elegantissima* 'Jacqueline Hillier') is a small, dense, slow-growing shrub and the somewhat flattened branches give the impression of fronds. The toothed leaves are rough to touch, to 4 cm (1½ in.) long. It is useful as background to a border or as a low hedge. Size: to 2.5 × 2.5 m (8 × 8 ft.). Zone 5.

Vaccinium (Ericaceae) bilberry, whortleberry

A very large genus of deciduous and evergreen shrubs with bell- or urn-shaped flowers in late spring and early summer. Many of the shrubs have good autumn foliage colour and several are grown commercially for their edible spherical berries. They will grow in sun or partial shade in very acid moist soils but will not tolerate any chalk or lime. Prune deciduous species in winter and evergreens in spring if necessary.

Vaccinium glaucoalbum 🏆 from the Himalayas is an upright shrub with large ovate leaves to 6 cm (2½ in.) long which are a bright blue-white underneath. The pink flowers are in short pendulous racemes to 7.5 cm (3 in.) long and are followed by edible black fruits covered with a white bloom 8 mm (¼ in.) across. Size: to 1.2 × 1 m (4 × 3 ft.). Zone 8.

Vaccinium vitis-idaea (cowberry, lingberry, mountain cranberry), a low-growing, evergreen, creeping shrub from northern Europe, Asia and North America, has pink-tinged, white flowers through the summer and red berries to 6 mm (¼ in.) across. Koralle Group 🏆 is exceptionally free fruiting with slightly larger, brighter red berries. Size: to 25 cm (10 in.) tall but will spread as far as it is allowed. Zone 5.

Vestia (Solanaceae)

Vestia foetida 🏆 (synonym *V. lycioides*) from Chile is the only species in this genus. It is a small, erect, evergreen shrub with glossy, bright green leaves to 5 cm (2 in.) long which are unpleasantly scented. From midspring to midsummer, it bears attractive, nodding, tubular, yellow flowers to 3 cm (1½ in.) long with swept back petals and long protruding stamens, followed by greenish yellow nonedible fruits. Grow in sun or partial shade. In colder areas, it could be grown in a container and put outdoors during the summer. Cut back in spring. Size: to 2 × 1.5 m (6 × 5 ft.). Zone 9.

Viburnum opulus 'Roseum' →

Viburnum (Caprifoliaceae)

A large genus of deciduous and evergreen shrubs and even small trees, many of which are cultivated for their flowers, often sweetly scented, and sometimes for their fruit and foliage as well. The flowers are small but produced in large clusters. In some species the outer flowers are large, showy and sterile, while the inner are smaller, fertile and produce seeds. Grow in sun or partial shade. Most species can be pruned hard to keep smaller; evergreens in late winter and deciduous ones after flowering. The following is a selection from the many species and cultivars available.

Viburnum ×bodnantense is an upright deciduous shrub with strongly scented, pink flowers forming from any time after midautumn and through the winter. Several cultivars are grown such as 'Deben' 🏆 with pink-flushed, white flowers. Size: to 3 × 2 m (10 × 6 ft.). Zone 7.

Viburnum ×carlcephalum 🏆 is one of the most sweetly scented viburnums. It is a fairly rounded, deciduous shrub with heart-shaped leaves and large almost spherical heads to 15 cm (6 in.) across of white flowers opening from pink buds in late spring. Size: to 3 × 3 m (10 × 10 ft.). Zone 5.

One parent of *V. ×carlcephalum* is ***Viburnum carlesii*** from Korea and Japan which is shorter and has smaller but equally fragrant flowers slightly earlier in the year. In autumn, the fruits are black and the foliage red. 'Aurora' 🏆 is a popular cultivar with red buds opening to pink flowers. Size: to 2 × 2 m (6 × 6 ft.). Zone 6.

↑ *Viburnum ×carlcephalum*

Viburnum davidii 🏆 from China is a small, compact, evergreen shrub with dark green, leathery leaves deeply indented by 3 veins. It bears small white flowers in early summer but is more usually grown for the foliage and the metallic blue ovoid fruits to 6 mm (¼ in.). To ensure good fruiting, it is advisable to plant more than one plant to ensure cross pollination. Size: to 1.5 × 1.5 m (5 × 5 ft.) but often less. Zone 7.

Viburnum opulus (guelder rose) from Europe and Asia is a deciduous shrub with maple-like leaves turning red before falling. The white flowers in late spring and early summer are produced in flattened inflorescences to 8 cm (3 in.) across with fertile central flowers surrounded by larger sterile ones. These are followed by pendulous clusters of spherical, glistening, fleshy, red fruits each to 8 mm (¼ in.) across. 'Xanthocarpum' 🏆 has translucent yellow fruits. 'Roseum' 🏆 (synonym 'Sterile'; snowball tree) has impressive balls to 6 cm (2½ in.) across of totally white sterile flowers but consequently does not produce fruit. Size: to 5 × 4 m (15 × 12 ft.). Zone 3.

Viburnum plicatum from China and Japan is a deciduous shrub. It has resulted in many cultivars popular in the garden. Those with balls of completely sterile flowers to 8 cm (3 in.) across are referred to as forma *plicatum* and do not bear fruit. These may be distinguished from *V. opulus* 'Roseum' by the toothed leaves which are not maple-shaped. *Viburnum plicatum* 'Popcorn' is a striking, large-flowered, new cultivar. Cultivars with flattened heads to 10 cm (4 in.) across of white, sterile and fertile flowers in late spring and followed by black fruits are referred to as forma *tomentosum*. One of the best known is 'Mariesii' 🏆 which has a very characteristic habit of tiered layers of branches, each bearing erect flattened flower heads. 'Nanum Semperflorens' (synonym 'Watanabe') is a smaller, more delicate, compact cultivar to about 2 m (6 ft.) tall which flowers right through the summer. Size: to 3 × 4 m (10 × 12 ft.). Zone 4.

Vinca minor 'Illumination' with *Artemisia* →

***Viburnum sargentii* 'Onondaga'** 🏆 has pinkish central flowers surrounded by white sterile ones opening in late spring as the dark bronze-purple foliage unfolds. In autumn, the leaves turn reddish purple. Size: to 3 × 2 m (10 × 6 ft.). Zone 4.

Viburnum tinus (laurustinus) from the Mediterranean is an evergreen shrub with dark green ovate leaves to about 10 cm (4 in.) long with white flowers to 6 mm (¼ in.) across formed in flattened clusters to about 10 cm (4 in.) across in winter and early spring which are followed by ovoid, almost black fruits to 6 mm (¼ in.) long. It makes a useful hedge and can be trained as a standard. Size: to 3 × 3 m (10 × 10 ft.). Zone 7.

Vinca (Apocynaceae) periwinkle

From this genus of shrubs and herbaceous plants, two evergreen shrubby species may be grown in sun or shade for their foliage and their large open flowers. They make effective ground cover but beware as these plants root very freely and can spread indefinitely. Keep them under control in a restricted space and cut back hard each spring. All parts of the plant are mildly poisonous.

Vinca minor (lesser periwinkle) from Europe and western Asia has blue flower to 3 cm (1½ in.) across. It flowers intermittently through spring to summer. Many cultivars with different flower and leaf variegation are available. 'Atropurpurea' 🏆 has dark reddish purple flowers. 'Azurea Flore Pleno' 🏆 has pale blue, double flowers. 'Gertrude Jekyll' 🏆 has pure white flowers. The leaves of 'Illumination' have a very prominent golden centre. Height: to 15 cm (6 in.) with an indefinite spread. Zone 4.

Vinca major (greater periwinkle) is very vigorous and larger in all parts.

Vitex (Verbenaceae)

A very large genus of usually evergreen trees and shrubs from the tropical regions of the world, a few of which are cultivated in temperate gardens. Grow in a well-drained soil in full sun with the protection of a wall in cooler areas. Prune in late winter to remove old flowering shoots if needed.

Vitex agnus-castus (chaste tree) from the Mediterranean to Asia is deciduous, and one of the few which has long been grown for its aromatic foliage and fragrant flowers. The palmate leaves have 5–7 narrow leaflets to about 10 cm (4 in.) long. In early to midsummer, the small, purplish blue flowers are formed in large branching panicles to about 15 cm (6 in.) tall. It can be a skin irritant to those who are sensitive. Size: to 4 × 4 m (12 × 12 ft.) or more in favourable conditions. Zone 8.

↑ *Vitex agnus-castus*

Vitis (Vitaceae) vine, grape vine

These vines which climb by tendrils can be very vigorous and should only be grown if they can be kept under control by regular hard pruning in winter and again in summer if necessary. The tiny flowers are of little interest but the leaves can be dazzling in autumn. Several, including *Vitis vinifera*, produce edible grapes even in a fairly small space, although specialist cultivation and pruning regimes are needed to be successful. Grow in full sun on a trellis, wall or pergola, through a large tree or to cover a shed, but remember that these vines will not respect boundaries and could invade your neighbour's garden.

***Vitis* 'Brant'** 🏆 is an old popular cultivar with vine-shaped leaves and sweet, edible, blue-black fruits as well as excellent red and purple autumn colour. Height: 7 m (20 ft.). Zone 3.

Vitis coignetiae 🏆 from Japan and Korea has heart-shaped leaves to 30 cm (1 ft.) across turning a brilliant bright red in autumn. It could be used as a screen or background. The fruits are not palatable. CLARET CLOAK 'Frovit' is closely related with purple young foliage changing to dramatic shades of scarlet and red in autumn. Height: 15 m (50 ft.). Zone 5.

***Vitis vinifera* 'Purpurea'** 🏆 has vine-shaped leaves to 15 cm (6 in.) across which are purplish red when young and turn to purple and deeper purple in autumn. Unfortunately, the fruits are not very tasty. Height: to 7 m (20 ft.) if unpruned. Zone 6.

Weigela (Caprifoliaceae)

A genus of deciduous shrubs grown for their early summer funnel- or bell-shaped flowers. There are many cultivars from which to choose with white, pink or red flowers, and purple, green or yellow foliage. They are generally easy to grow in sun or partial shade, are tolerant of industrial air pollution and also attract bees. Prune after flowering by cutting out old flowering shoots. Large and vigorous plants can be cut nearly back to hardwood to keep within the space allotted. Size (unless stated otherwise): to 2.5 × 2.5 m (8 × 8 ft.). Zone 5.

↑ *Weigela* 'Florida Variegata'

Weigela florida from China and Korea has clusters of pink, funnel-shaped flowers to about 3 cm (1½ in.) long in late spring and early summer. This species is probably the most important in the parentage of the many cultivars grown in gardens. 'Foliis Purpureis' 🏆 has bronze-purple flushed foliage and is slightly smaller to about 1.2 m (4 ft.). 'Java Red' is a newer compact cultivar not much over 1 m (3 ft.) with bronze-tinged leaves and deep red buds opening to deep pink. WINE AND ROSES 'Alexandra' has red flowers and leaves. 'Bristol Snowflake' has white flowers tinged pale pink.

***Weigela* 'Florida Variegata'** 🏆 can be grown for its foliage alone which is grey-green and bordered with creamy white. The flowers are bright rose-pink, paler inside and open from deep pink buds. *Weigela* 'Candida' has pure white flowers, even in bud. 'Looymansii Aurea' with yellow foliage is useful in a shadier corner as the foliage is affected by strong sun. 'Red Prince' 🏆 has narrower bright red flowers.

Weigela coraeensis from Japan is less frequently grown but worth considering for the multicoloured effect of the bell-shaped flowers to 4 cm (1 ½ in.) long, which open white changing through pink to deep pink to red as they age. Zone 6.

↑ *Wisteria sinensis*

Wisteria (Papilionaceae)

A very popular group of vigorous, deciduous, twining climbers which once established should produce a brilliant display of flowers each season. The pea-like, fragrant flowers are formed in long pendulous racemes in late spring and early summer, and sometimes again in late summer. They have large pinnate leaves to 30 cm (1 ft.) or more long which often become a good yellow in autumn. Many of the cultivars are probably hybrids so the common perception that different plants can be recognized by their clockwise or anticlockwise twining becomes confused. A large number of the cultivars have been raised in Japan and have Japanese names which, although more difficult for English-speaking gardeners, are in fact the correct ones to use. A common problem is plants which do not flower. To have the best chance of flowering, obtain named, vegetatively propagated cultivars from a reliable source and allow time for them to establish. Effective pruning at the right time of year is also important. Lush vegetative growth will be at the expense of flower. Early flowers may be affected by late frosts. Train against a wall, on pergolas or trellises, up trees or even as a free standing standard, although this last option needs careful attention to training and pruning. Grow in sun or partial shade, in a fertile but well-drained soil. In summer, after flowering, and once the main spread of the plant is reached, the very long, vigorous, leafy shoots may be cut back to within about 15 cm (6 in.) of the main branches. In winter, these shoots may be reduced further. Height depends on the training and pruning regime but can reach to 10 m (30 ft.) or more if unchecked.

Wisteria brachybotrys (synonym *W. venusta*; silky wisteria) from Japan has silky, hairy leaves. 'Shiro-kapitan' has large, pure white scented flowers. Zone 5.

***Wisteria* 'Caroline'** has fragrant lavender-blue flowers and will bloom when still quite a young plant. Zone 5.

Wisteria floribunda (Japanese wisteria) from Japan has flowers which open successively along a single raceme. 'Violacea Plena' (synonyms 'Yae Fuji', 'Black Dragon' and lots more) is a very old cultivar and considered the only one with double, violet-blue flowers. 'Rosea' 🏆 (synonyms 'Pink Ice', 'Honbeni') has pink flowers on very long racemes to 45 cm (1½ ft.). 'Multijuga' 🏆 (synonym 'Macrobotrys') has probably the longest racemes to over 1 m (3 ft.) of fragrant lilac and blue-purple flowers. Zone 4.

Wisteria sinensis 🏆 (synonym *W. chinensis*; Chinese wisteria) from China has flowers which tend to open at the same time along the raceme. 'Amethyst' has reddish purple flowers with a very good scent. Zone 5.

Xanthoceras (Sapindaceae)

Xanthoceras sorbifolium 🏆 from North China is the only species in this genus. It eventually makes a beautiful, spreading, deciduous shrub or small tree, although it is not often seen in private gardens and deserves to be better known. The glossy green leaves are pinnate to 30 cm (1 ft.) long with up to 17 toothed leaflets. In late spring or early summer, it produces large, upright, branched inflorescences to 20 cm (8 in.) of numerous, scented, white flowers about 2.5 cm (1 in.) across with a yellow mark at the base of each petal which gradually changes to carmine red as the flowers age. Although hardy, it is best placed in a sheltered position in full sun as it needs a warm summer to encourage flowering the following year. Late frosts may damage flower buds in susceptible areas. Grow in a good fertile soil. Prune in late winter only if there are dead or weak branches. Size: to 4 × 3 m (12 × 10 ft.). Zone 6.

Yucca (Agavaceae)

A genus of about 40 species of woody and herbaceous plants with or without stems, and with long, narrow, often stiff, sword-shaped leaves. The flowers, some scented, are usually white or creamy white, bell-shaped or rounded with 6 fleshy petals, produced in very tall racemes or branched inflorescences. These are incredible in flower and can be used to create an exotic tropical-looking garden in warm courtyards or

↑ *Yucca gloriosa* 'Variegata'

seaside gardens, but they could eventually fill a small front garden. Grow in a hot, dry, sunny position in well-drained soil. Be aware that the leaves of many are stiff and sharply pointed. Remove dead stems after they have flowered.

Yucca filamentosa 🏆 (Adam's needle, needle palm) from eastern USA is more or less stemless spreading to form large clumps. The narrow leaves may reach 75 cm (2½ ft.) long by 10 cm (4 in.) wide. In midsummer, nodding, creamy white flowers to 5 cm (2 in.) are produced on tall branching stems. 'Bright Edge' 🏆 is slightly smaller with striking golden-edged foliage. Size (in flower): to 2 × 1 m (6 × 3 ft.). Zone 5.

Yucca gloriosa 🏆 (Spanish dagger, Roman candle, palm lily) from eastern USA is similar in flower but has a stout stem and blue-green, very sharp, spine-tipped leaves reaching 60 cm (2 ft.) long by 10 cm (4 in.) wide. 'Variegata' 🏆 has leaves margined creamy yellow fading to creamy white. Size (in flower): to 2.5 × 2 m (8 × 6 ft.). Zone 8.

Zauschneria synonym *Epilobium*
(Onagraceae) California fuchsia

Bushy, evergreen or semi-evergreen subshrubs in a small genus of plants which are useful for

↓ *Zauschneria californica*

the front of a border. They flower over a long period from late summer to autumn but need a sunny position and shelter from cold winds. Cut back shoots in spring.

***Zauschneria californica* 'Dublin'** 🏆 (synonym 'Glasnevin') from western North America and Mexico is more or less deciduous with narrow, grey-green, hairy leaves and narrow, tubular, scarlet flowers to 4 cm (1½ in.) long in loose spikes. Size: to 25 × 30 cm (10 × 12 in.). Zone 8.

Zenobia (Ericaceae)

Zenobia pulverulenta from southeastern USA, the only species in this genus, is a deciduous shrub with blue-green leaves to 7.5 cm (3 in. long). In early summer, it bears numerous nodding, scented, bell-shaped, pure white flowers to 1.5 cm (½ in.) long on upright racemes to 20 cm (8 in.) tall. It needs an acid, preferably moist soil, in partial shade. Remove old flowering shoots after flowering. Older plants can be cut back quite substantially if they become too large. 'Blue Sky' has exceptionally silvery blue young leaves. 'Raspberry Ripple' is a very new cultivar which has pink-flushed flowers. Size: to 2 × 1.5 m (6 × 5 ft.). Zone 5.

Choosing Woody Plants

These guides provide a quick reference to the horticultural features of the genera of trees and shrubs described in more detail in the A to Z of Trees and Shrubs. The charts are ordered by colour, size and season of bloom, except for the final three charts which show plants with attractive foliage, plants with attractive fruits and plants grown for their habit or other feature. Unless otherwise mentioned, all have a hardiness rating of Zone 8 or below and therefore will survive in the greater part of the British Isles. Those described as slightly tender have a rating of Zone 9 and if tender, a rating of Zone 10. An * next to the plant name indicates that it can be pruned to keep smaller.

In the reference guides, the shrub sizes are as follows:

- dwarf shrubs, under 0.5 m (1 ½ ft.)
- small shrubs, 0.5–1.5 m (1 ½ –5 ft.)
- medium shrubs, 1.5–3 m (5–10 ft.)
- large shrubs, over 3 m (10 ft.)

Flowers in shades of blue

plant	season of bloom	site	other
dwarf shrubs			
Erinacea	spring	sun	spiny stems; evergreen
Vinca	late spring to early summer	sun or shade	evergreen ground cover; some with white or purple flowers; some variegated leaves
Parahebe	summer	sun	some with white or pink flowers
small shrubs			
*Rosmarinus**	spring	sun	aromatic evergreen leaves; culinary herb
Hyssopus	summer	sun	aromatic leaves; culinary herb
Perovskia	summer	sun	aromatic grey foliage
Teucrium	summer	sun	grey foliage
Ceratostigma	summer to early autumn	sun	red autumn foliage
Caryopteris	late summer to early autumn	sun	grey-green foliage
medium shrubs			
*Ceanothus**	late spring to early summer	sun	some evergreen and some smaller shrubs
*Hydrangea**	summer	sun or part shade	flower colour depends on pH; some white or red
large shrubs			
*Vitex**	late spring to early summer	sun	aromatic foliage
climbers			
Clematis	winter to autumn	sun or part shade	deciduous and evergreen species; many cultivars in a range of colours and sizes
Wisteria	early summer	sun	many scented; some white or pink flowers; good yellow autumn colour
Passiflora	summer	sun or part shade	large, ovoid, orange but nonedible fruits
Solanum	summer	sun	also with white flowers
Sollya	summer	sun or part shade	tender, suitable for containers; evergreen

*Can be pruned to keep smaller

Flowers in shades of yellow

plant	season of bloom	site	other
dwarf shrubs			
Jasminium	early summer	sun	evergreen; also climbers
Linum	summer	sun	evergreen
small shrubs			
Edgeworthia	early spring	sun or part shade	attractive peeling bark
Coronilla	spring to summer	sun	evergreen
Cytisus	spring to summer	sun	many multicoloured cultivars and various sized shrubs
Genista	spring to summer	sun	grows in poor soils; some smaller
Halimium	late spring to summer	sun	evergreen
Potentilla	late spring to summer	sun or part shade	cultivars with red, white and pink flowers
Brachyglottis	summer	sun	silver evergreen foliage
Euryops	summer	sun	evergreen
Helichrysum	summer	sun	useful for dried flowers; aromatic leaves
Hypericum	summer	sun or part shade	red or black fruits; many smaller
Medicago	summer	sun	slightly tender; evergreen
Ruta	summer	sun or part shade	can be a skin irritant; evergreen
Santolina	summer	sun	evergreen; aromatic leaves
Amicia	autumn	sun	slightly tender; attractive foliage
medium shrubs			
Mahonia	winter and spring	part shade or shade	evergreen; spiny leaves; some smaller
*Berberis**	spring	sun or part shade	spiny; some evergreen; some larger or smaller; red or black fruits
*Corylopsis**	spring	part shade	lime-free soil for some
*Forsythia**	spring	sun or part shade	useful hedge
*Stachyurus**	spring	sun or part shade	one with variegated foliage
*Ulex**	spring	sun or part shade	very spiny shoots
*Corokia**	late spring	sun	evergreen; flowers fragrant; orange fruits
*Kerria**	late spring to early summer	sun or part shade	suckers need to be removed
Lupinus	late spring to early summer	sun	may be short lived
*Bupleurum**	summer	sun	good coastal plant; evergreen

*Can be pruned to keep smaller

plant	season of bloom	site	other
medium shrubs (continued)			
Dendromecon	summer	sun	evergreen
*Spartium**	summer	sun	green stems but few leaves
*Vestia**	summer	sun or part shade	slightly tender; evergreen
large shrubs			
*Hamamelis**	winter	sun or part shade	good autumn colour
*Acacia**	winter and spring	sun or part shade	evergreen; slightly tender
*Azara**	winter and spring	sun	evergreen; lime-free soil
Sophora	spring	sun	slightly tender; evergreen
*Fremontodendron**	summer	sun	best against a wall; evergreen; can be an irritant
trees			
Laburnum	late spring	sun	seeds poisonous
Koelreuteria	summer	sun	good yellow autumn foliage
climbers			
Jasminum	winter and summer	sun or part shade	also white-flowered climbers and yellow-flowered shrubs

Flowers in shades of pink and purple

plant	season of bloom	site	other
dwarf shrubs			
Daboecia	summer	sun or part shade	different flower colours; evergreen; lime-free soil
Lotus	summer	sun	silver foliage
Penstemon	summer	sun	also with yellow flowers; evergreen
Thymus	summer	sun	aromatic foliage; many culinary
Persicaria	late summer	sun or part shade	creeping; evergreen
Calluna and *Erica*	summer to early spring	sun	cultivars with coloured foliage and different flower colours; evergreen; lime-free soil

*Can be pruned to keep smaller

plant	season of bloom	site	other
small shrubs			
Daphne	late winter to spring	sun or part shade	highly scented flowers; some evergreen; some larger
Correa	spring	sun	slightly tender; evergreen; lime-free soil
Anisodontea	summer	sun	tender; useful for containers
Fabiana	summer	sun	evergreen
Hebe	summer	sun	evergreen; other colours and larger shrubs
Jovellana	summer	sun or part shade	slightly tender; can grow in containers
Lavandula	summer	sun	aromatic; flowers can be dried; can use for hedging; evergreen
medium shrubs			
*Kolkwitzia**	late spring to early summer	sun	attractive peeling bark
Paeonia	late spring to early summer	sun or part shade	various shades of pink, red, yellow and white
*Robinia**	late spring to early summer	sun or part shade	also as a tree for foliage
*Weigela**	late spring to early summer	sun or part shade	red, pink and white flowers
*Spiraea**	spring or summer	sun	also white flowers and coloured foliage
*Kalmia**	early summer	part shade	evergreen; lime-free soil
*Abelia**	summer	sun	some with scented flowers
*Amorpha**	summer	sun	flowers purplish blue
*Lavatera**	summer	sun	long flowering period
*Nerium**	summer	sun	slightly tender; various flower colours; poisonous
Indigofera and *Lespedeza**	summer to autumn	sun	graceful habit
*Hibiscus**	late summer	sun	wide colour range
large shrubs			
*Camellia**	spring	sun or part shade	evergreen; flowers pink, red and white; various shapes; lime-free soil
*Magnolia**	late spring to early summer	sun or part shade	flowers pink or white; rarely yellow; some smaller or evergreen
*Syringa**	late spring to early summer	sun or part shade	cultivars in several other colours
*Tamarix**	spring or summer	sun	good coastal plant

*Can be pruned to keep smaller

plant	season of bloom	site	other
large shrubs (continued)			
*Neillia**	early summer	sun or part shade	remove suckers
*Buddleja**	summer	sun	cultivars in other colours
*Lagerstroemia**	summer	sun	slightly tender
*Clerodendrum**	late summer	sun	scented flowers; very dark stems
trees			
Cercis	spring	sun	some grown for foliage and coppiced
climbers			
Hardenbergia	spring to summer	sun or part shade	slightly tender; suitable for containers
Rhodochiton	summer	sun or part shade	slightly tender
Mutisia	summer to autumn	sun	evergreen

Flowers in shades of green

plant	season of bloom	site	other
small shrubs			
Euphorbia	spring to early summer	sun or part shade	evergreen; avoid sap
medium shrubs			
*Cestrum**	summer	sun or part shade	slightly tender; night-scented flowers
large shrubs			
*Garrya**	winter	shade or part shade	evergreen; useful on a north wall
*Itea**	summer	part shade	evergreen or deciduous

*Can be pruned to keep smaller

Flowers in shades of red, orange and deep pink

plant	season of bloom	site	other
dwarf shrubs			
Helianthemum	summer	sun	red, orange, yellow and white flowers
Zauschneria	summer to autumn	sun	grey foliage
small shrubs			
Agapetes	late spring	sun or part shade	slightly tender; evergreen; lime-free soil
Desfontainia	summer	part shade	lime-free soil; spiny leaves; evergreen
Fuchsia	summer	sun	many variations of red, purple and pink
Phygelius	summer	sun	also yellow flowers
Salvia	summer	sun	red, cream and blue-purple flowers; aromatic foliage; some culinary
Mimulus	late summer	sun or part shade	orange, red and yellow flowers
Mitraria	late summer	part shade	slightly tender; evergreen; lime-free soil
Philesia	late summer	part shade	slightly tender; lime-free soil
Leonotis	autumn	sun	slightly tender
medium shrubs			
Cantua	spring	sun	slightly tender; semi-evergreen
*Chaenomeles**	spring	sun or part shade	various shades of pink, red and white; thorny
*Grevillea**	spring	sun	slightly tender; evergreen; lime-free soil
*Ribes**	spring	sun or part shade	some green- and yellow-flowered shrubs
*Leptospermum**	late spring to early summer	sun	evergreen; many colours; lime-free soil
*Abutilon**	summer	sun	slightly tender; various colours
*Callistemon**	summer	sun	evergreen
*Escallonia**	summer	sun	evergreen; also white and pink
*Leycesteria**	summer	sun or part shade	white flowers in red-purple bracts
Rosa	summer	sun or part shade	very variable; some climbers; flowers in all shades except blue
*Colquhounia**	late summer	sun	evergreen
*Rhododendron**	winter to summer	sun or part shade	mainly evergreen; shrubs of all sizes; flowers of all colours; lime-free soil

*Can be pruned to keep smaller

plant	season of bloom	site	other
large shrubs			
*Crinodendron**	late spring	sun	evergreen; lime-free soil
*Embothrium**	late spring	sun or part shade	evergreen; lime-free soil
climbers			
Asteranthera	early summer	part shade	slightly tender; evergreen; lime-free soil
Clianthus	early summer	sun	slightly tender; evergreen
Campsis	late summer	sun	also with orange flowers
Berberidopsis	late summer	part shade	evergreen; lime-free soil

Flowers in shades of white and cream

plant	season of bloom	site	other
dwarf shrubs			
×*Halimiocistus*	summer	sun	avoid heavy wet soils; evergreen
small shrubs			
Sarcococca	winter	shade or part shade	very scented flowers; evergreen; black or red fruits
Skimmia	late winter	shade or part shade	red fruits; evergreen; need male and female plants for fruiting; very fragrant
Vaccinium	late spring to early summer	sun or part shade	lime-free soil; some with edible fruits
Convolvulus	late spring to summer	sun	useful for containers; evergreen silver foliage
Cistus	summer	sun	white or pink flowers; evergreen
Prostanthera	summer	sun	slightly tender; aromatic foliage; evergreen
medium shrubs			
*Abeliophyllum**	late winter to spring	sun	some with pale pink flowers
*Lonicera**	early spring	sun or part shade	variable genus; some evergreen; some climbers
*Aronia**	spring	sun or part shade	red or black fruits; good autumn foliage
Fothergilla	spring	sun or part shade	lime-free soil; autumn colour

*Can be pruned to keep smaller

plant	season of bloom	site	other
medium shrubs (continued)			
*Pieris**	spring	sun or part shade	evergreen; lime-free soil
*Acradenia**	late spring	part shade	evergreen
*Choisya**	late spring to summer	sun	evergreen; scented flowers; some for foliage
*Exochorda**	late spring to summer	sun or part shade	avoid very alkaline soils
*Viburnum**	spring to summer	sun or part shade	some evergreen; some with pink or scented flowers; smaller and larger shrubs; some with attractive fruit
*Philadelphus**	early summer	sun or part shade	highly scented flowers
*Carpenteria**	summer	sun	evergreen
*Deutzia**	summer	sun or part shade	some pink flowers
*Olearia**	summer	sun	silver evergreen foliage
*Ozothamnus**	summer	sun	silver evergreen foliage
Romneya	summer	sun	long flowering
Yucca	summer	sun	spine tipped leaves
*Zenobia**	summer	part shade	lime-free soil
Clethra	late summer	part shade	scented flowers; lime-free soil
Colletia	late summer	sun	unusual, triangular, green, spiny stems
large shrubs			
Chimonanthus	winter	sun	highly scented flowers
*Poncirus**	spring	sun	makes a good very thorny hedge
*Enkianthus**	late spring	sun or part shade	lime-free soil; autumn colour
Xanthoceras	late spring	sun	can be trained to a tree
*Osmanthus**	spring or summer	sun or part shade	evergreen; scented flowers; variegated foliage
Cornus	summer	sun or part shade	some pink or yellow; some can be coppiced
*Hoheria**	summer	sun or part shade	evergreen
*Eucryphia**	late summer	sun or part shade	some evergreen; lime-free soil
*Heptacodium**	late summer	sun or part shade	scented flowers
trees			
Amelanchier	late spring	sun or part shade	autumn fruit and foliage; lime-free soil
Crataegus	late spring	sun or part shade	some pink flowers; autumn fruits; thorny
Davidia	late spring	sun or part shade	takes several years to flower
Halesia	late spring	sun or part shade	lime-free soil; yellow autumn foliage

*Can be pruned to keep smaller

plant	season of bloom	site	other
trees (continued)			
Prunus	spring to summer	sun or part shade	flowers white and pink; some evergreen; some shrubs; some with autumn colour
Styrax	early summer	sun or part shade	yellow autumn foliage; lime-free soil
climbers			
Lonicera	summer	sun or part shade	many colours in different species; some shrubs; some evergreen
Schizophragma	summer	sun	pale pink forms available
Trachelospermun	summer	sun or part shade	white or cream; highly scented; evergreen; slightly tender unless against a wall
Pileostegia	late summer	sun or part shade	evergreen

Plants with attractive foliage (many foliage plants also have interesting flowers and/or fruits)

plant	season of interest	colour	site	other
small shrubs				
Artemisia	all year	silver	sun	aromatic foliage; some deciduous
Ballota	all year	silver	sun	evergreen; pink flowers
Leucothoe	all year	variegated	sun or shade	evergreen ground cover; white flowers; lime-free soil
Phlomis	all year	silver	sun	yellow or pink flowers
medium shrubs				
*Buxus**	all year	green	sun or shade	useful hedge; topiary
*Eucalyptus**	all year	blue-green	sun	evergreen; tree unless coppiced
Euonymus (evergreen)*	all year	many variegated	sun or part shade	evergreen; good hedging plant
*Loropetalum**	all year	purple	sun or part shade	slightly tender; pink flowers; others with green leaves and white flowers
Myrtus and *Luma**	all year	green	sun	aromatic foliage; can be trimmed and shaped; white flowers

*Can be pruned to keep smaller

plant	season of interest	colour	site	other
medium shrubs (continued)				
Aloysia	summer	green	sun	slightly tender; lemon-scented leaves; pale purple flowers
*Atriplex**	summer	silver	sun	good hedge and coastal plant
*Catalpa**	summer	yellow or purple	sun	very large tree unless coppiced
Melianthus	summer	blue-green	sun	slightly tender; evergreen
*Physocarpus**	summer	green, yellow or purple	sun or part shade	white flowers; attractive bark
*Aronia**	autumn	orange to red	sun or part shade	white flowers; red or black fruits
large shrubs				
*Aucuba**	all year	some variegated	sun or shade	tolerant of most conditions; evergreen
*Drimys**	all year	bluish green	sun or part shade	white scented flowers; evergreen, aromatic foliage
*Elaeagnus**	all year	many variegated	sun or part shade	scented autumn flowers
*Eriobotrya**	all year	green	sun	textured bold leaves; cream flowers
Fatsia	all year	green	shade or part shade	interesting foliage; late cream flowers
*Griselinia**	all year	some variegated	sun	good coastal and hedge plant
*Ilex**	all year	many variegated	sun or shade	also grown for autumn fruits; useful hedge and topiary
*Laurus**	all year	green	sun or part shade	aromatic culinary leaves; useful hedge and topiary
*Ligustrum**	all year	some variegated	sun or shade	useful hedge; white scented flowers
*Olea**	all year	silver	sun	can be container grown and trimmed to shape; slightly tender
Phormium	all year	variegated	sun or part shade	many shades of red, yellow, bronze, green; evergreen
*Photinia**	all year	red	sun or part shade	useful hedge; white flowers
*Pittosporum**	all year	some variegated	sun or part shade	useful hedge and flower arrangements; many leaf forms
Prunus (evergreen)*	all year	glossy green	sun or part shade	useful hedge; black fruits; white flowers
*Rhamnus**	all year	variegated	sun or part shade	evergreen
*Baccharis**	summer	grey-green	sun	good coastal plant; white flowers
*Sambucus**	summer	purple	sun or part shade	white flowers and black fruits

*Can be pruned to keep smaller

plant	season of interest	colour	site	other
medium shrubs (continued)				
Acer	summer and autumn	various; some variegated	sun or part shade	large variety of leaf shapes and colours all season; also some trees
*Cotinus**	summer and autumn	some purple; reds in autumn	sun or part shade	smoky plumes of feathery flowers and fruits in summer
*Disanthus**	autumn	red, orange	part shade	lime-free soil
trees				
Gleditsia	summer	yellow or red	sun	thorns on trunk
Ptelea	summer	yellow	sun or part shade	insignificant but very scented early summer flowers
Pyrus	summer	silver	sun or part shade	weeping habit
Robinia	summer	yellow	sun	can be coppiced
Cercidiphyllum	autumn	red, orange, yellow	sun or part shade	lime-free soil
Liquidambar	autumn	red, orange	sun or part shade	lime-free soil
Nyssa	autumn	red, orange	sun or part shade	lime-free soil
Parrotia	autumn	red, orange	sun or part shade	select a smaller cultivar
Rhus	autumn	red, orange	sun	suckers freely; spreading habit
climbers				
Hedera	all year	green or variegated	shade or sun	evergreen; wide range of leaf shape and variegation
Actinidia	summer	white, pink, green	sun	also one with edible fruits
Akebia	summer	light green	sun or shade	scented, reddish purple spring flowers
Parthenocissus	autumn	red	sun or part shade	very vigorous
Vitis	autumn	purple, red	sun	some with edible fruit

Plants with attractive fruits (many flowering or foliage plants also have attractive fruits)

plant	type	colour	site	other
Gaultheria	dwarf or small	red, pink, white, purple	shade or part shade	white flowers; evergreen; lime free soil
Danae and *Ruscus*	small	red	sun or part shade	useful for flower arranging

*Can be pruned to keep smaller

plant	type	colour	site	other
*Cotoneaster**	small to large	red	sun or part shade	white flowers; useful hedge; some evergreen
Callicarpa	medium	purple	sun or part shade	pink summer flowers
Euonymus (deciduous)*	medium	bright pink	sun or part shade	brilliant red autumn colour
*Nandina**	medium	red	sun	white flowers; good autumn colour
*Symphoricarpos**	medium	white or pink	sun or part shade	useful hedge
*Pyracantha**	large	red, orange, yellow	sun or part shade	useful evergreen, thorny hedge; flowers white
Arbutus	tree	red	sun or part shade	white flowers; attractive bark; evergreen; lime-free soil
Malus	tree	red, orange or yellow	sun or part shade	white and pink flowers; autumn foliage
Sorbus	tree	red, pink, white, yellow	sun or part shade	white flowers; good autumn colour
Celastrus	climber	red	sun	yellow autumn foliage

Plants grown mainly for their habit, stem effect or other feature

plant	type	other
Betula	tree grown for its stem effect	choose a named cultivar
Carpinus	tree grown for its habit	choose a small cultivar
Cornus	shrub grown for its winter stem effect	coppice regularly; others grown for flower
Corylus	large shrub grown for its interesting habit or coloured foliage	for edible nuts, choose a named cultivar; also grown for early spring catkins
Fagus	tree grown for its habit	useful as a hedge
Ginkgo	tree grown for its habit	unusual foliage with good autumn colour
Liriodendron	tree grown for its habit	unusual leaves and green flowers; choose a narrow, erect cultivar
Morus	tree grown for its habit	choose a small or pendulous cultivar
Quercus	tree grown for its habit	choose a small or narrow, erect cultivar; evergreen species may be used as a hedge
Rubus	arching shrub grown for its winter stem effect	coppice regularly
Salix	large shrub grown for its winter stem effect	coppice regularly; others grown for spring catkins
Tilia	tree grown for its habit and scented white flowers	choose a small or slow-growing species
Ulmus	tree grown for its habit	choose a small or slow-growing species

*Can be pruned to keep smaller

Where to Buy and Where to See Trees and Shrubs

The majority of trees and shrubs mentioned in this book should be available from the larger garden centres and nurseries, even if some have to be ordered.

The *RHS Plant Finder* lists where to find plants available in nurseries in the United Kingdom and the Republic of Ireland, and provides detailed information about nurseries including locations, catalogue costs, mail-order facilities and post and packing charges. Do remember, however, that it is not completely comprehensive as not all nurseries agree to be listed. Other plants may not be listed but are imported from other countries, especially the Netherlands, directly to garden centres where they are freely available to gardeners.

There is a similar publication known as *The Plant Locator: Western Region* (2004) covering 13 western states of the USA written by Susan Hill and Susan Narizny and published by Timber Press.

Nurseries specialising in a limited range of genera will have a wider selection of these plants, particularly the rarer species and cultivars, and may be worth contacting. They are often advertised in the horticultural press. The Internet is an invaluable fund of information about plants as well as suppliers of both rare and more common plants.

Many public gardens also sell plants and some of the more unusual species typically grown in specialist collections.

In the UK, it is worth visiting the gardens of the National Trust and National Trust for Scotland. Other smaller gardens are listed by local tourist offices, and gardens open for charity can be found in the annually published *Yellow Book of the National Gardens Scheme*. The National Plant Collections of NCCPG (National Council for the Conservation of Plants and Gardens) is another source of specialist plants collected by enthusiasts.

The American Horticultural Society has recently produced two volumes on gardens entitled *Gardens Across America Volume I: East of Mississippi* (2005) and *Gardens Across America Volume II: West of Mississippi* (2006) by John J. Russell and Thomas P. Spencer and published by Taylor Trade. There are two older books, *The American Garden Guidebook* (1987) by Everitt L. Miller and Jay S. Cohen and published by M. Evans and Company and *The Traveler's Guide to American Gardens* (1988) edited by Mary Helen Ray and Robert P. Nicholls and published by University of North Carolina Press which are sometimes available.

Details of national arboreta and the larger gardens may be found by searching the Internet which can also be used to locate gardens in which to see tree and shrubs.

Europe Hardiness Zones

Centigrade		Fahrenheit
–45.6° and below	Zone 1	below –50°
–45.5° to –40.0°	Zone 2	–50° to –40°
–40.0° to –34.5°	Zone 3	–40° to –30°
–34.4° to –28.9°	Zone 4	–30° to –20°
–28.8° to –23.4°	Zone 5	–20° to –10°
–23.3° to –17.8°	Zone 6	–10° to 0°
–17.7° to –12.3°	Zone 7	0° to 10°
–12.2° to –6.7°	Zone 8	10° to 20°
–6.6° to –1.2°	Zone 9	20° to 30°
–1.1° to 4.4°	Zone 10	30° to 40°
4.5° and above		40° and above

average annual minimum temperatures

USA Hardiness Zones

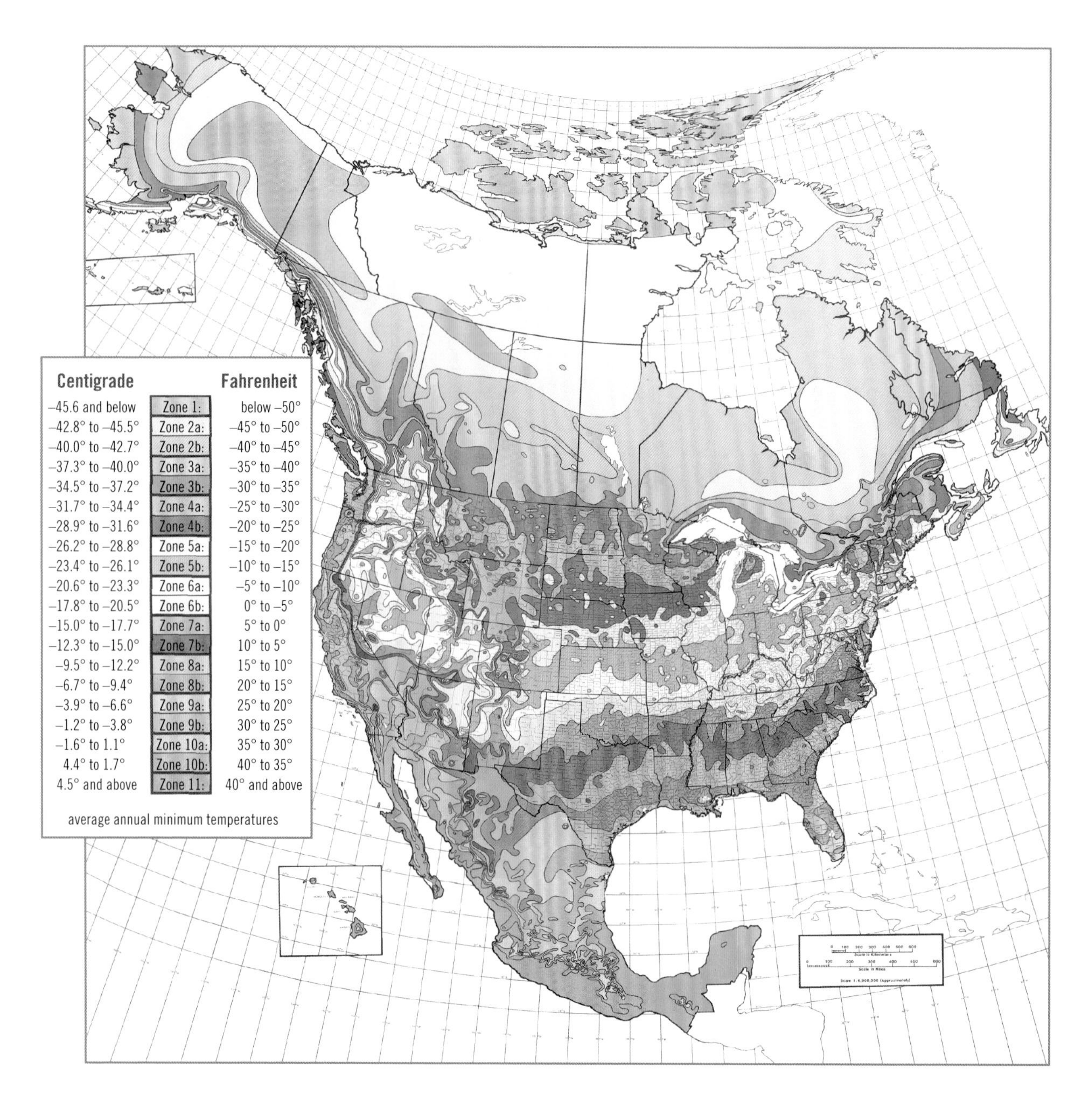

Glossary

acid soil: A soil without lime or chalk, often, but not always, sandy or peaty, with a pH below 7.

alkaline soil: A soil containing lime or chalk with a pH above 7.

anther: The part of the stamen which bears the pollen.

bare-rooted: Describes a plant which is sold without soil around the roots.

bigeneric hybrid: A hybrid between two genera—for example, ×*Fatshedera*.

bract: A structure found under the flower or inflorescence which is sometimes large, coloured and petal-like or large, green and leaflike.

calyx (pl. calyces): The outer whorl of flower parts which protect the flower in bud before it opens. These are usually green but may sometimes be coloured. The individual segments are known as sepals.

capsule: A dry, not fleshy, seed pod which splits open to release the seeds.

columnar: Narrow and column-shaped, usually referring to a tree.

coppicing: A method of regular and severe pruning almost to ground level performed to encourage the growth of new stems. Also known as stooling.

corolla: The petals of an individual flower. Sometimes the petals are joined and sometimes separate.

corolla tube: When the petals of the flower are joined together, the joined part below the lobes is known as the corolla tube.

cultivar: A distinct variety selected, named and propagated for horticultural use.

cutting: A section of stem (or root) used for rooting as a means of propagation.

dead head: To remove the faded flowers after flowering.

deciduous: A plant which drops its leaves annually, usually in autumn.

evergreen: A plant which retains its leaves through the winter but will drop the older leaves intermittently throughout the year.

forma: A subdivision of a species.

fruit: The part of the plant containing the seeds. Fruits may be dry or fleshy and not necessarily edible.

genus (adj. generic; pl. genera): A category of plant classification which includes species and cultivars.

grafting: A method of propagation where a cut stem of one plant is bound onto a stem of a rooted plant so that the two parts eventually fuse and produce a new plant.

group: A number of related cultivars.

hardwood cutting: A cutting taken from a stem which is fully woody, usually made in late autumn or early winter after the leaves have fallen.

hybrid: A cross between two distinct plants to create a new plant. A hybrid may be created artificially by man or formed naturally.

inflorescence: A collection of flowers on a single stem.

lanceolate: A narrow leaf 3–6 times as long as wide.

lime-free soil: An acid or neutral soil with a pH of 7 or below.

lobed margin: The edge of a leaf (or petal) with rounded lobes.

mulch: A covering of material spread on the soil and used to suppress weeds, retain water and also as additional protection for the base of tender plants during winter. The mulch may be organic such as compost, shredded bark or leaf mould, or of an artificial material such as black polythene sheeting.

ovary: The female part of the flower which develops into the fruit containing the seeds.

ovate: Oval, broader below the middle.

ovoid: Egg-shaped.

palmate, palmately divided: A leaf composed of several leaflets joined to the end of the leaf stalk.

palmately lobed: A leaf divided into lobes but not into distinct leaflets.

panicle: A branching inflorescence of several racemes.

pH: A measure of the acidity of soils: pH 7 is neutral, above 7 is alkaline and below 7 is acid.

phyllode: A flattened leaflike stem which takes over the function of a leaf. When phyllodes are present, the leaves are usually minute or fall soon after unfolding as a means of conserving water.

pinnate: A leaf with several leaflets joined on either side of a central axis.

pollinate: The process by which the pollen is passed from one flower to another. Once the flower is pollinated, the seeds and fruits will develop.

pot-bound: When a pot-grown plant's roots have become too crowded.

raceme: An inflorescence with the oldest flowers at the bottom and the younger opening in succession towards the top.

root ball: The roots and soil around them when a plant is dug up from the ground.

semi-evergreen: A plant which retains some or most of its leaves through the winter.

semi-ripe cutting: A cutting taken from a stem which is not fully woody, usually made in mid to late summer.

sepal: One segment of the calyx.

shrub: A woody plant without a distinct trunk. By pruning the lateral stems and retaining a single stem, it is possible for some shrubs to be treated as trees.

softwood cutting: A cutting taken from a young, non-woody stem, usually made in spring or early summer.

species (adj. specific; pl. species): The basic category of plant classification.

specimen tree or shrub: A tree or shrub grown on its own, usually as a feature in the garden.

spike: A raceme where the flowers are without stalks or with exceedingly short stalks.

stamen: The male part of the flower bearing the anther.

subshrub: A plant with a woody base but with less woody stems which may or may not die back in winter.

sucker: A shoot arising from the underground roots or a shoot arising from below the graft of a plant.

tepal: When the petals and sepals cannot be differentiated.

tomentum (adj. tomentose): A dense hairy covering, usually used to describe hairy leaves or stems.

toothed margin: The edge of the leaf which is sharply serrated.

tree: A single stemmed woody plant with a distinct trunk.

trifoliate: A leaf composed of 3 leaflets.

umbel: A flat-topped inflorescence of several flowers whose stalks arise from the top of the flowering stem.

variety: A subdivision of a species.

Illustrated Glossary

Leaves

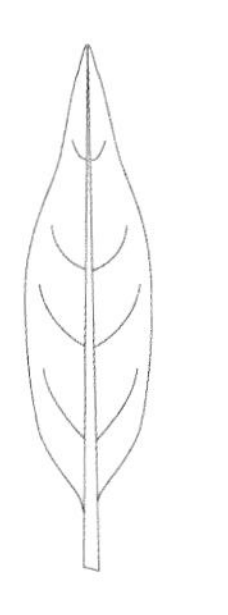

lanceolate

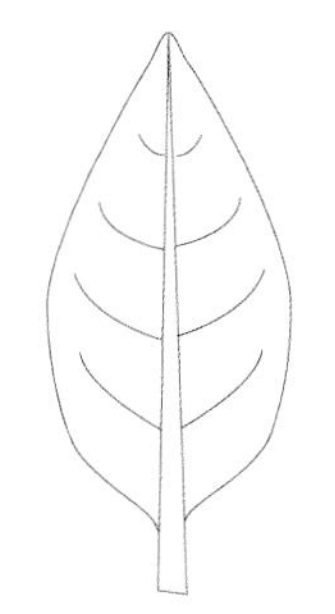

ovate

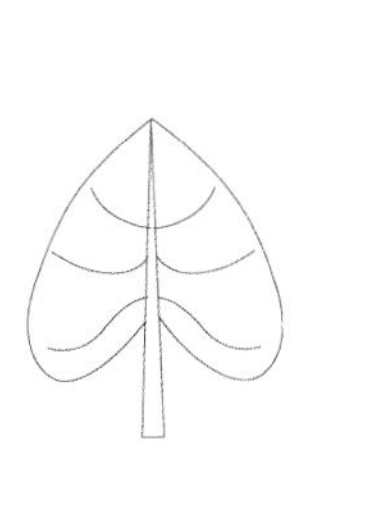

heart-shaped

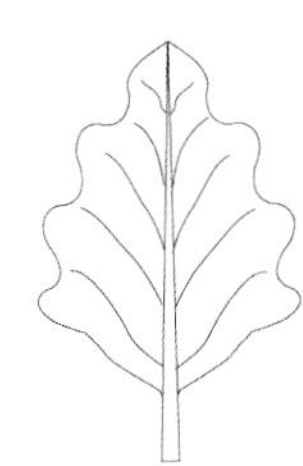

lobed margin

toothed margin

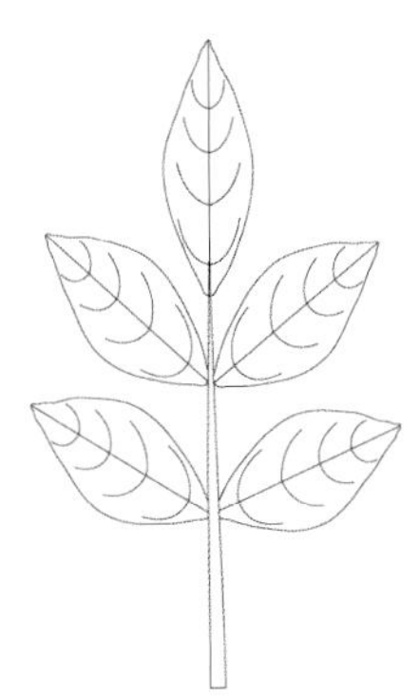

pinnate

palmate

trifoliate

palmately lobed

Parts of a flower

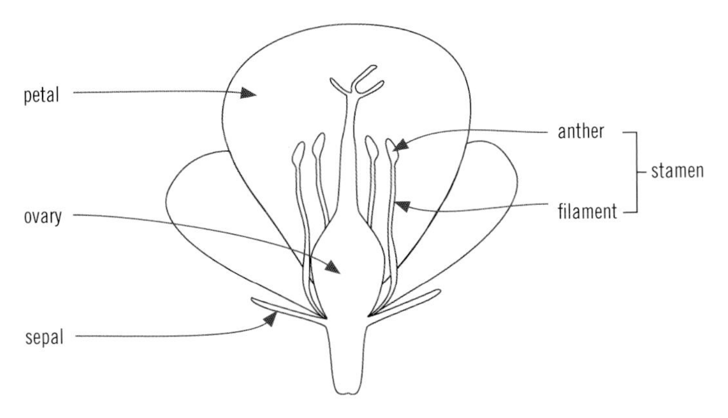

Inflorescence types

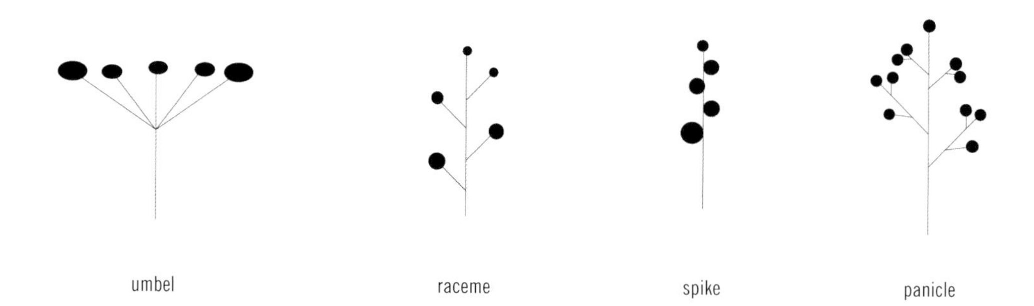

Flower shapes

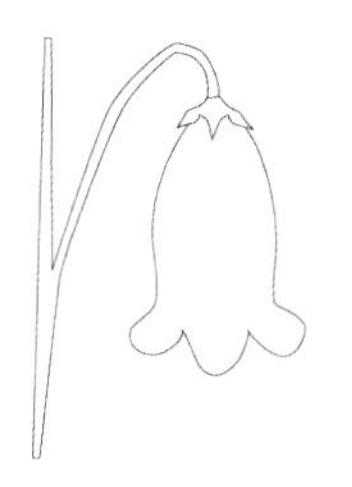

bell-shaped

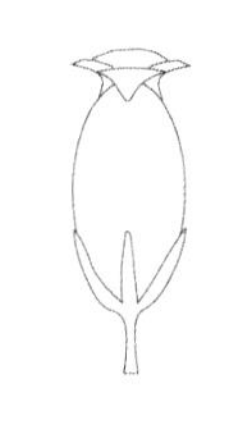

urn-shaped

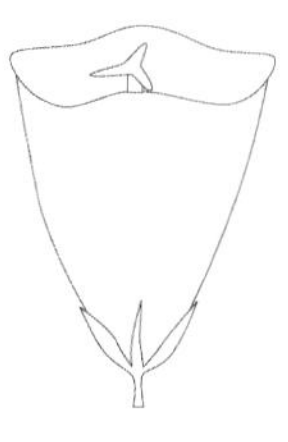

funnel-shaped

tubular

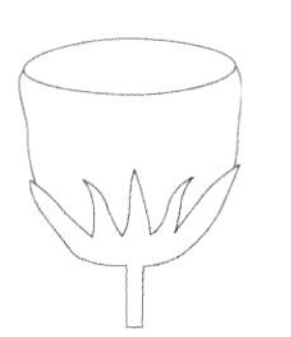

bowl-shaped

open, saucer-shaped

corolla tube

two-lipped

Further Reading

General Gardening

Bean, W. J. 1970–1980. *Trees and Shrubs Hardy in the British Isles*. 8th ed. London: John Murray.

Bevie, S. 1999. *The Encyclopedia of Trees in Canada and the United States*. Toronto: Key Porter Books.

Bird, R. 2001. *How to Plan a Small Garden*. London: Hamlyn.

Brickell, C., ed. 2002. *RHS A to Z Encyclopedia of Gardening*. London: Dorling Kindersley.

Brickell, C., ed. 2003. *RHS A to Z Encyclopedia of Garden Plants*. London: Dorling Kindersley.

Brickell, C., ed. 2003. *The American Horticultural Society Encyclopedia of Gardening*. New York: Dorling Kindersley.

Brickell, C., and H. M. Cathey, eds. 2004. *The American Horticultural Society A to Z Encyclopedia of Garden Plants*. New York: Dorling Kindersley.

Brooks, A., and A. Halstead. 2005. *Garden Pests and Diseases*. London: Mitchell Beazley.

Brown, G. E., and T. Kirkham. 2004. *The Pruning of Trees, Shrubs and Conifers*. 2d ed. Portland, Oregon: Timber Press.

Capon, B. 2005. *Botany for Gardeners*. Portland, Oregon: Timber Press.

Dirr, M. A. 1997. *Dirr's Hardy Trees and Shrubs: An Illustrated Encyclopedia*. Portland, Oregon: Timber Press.

Hessayon, D. J. 2005. *The Tree and Shrub Expert*. London: Expert Books.

Hillier, J., and A. Coombes, eds. 2002. *The Hillier Manual of Trees and Shrubs*. Newton Abbot, Devon: David and Charles.

Houtman, R. 2004. *Variegated Trees and Shrubs*. Portland, Oregon: Timber Press.

Joyce, D. 2006. *RHS Pruning and Training*. London: Dorling Kindersley.

National Gardens Scheme. [Annual.] *The Yellow Book: NGS Gardens Open for Charity*. East Clandon, Surrey: National Gardens Scheme Trust.

Phillips, R., and M. Rix. 1994. *Shrubs*. London: Pan Books.

Quest-Ritson, C. [Annual.] *RHS Garden Finder*. London: Think Books.

Rice, G. 2004. *The Ultimate Book of Small Gardens*. London: Cassell Illustrated.

Royal Horticultural Society. [Annual.] *RHS Plant Finder*. London: Dorling Kindersley.

Stearn, W. T. 1996. *Stearn's Dictionary of Plant Names for Gardeners*. London: Cassell.

Toogood, A. 2006. *RHS Propagating Plants*. London: Dorling Kindersley.

White, J., J. White, and S. M. Walters. 2005. *Trees*. Oxford: Oxford University Press.

Plant Monographs

Acer – Vertrees, J. D., and P. Gregory. 2001. *Japanese Maples: Momiji and Kaede*. 3d ed. Portland, Oregon: Timber Press.

Buddleja – Stuart, D. D. 2006. *Buddlejas*. Portland, Oregon: Timber Press.

bamboos – Whittaker, P. 2005. *Hardy Bamboos: Taming the Dragon*. Portland, Oregon: Timber Press.

Calluna and *Erica* – Underhill, T. L. 1971. *Heaths and Heathers*. Newton Abbot, Devon: David and Charles.

Camellia – Rolfe, J., and Y. Cave. 2003. *Camellias: A Practical Gardening Guide*. Portland, Oregon: Timber Press.

Ceanothus – Fross, D., and D. Wilken. 2006. *Ceanothus*. Portland, Oregon: Timber Press.

Cistus – Bygrave, P. 2001. *Cistus*. Wisley, Surrey: National Council for the Conservation of Plants and Gardens.

Clematis – Evison, R. 2005. *The Gardener's Guide to Growing Clematis*. Newton Abbot, Devon: David and Charles.

Clematis – Toomey, M. K., and E. Leeds. 2001. *An Illustrated Encyclopedia of Clematis*. Portland, Oregon: Timber Press.

conifers – Bitner, R. L. 2007. *Conifers for Gardens: An Illustrated Encyclopedia*. Portland, Oregon: Timber Press.

Cornus – Cappiello, P., and D. Shadow. 2005. *Dogwoods: The Genus Cornus*. Portland, Oregon: Timber Press.

Daphne – White, R. 2006. *Daphnes: A Practical Guide for Gardeners*. Portland, Oregon: Timber Press.

Fuchsia – Bartlett, G. 2000. *Fuchsias: The New Cultivars*. Malborough, Wiltshire: Crowood Press.

Hamamelis – Lane, C. 2005. *Witch Hazels*. Portland, Oregon: Timber Press.

Hebe – Metcalf, L. 2006. *Hebes: A Guide to Species, Hybrids, and Allied Genera*. Portland, Oregon: Timber Press.

Hedera – Rose, P. Q. 1996. *The Gardener's Guide to Ivies*. Newton Abbot, Devon: David and Charles.

Hydrangea – Dirr, M. A. 2004. *Hydrangeas for American Gardens*. Portland, Oregon: Timber Press.

Hydrangea – van Gelderen, C. J., and D. M. van Gelderen. 2004. *Encyclopedia of Hydrangeas*. Portland, Oregon: Timber Press.

Ilex – Bailes, C. 2006. *Hollies for Gardeners*. Portland, Oregon: Timber Press.

Lavandula – Andrews, S., and T. Upson. 2004. *The Genus Lavandula: A Botanical Magazine Monograph*. Portland, Oregon: Timber Press.

Magnolia – Gardiner, J. 2000. *Magnolias: A Gardener's Guide*. Portland, Oregon: Timber Press.

Malus – Fiala, Fr. J. L. 1994. *Flowering Crabapples: The Genus Malus*. Portland, Oregon: Timber Press.

Passiflora – Vanderplank, J. 1996. *Passion Flowers*. London: Cassell.

Paeonia – Page, M. 2005. *The Gardener's Peony: Herbaceous and Tree Peonies*. Portland, Oregon: Timber Press.

Prunus – Kuitert, W. 1999. *Japanese Flowering Cherries*. Portland, Oregon: Timber Press.

Rhododendron – Cox, P. A. 1985. *The Smaller Rhododendrons*. London: B. T. Batsford.

Rhododendron – Riley, H. E. 2004. *Success with Rhododendrons and Azaleas*. Portland, Oregon: Timber Press.

Rosa – Moody, M. ed. 1992. *The Illustrated Encyclopedia of Roses*. Portland, Oregon: Timber Press.

Rosa – Phillips, R., and M. Rix. 2005. *The Ultimate Guide to Roses*. London: Macmillan.

Salix – Newsholme, C. 1992. *Willows: The Genus Salix*. London: B. T. Batsford.

Sorbus – McAllister, H. 2005. *The Genus Sorbus*. Richmond, Surrey: Royal Botanical Gardens Kew.

Syringa – Fiala, Fr. J. L., and F. Vrugtman 2008. *Lilacs: A Gardener's Encyclopedia*. Portland, Oregon: Timber Press.

Viburnum – Kenyon, L. 2001. *Viburnum*. Wisley, Surrey: National Council for the Conservation of Plants and Gardens.

Wisteria – Valder, P. 1995. *Wisterias: A Comprehensive Guide*. Balmain, New South Wales: Florilegium.

Two useful Internet addresses which are invaluable sources of further information:

The Royal Horticultural Society www.rhs.org.uk

The American Horticultural Society www.ahs.org

Plant Index

Page numbers in *italic* include photographs.

A

B

C

F

G

H

I

M

N

O

P

Q

R

S

T

U

V

W

X

Y

Z